MOST MOVED MOVER
A Theology of God's Openness

Didsbury Lectures, 2000

MOST MOVED MOVER
A Theology of God's Openness

Clark H. Pinnock

 Baker Academic
A Division of Baker Book House Co
Grand Rapids, Michigan 49516

�; Clark Pinnock

First published in 2001 by Paternoster Press in the UK
and by Baker Book House in the USA

Paternoster Press is an imprint of Paternoster Publishing,
P.O. Box 300, Carlisle, Cumbria, CA3 0QS, UK
http://www.paternoster-publishing.com

British Library Cataloguing in Publication Data
A catalogue record for this book is available from the British Library

ISBN 1-84227-014-1

Library of Congress Cataloging-in-Publication Data

Pinnock, Clark H., 1937-
    Most moved mover: a theology of God's openness
/Clark H. Pinnock.
        p. cm. -- (The Didsbury lectures)
    Includes bibliographical references (p.).
    ISBN 0-8010-2290-8 (paper)
    1. God--Love. 2. God--Attributes. I. Title. II. Series.

BT140 .P5 2001
231--dc21
                                                                2001025313

Typeset by WestKey Ltd, Falmouth, Cornwall, England
Printed in the United States of America

A Prayer

Lord, give me weak eyes for things that are of no account,
But clear eyes for all thy truth.

Søren Kierkegaard

Contents

Preface

Over the course of my life as a theologian, I have been a pilgrim and have sought to grow as a hearer of God's word. Theology has been for me a journey of discovery and, though I have respected them, I have not regarded traditional views as beyond reform. Tradition has not stopped me from thinking or suppressed new sources of insight. One's theology is a work of human construction, even when based in divine revelation, and interpretation requires strenuous effort. Our interpretations are provisional and truth is, to some extent, historically conditioned and ultimately eschatological. To paraphrase St Paul, 'Now we know in part; then we will know fully' (1 Cor. 13:12). The truth claims that we make are all open to discussion and we ought to be teachable and ready to learn because none of our work rises to the level of timeless truth. There will always be multiple models and any one of them may be valuable in expressing the richness of the divine mystery. I think there is always a place for asking questions and for challenging assumptions. Our God-talk is always open to re-evaluation because mistakes can be made and need correcting. The prophet Hosea was not alone in alleging that the theologians of Israel had failed in their task of instructing people (Hos. 4:4–10). An orientation to reform, I realize, does not go down well with those who privilege certain traditions as practically beyond discussion and certainly beyond improving. I have found that one cannot engage in the task of reforming post-fundamentalist thought and escape criticism. Appreciation from some and hostility from others comes with the territory.

I did not for a moment imagine in 1994 that our book on 'the openness of God' would create such interest and provoke such controversy, particularly in the evangelical community. I suppose it did so because it was a fresh proposal with a certain appeal and because it created an agenda that others had to reply to. For some years the nature of God and God's relationship with the world had been an area of reflection and debate in theology. Among evangelicals this was fostered by a felt tension between our belief in the living God implied in the biblical story and experienced in the life of faith and our received traditions that communicate a certain inertness in God. There are many ways to approach the divine mysteries and the open view favors thinking of God as open, loving and personal. Too often in the past we have thought of God as unchangeable substance or an all-controlling power: too seldom as a triune communion of love, internally relational and involved with creatures. We are not alone in calling for a measure of reform in this area; many are now attempting to do greater justice to the 'dual aspect' of the divine nature. They sense the need to respect God's everlasting nature and relational dealings, and understand that he is ontologically transcendent and genuinely responsive. We have heard much in the past about God's transcendence, we now need to hear more about God's condescendence. We need to view God as participating in human affairs and vulnerable for the sake of love; he is not an invulnerable onlooker.

The open view of God invites believers to consider a new perspective on God in relation to the world. It asks us to imagine a response-able and self-sacrificing God of changeable faithfulness and vulnerable power. It invites us to see God as the power of love that creates personal agents able to freely love him. It is not a naked power. Love is God's essence and power only an attribute. His power, however great in physical terms, is an expression of love. And because love involves suffering, it is a power which, having loved to the end, takes up a towel and washes feet. God's power is even great enough to transform a wicked heart, which no tyranny, however complete, can accomplish. The open view of God is about celebrating the loving project that God has set in motion and entered into; it is not about human beings demanding autonomy from God.

The openness proposal was an idea that we thought might generate fruitful discussion and contribute to theological understanding. I had also hoped that it might make belief in God more intelligible and even nourish a more vital faith relationship. At the same time, I recognize the inadequacy of my mind to comprehend God and, therefore, engage in open-ended thinking, offering tentative conclusions. To err is human, and I am certainly ignorant of and possibly mistaken about many things. Therefore, I welcome diversity of opinion and look to others to help me build on insights of the past.

For many who encountered it, the open view did not cause any particular consternation. It was seen as a species of free will theism, which can be traced back to the fathers before Augustine and which has flourished in Wesleyan, Arminian and Pentecostal circles of Protestantism in recent years. Though the proposal challenges aspects of these traditions too, and requires some rethinking even from them (e.g. as regards the nature of divine eternity and the extent of divine knowledge), nevertheless it lifts up themes familiar and precious to them (e.g. universal divine love and genuine relationality) and has created a new context for an enriching conversation. Despite the differences, few in these circles have wanted to silence any discussion of the openness model and many have even found it promising and a credible development of their own traditions. On the spectrum of divine control, of course, they were already theological minimalists and on the subject of tradition, already reformers of classical Protestantism.

There have been others, however, who find the open view of God totally unacceptable, subversive and threatening. They did not welcome an initiative that challenged conservative Reformation thinking and fell like a bombshell on the theological playground (to recall Barth's expression). For those with the conventional presuppositions found in Augustine, Thomas Aquinas, Luther and Calvin the model was too radical and impossible to accept. By breaking with a number of long-accepted ideas, it waved a red flag in their faces. I have to be sanguine, how could one expect those, who have only recently come to tolerate Arminian thinking, to stomach a more radical version of it? How could one expect criticism of central pillars of conventional theology – in particular, the strong immutability central to the Thomistic model and the all-controlling sovereignty fundamental to the Calvinist view – to escape controversy? The fact is that the openness model diverges from historic Protestant and Catholic thought at several important points and inevitably becomes a target for criticism. It is no accident that 'this now infamous openness of God movement', as one critic has characterized it, has become a hot topic among, in particular, traditionalist and mostly Calvinist conservative evangelicals. Why would that surprise anybody? Of course, I would prefer a sweeter spirit from some of these critics but I am not surprised that they are adamant in opposition.

I am not particularly concerned about my reputation as an evangelical theologian, having advanced new proposals in the past and taken the heat of criticism before, though not to the extent of being called a heretic. I understand why I am viewed in certain quarters as a danger to sound theology. I do not like it because it is painful to be anathematized. Apparently the fact that I confess Jesus Christ as Lord and believe in my heart that God raised him from the dead is of less importance to some critics than my questioning of certain traditions and constructs. Still, I ask for an amicable conversation about the nature of God and God's relationship to the world. Like my critics, I too seek rightly to divide the word of truth and bring glory to God. I even agree with them that God's immanence should not be stressed at the expense of his transcendence. My concern is that we also consider another possibility: God's transcendence can be emphasized at the expense of his involvement in the world; that placing too much distance between God and creation takes away from God's glory too, if it obscures the freely chosen relationships that God seeks to have with creatures. Some of my critics do not think so, but surely there is room in the evangelical big tent for such discussions. A conversation among us might just be mutually beneficial and the situation an opportunity rather than a crisis. Evangelicalism has always had a transdenominational character that makes it possible in principle to appreciate what others are saying. Perhaps our differences could be experienced as a gift. Perhaps the evangelical Calvinist might be able not only to accept the open theist as brother or sister, but even read them with profit and learn from them, and vice versa. Has it not already happened that the doctrine of God has become the subject of more serious discussion among evangelicals? Maybe we will find that the problem lies in the swing of the pendulum, in the tendency to emphasize transcendence and/or immanence; in our being insufficiently dialectical and too one-sided.

What has happened is that an alternative position, the open view of God, has been placed alongside the time-honored Calvinist (and sister) models, creating vigorous debate. The stakes are high and the passions exceedingly warm because both models are quite coherent in themselves and the issues they raise are weighty and not at all trivial. On the one hand, it has led to some mutually beneficial conversation, as I had hoped, but it has also stirred up opposition among the guardians of a brand of orthodoxy that pretends to own the movement theologically. Without meaning to, the openness initiative has become part of a political struggle within evangelicalism and we need to conduct ourselves carefully. It would be helpful if we discussed matters as seekers after truth rather than as gatekeepers obsessed by who is in and who is out of the evangelical movement. Charity dictates that we recognize that some among us are more like pilgrims who are comfortable with change, and others are more like settlers who find change difficult.

The open view of God continues the much older debate between theological determinists, like Calvin, and free will theists, like Wesley, but also adds something new. It makes the choices even sharper and clearer, being itself a more coherent alternative to Calvinism than Arminians have presented before. At any rate, it has opened up a passionate discussion and created the need to explore the topic further. Not only is there more work to be done, we need to understand better why the proposal is considered so positively by some but so negatively by others. How could a vision of God so close to the Bible and so near the grain of evangelical piety be rejected, I wonder, so wholeheartedly by some and not even be considered a worthy topic for discussion? I must try to shed some light on these matters, if only for myself. In doing so I must also make an effort not to be obsessed by intemperate critics when there are more who are not extreme and who voice concerns more calmly. Evangelicals are not famous for the quality of their theological work. The scandal of the evangelical mind, i.e. the lack of thoughtfulness, extends to theology as well and will be evident as we proceed. Though it is a good subject to pursue, we will come across many examples of ignorance, malice, and poor taste. But it also affords us an opportunity to improve our game. I know it has helped me to take account of more factors to guide my own reflection. Many others will benefit too.

On a personal note, I am delighted to have the opportunity of returning to Manchester where, thirty-seven years ago, I received my doctorate in New Testament under the supervision of F.F. Bruce, the first Didsbury lecturer. It is pleasant to return to West Didsbury, where I lived in Needham Hall on Spath Road, and to the Nazarene Theological College where I enjoyed fellowship many years ago. I thank the College for the honour of asking me to deliver the Disbury Lectures this year and thank Paternoster Publishing for issuing the lectures as a whole book.

Introduction

Responsible faith always asks questions and theology is done when the community takes a real interest in the truth. Every believer is a theologian at some level and together we can engage in the search for the fullness of the truth made known in Jesus Christ. It is not enough to repeat traditional formulations of doctrine, which may be adequate or inadequate. We must persist in searching for the truth to which our traditions point but which they only partially express. We must make every effort to be true to the self-revelation of God attested in Scripture and attend most seriously to the doctrine of God, which is the principle category of theology. God is mystery and the ultimate reality, the source and foundation of everything that exists. Every generation needs to think about its conception of God – is it true to the gospel, does it communicate and is it adequate for living?[1]

Some people reject faith on account of misunderstanding the nature of God. Many do so because they have the impression, for example, that God is primarily a punitive authority or a metaphysical immobility or an all-controlling power. There exist conceptions of God that fall a long way short of representing God's true beauty, and they alienate people. We theologians sometimes falter when we translate the word of God into human concepts and actually make it more difficult for them to believe. How can people, whether inside or outside the churches, be expected to believe in God if they view God as an alienating being who exists at their expense? What if a person thought God was the author of evil, would that not make atheism a reasonable belief? Might it not be more pious not to believe than to believe? When persons take leave of God, we need to ask what sort of God did they take leave of? What if they thought of God as, in Dallas Willard's words, 'an unblinking

---

[1] On the task of theology, see D.L. Migliore, *Faith Seeking Understanding: An Introduction to Christian Theology*, ch. 1. I gravitate to the image in M. Bauman's title, *Pilgrim Theology: Taking the Path of Theological Discovery*.

cosmic stare?'[2] Surely it is better that there be no belief in God than that the God who is believed in be an idol who diminishes and humiliates people. We should not forget that God's commandments identify idolatry not atheism as the primary sin.

We assume in the western world that people know what the word 'God' means, whether they believe or not. They think 'God' refers, perhaps, to an all-controlling, dominating and aloof patriarch. One's impression of the great atheists in modern times – Feuerbach, Marx, Freud, Durkheim and Nietzsche – is that they denied an intellectual idol and not the God of Jesus Christ. What strikes one is not their denial of God's existence, but the fact that not a single one of them had the faintest idea of who God really is as a loving and relational person. When they speak about the God whom they reject, I see little resemblance to the God of the Bible, though I do see a resemblance to the God of conventional theism. Atheism is, in part, an unpaid bill of the church which has too often presented God as an alienating substance, remote and unsympathetic, and who exists at humanity's expense. Many of the difficulties with faith are due to problems inherent in conventional theism. Atheists have not been told about the God of the gospel who loves us freely, wants a relationship with us and wants to empower us, not foster our weakness. They do not know about the God who chooses to act faithfully in the midst of the world and does not dwell in lonely isolation. They do not know about the Lord who encourages other creaturely agents to be energetic, creative, and sovereign themselves.[3] The challenge of atheism, and the nihilism that so often accompanies it, is best countered by a clearer vision of God's fair beauty, not by intellectual arguments.[4] In the gospel we encounter a God who loves and takes risks, becomes vulnerable even to the point of suffering, and reveals himself in a man of sorrows who was acquainted with grief. This is a God one can believe in.[5]

We theologians should not produce misconceptions of God and then blame peoples' lack of belief in God. Of course, humanity without God

---

[2] D. Willard, *The Divine Conspiracy: Rediscovering Our Hidden Life in God*, 244–5.

[3] J.J. O'Donnell, *Trinity and Temporality: The Christian Doctrine of God in the Light of Process Theology and the Theology of Hope*, 17–23.

[4] H. Küng speaks about these heresiarchs and helps recover faith in God as a possibility in our time in *Does God Exist? An Answer for Today*. Further on atheism and the models of God which we hold, see J. Moltmann, *The Crucified God: The Cross of Christ as the Foundation and Criticism of Christian Theology*, 219–27.

[5] See W.C. Placher, *Narratives of a Vulnerable God: Christ, Theology, and Scripture*.

is dehumanized, but this truth will never strike home as long as God is conceived of after the manner of conventional theism. God is not dead, but some of the ways we have presented God are dead. By distancing God so far from the world and from human affairs, theology has prepared the way for secularism and atheism. Of course, the living God is not dead. He is the God of the Bible, the one who is genuinely related to the world, whose nature is the power of love and whose relationship with the world is that of a most moved, not unmoved, Mover.[6]

The Openness of God

In order to bring out the truth of God's rule over the world, the dynamic character of his nature and the openness of his loving relationships more effectively, myself and some colleagues offered the 'openness of God' model, so-called because it was an appealing and unused term. In it we portrayed God as a triune communion who seeks relationships of love with human beings, having bestowed upon them genuine freedom for this purpose. Love and not freedom was our central concern because it was God's desire for loving relationships which required freedom. In a controversial move, we also envisaged God making a world, the future of which was not yet completely settled, again to make room for the input of significant creatures.[7]

This was the perspective I saw reflected in Jesus' intimate address to God. His use of *Abba,* an Aramaic word suggesting 'daddy' (Mk. 14:36), expressed the heart of his relationship to God – the God of boundless grace and mercy.[8] This is spelled out in the parable in which Jesus represents God as a father longing for a loving relationship with two sons (Lk. 15:11–32). The boys enjoyed real freedom and were free to leave home and reject the father's love, if they chose to. God took an enormous risk in giving them such a freedom and exposed himself to the pain of rejection, should they turn their backs. At the same time, he also

---

[6] M. Welker even wonders if re-thinking the doctrine of God in this way might not herald a new beginning for theology itself, see 'Christian Theology: Which Direction at the end of the Second Millennium?' in M. Volf, C. Krieg and T. Kucharz (eds.), *The Future of Theology: Essays in Honor of Jurgen Moltmann,* 75–6.

[7] C.H. Pinnock, R. Rice, J. Sanders, W. Hasker and D. Basinger, *The Openness of God: A Biblical Challenge to the Traditional Understanding of God.* My own definition of the open view is found on pages 103–4 and it features love as the highest value, not freedom.

[8] J. Jeremias, *New Testament Theology: The Proclamation of Jesus,* 61–8.

made possible the joy of reconciliation, should they decide to return. The pathos is profound: the father longs and waits and does not know what the sons will do and the parable ends with suspense: will the older son return home? The story is about the power of love, not about any love of power. It portrays God as not wanting to control everything, but choosing to give the creature room to exist and freedom to love. It depicts God as personal in his dealings and as one who does not treat people like puppets. Though there were risks in creating this kind of a world, we presume that it was better to have a world where creatures were free to love God than to have a world in which God always gets his way. The parable dramatizes the truth of the open view of God: he is a loving person who seeks freely chosen relationships of love with his creatures; he is not a pillar around which everything else moves (Thomas Aquinas) or an all-controlling despot who can tolerate no resistance (Calvin).

According to the openness model, God in grace sovereignly granted humans significant freedom to cooperate with or to work against God's will for their lives and to enter into dynamic, give-and-take relationships with himself. It places the emphasis upon the genuine interactions that take place between God and human beings: how we respond to God's initiatives and how he responds to our responses. It implies that God takes risks in such give-and-take relationship but is endlessly resourceful and competent still to work toward his ultimate goals. Sometimes God alone decides how to accomplish these goals and sometimes he works with human decisions, adapting his own plans to fit changing situations. God wants input from creaturely agents and does not control everything that happens. God invites us to participate with him in loving dialogue, to bring the future into being.[9]

John Sanders, who is a leading openness theologian, has delineated four major points in the model. First, God loves us and desires for us to

[9] Earlier essays of mine along these lines were entitled: 'The Need for a Scriptural and Therefore a Neo-Classical Theism' in K.S. Kantzer and S.N. Gundry (eds.), *Perspectives on Evangelical Theology: Papers from the Thirtieth Annual Meeting of the Evangelical Theological Society*, 37–42; 'Between Classical and Process Theism' in R. Nash (ed.), *Process Theology*, 313–27; and 'God Limits his Knowledge' in D. Basinger and R. Basinger (eds.), *Predestination and Free Will: Four Views of Divine Sovereignty and Human Freedom*, 143–62. The latter also contains expositions of the Augustinian model by J. Feinberg, of Thomism by N.L. Geisler, and of classical Arminianism by B. Reichenbach, together with interaction between the four scholars. For a reflection on how the idea of openness took shape in my mind over the years see C.H. Pinnock (ed.), *The Grace of God, The Will of Man*, 15–30.

enter into reciprocal relations with him and with our fellow creatures. The divine intention in creating us was for us to experience the triune love and respond to it with love of our own. In this, we would freely come to collaborate with God toward the achievement of God's goals. Second, God has sovereignly decided to make some of his actions contingent on our requests and actions. God establishes the project and elicits our collaboration in it. Hence there is conditionality in God, in that he truly responds to what we do. Third, God chooses to exercise a general rather than a meticulous providence, allowing space for us to operate and for God to be resourceful in working with it. Fourth, God granted us the libertarian freedom necessary for personal relationships of love to develop. God freely enters into give and take relations with us which are genuine and which entail risk-taking on his part, because we are capable of letting God down.[10]

According to the open view, God freely decided to be, in some respects, affected and conditioned by creatures and he established things in such a way that that some things he desires may not happen. For example, God may want everyone to receive his love but apparently not all do so. God does not control everything that happens but sovereignly decided to make a world in which creatures could respond to God and where he would make himself available for such relationships. Creation, then, is an open project with which God has decided to be open himself.[11]

Herein we glimpse, I believe, the true glory of God as the one who wills and is committed to creatures. It would be far off the mark to speak of it as a diminishing of God's reputation.[12] This is a God who creates a world that is not just a mechanical expression of his own purposes but an environment for other free, though finite, agents to exist with a degree of autonomy and a measure of real freedom. This is a God who loves being in covenant partnership with the creature and longs to draw us into a community of love, both with God and among ourselves. God's perfection is not to be all-controlling or to exist in majestic solitude or to be infinitely egocentric. On the contrary, God's fair beauty according to

---

[10] J. Sanders, *The God Who Risks: A Theology of Providence*, 282.

[11] D. Basinger clarifies the openness model within the larger category of free will theism and in contrast to both classical and process theism; see *The Case for Freewill Theism: A Philosophical Assessment*.

[12] Contra B.A. Ware, 'God's Lesser Glory: Open Theism's Diminutive Conception of Divine Providence'. Ware is able to describe the model quite fairly, see *God's Lesser Glory: The Diminished God of Open Theism*, ch. 3. At the same time, he writes, 'The God of the Bible is not the limited, passive, hand-wringing God open theism portrays,' 216.

Scripture is his own relationality as a triune community. It is God's gracious interactivity, not his hyper-transcendence and/or immobility,
which makes him so glorious. According to the gospel, God is free and
self-communicating love, not a solitary monad. He is not a supreme will
to power, but a will to community in which both life and power are
shared. He is the power whose very nature it is to give and receive love,
and his rule, as the triune God, is one of love and not force. The power of
God is creative, sacrificial and empowering, not coercive, and his glory
consists in sharing life with, not dominating, others. God is for us and
with us. He is not a metaphysical abstraction, but the one who makes his
presence felt – actively, responsively, relationally, dynamically, and
reciprocally. God is transcendent, but does not exist in isolation from
the world. He is unchangeable in character, but is not unchanging in his
relations with us.[13]

Conventional theology did not leave enough room for relationality in
God's essence. It favored a view of the divine nature as something in
which nothing accidental could inhere. While the creatures can be relational, God's essence cannot be involved in real relationships with a
changing world, lest it change too. Relations can be real on the side of
the creature, but not on the side of God, and not in a mutual way,
because that would introduce change into him. Thus it is hard for conventional theism to deal with a relational and personal God, with a God
really involved in the world, in short, with the God of the Bible. It has led
to thinking of God, in Walter Kasper's poignant phrase, when speaking
of what has become known in recent years as 'classical' theism, as 'a solitary narcissistic being, who suffers from his own completeness.'[14]

In the tradition there was an attempt to fuse two very different ideals
of divine perfection in what Donald Bloesch calls a biblical-classical synthesis.[15] H.P. Owen writes, 'As far as the western world is concerned,
(classical) theism has a double origin in the Bible and Greek philosophy.'[16] What took place was that the attributes of God contained in
Scripture were shaped and amplified under the influence of Greek

---

[13] See T. Tiessen's excellent summary of the openness model in the course of his
exposition of the alternative positions, *Providence and Prayer: How Does God
Work in the World?*, chs. 4–5. Here is a Reformed scholar who can set forth the
open view accurately and without rancor. May his tribe increase.
[14] W. Kasper, *The God of Jesus Christ*, 306. The term 'classical theism' is a
recent neologism that conveys more respect than is deserved and implies more
agreement among its exponents than there is. It is better to call it conventional,
a traditional view among others.
[15] D.G. Bloesch, *God the Almighty: Power, Wisdom, Holiness, Love*, ch. 8.
[16] H.P. Owen, *Concepts of Deity*, 1.

thought. On the one hand, there was a Hellenic ideal of God as absolute, timeless and unchangeable being, a view which assumes God to be unconditioned, unchanging, impassible and totally in control; a Being that cannot be affected by anything outside of itself. On the other hand, there was the biblical ideal of God as a dynamic, relational person; vulnerable, sympathetic, accessible and committed to relationships. This is the picture of a God who loves covenant and chooses dialogue over monologue. These two ideals, the Hellenic and the biblical, cannot really be fused successfully. A decision needs to be made whether to go with one or the other, with the philosophers or with God's self-disclosure in Jesus Christ.[17] The tendency of conventional theism is to deny the dynamism of the world in order to preserve the absoluteness of God. It is the result of a biblical/philosophical synthesis.[18]

I entitled the book *Most Moved Mover* because, even though for many it would be a little obscure, it contrasts what the Bible highlights as to the nature of God and what, in this case, Aristotle suggested as a representative Greek philosopher. Aristotle spoke of God as an unmoved mover, which contrasts sharply with the God of Abraham, Isaac, and Jacob. Aristotle believed God moves other beings by being an object of desire and thought, without moving itself. God serves as the final cause for worldly activities, while remaining completely unchangeable in itself. Echoing Plato, Aristotle denied any kind of change in God, because, he thought, any change in a perfect being would have to be change for the worse. The only activity, therefore, which God could engage in would be the 'activity' of self-contemplation. How very different is this immobile substance from the living God of biblical revelation. What different views of the divine perfection are found here! It requires us to decide whether God is perfect by virtue of unchangeability, as the philosopher says, or perfect by virtue of relationality, as the Bible indicates.

The traditional way of thinking about God has some appeal. Not only is it ancient, it portrays God as majestic and unchanging, far beyond the world, enthroned above the rough and tumble, untouched by turbulence and pain. But it is one sided in its preference for God's magnificent otherness over his loving condescension and it makes it difficult to speak adequately about a personal God. God is not like a stone

---

[17] C. Hartshorne calls attention to the different models of perfection in *Omnipotence and Other Theological Mistakes*, ch. 1; as does C.E. Gunton in *Becoming and Being: The Doctrine of God in Charles Hartshorne and Karl Barth*, ch. 1.

[18] G.F. O'Hanlon, *The Immutability of God in the Theology of Hans Urs von Balthasar*, 1.

pillar, in no way affected by the world and alien to real relatedness and reciprocity; God's sovereignty is not all-controlling such that everything is decided and historical reality is squashed. It is not helpful to think of divine eternity as timelessness, jeopardizing God's freedom to act in time. It is unsound to think of exhaustive foreknowledge, implying that every detail of the future is already decided. More justice can be done to Scripture to bring the truth of the living God into better theological expression.

Conventional theism is not a single model but comes in different versions. Thomism, for example, places emphasis on God's immutability and must be criticized for threatening real relationships, while Calvinism, on the other hand, guards the absolute sovereignty of God and has to be opposed for threatening the reality of creaturely actions. These represent different priorities within a basically shared commitment. But since it is the Calvinist model that is the form of conventional theism which one encounters most in the evangelical context, it will be the version most interacted with here. It is the model in which the omnicausality of God is central and in which God is seemingly the solo performer.

We ought to remember, however, that this tradition is multi-stranded and not uniform though. There are those who speak of themselves as truly Reformed, e.g. the Association of Confessing Evangelicals, there are in fact Calvinists who are not theological determinists, e.g. Hendrikus Berkhof, Vincent Brummer, Adrio König, Alvin Plantinga, Nicholas Wolterstorff and Kelly J. Clark.[19] There are many I talk to who are troubled by the Canons of the Synod of Dort (AD 1618–19) and its notions of God's giving and withholding of faith according to his eternal decree and of Christ's atonement being limited. Thus, a work of revision goes on in the tradition that is genuinely Calvinist. When the covenant between God and humankind is stressed, the element of partnership comes to the fore and works against determinism in the system. When God created us, he wanted more than an instrument, he wanted a covenant partner who could respond. God wanted to make promises that we by faith could hold him to. God who is always greater was willing to limit his own scope of activity in order to make room for the significant other, humanity. In this mode Calvinists are not obliged to be determinists.

Nevertheless, many Calvinists, especially among the conservative evangelicals, are theological determinists and they are the ones who dislike the openness model most intensely. Such determinism is what I

---

[19] K.J. Clark holds to libertarian human freedom, see *When Faith Is Not Enough*, 85–6; *Return to Reason*, 68–77.

myself learned from Calvin and from disciples like Charles Hodge, B.B. Warfield, Louis Berkhof, Cornelius Van Til, James I. Packer, R.C. Sproul and Paul Helm. It is the variety of Calvinism which not only I but many others have had to distance themselves from.

I do not presume to judge what Calvin really meant but I am alarmed by the omnicausality that is associated with his name and with some justification. Calvin seems to have taught that God wills and determines everything that happens in the world. He writes, 'Whatever happens in the universe is governed by God's incomprehensible plans.'[20] 'God so regulated all things that nothing takes place without his deliberation.'[21] 'Nothing is more absurd than that anything should happen without God's ordaining it.'[22] It is not just inanimate objects that are controlled by God, 'but also the plans and intentions of men.'[23] There are not multiplicities of agents, things occur ultimately because of 'the sole decision of God's will.'[24] 'God regulates all things according to his secret plan which depends solely upon itself.'[25] Things do not happen partly as a result of God's will and partly as a result of our wills, things happen because God ordains them. The reason God knows the future is because he decreed it. As the *Westminster Confession* puts it, 'God from all eternity did by the most wise and holy counsel of his will freely and unchangeably ordain whatsoever comes to pass.'[26] This is surely omnipotence without obfuscation and it is what openness theology has chiefly to oppose.[27]

This present book aims to re-present the open view of God in the light of many useful criticisms and a few fresh reflections. It aims at keeping the conversation alive and hopes to contribute further to it. Theologically, I see the need to highlight the relationality of God as Scripture presents it and hope that the openness model will help us communicate belief in God more intelligibly to people at large and liberate believers to love God more passionately.

---

[20] J. Calvin, *Institutes of the Christian Religion* I.,17.2.

[21] Ibid., I, 16.3.

[22] Ibid., I, 16.8.

[23] Ibid.

[24] Ibid., III, 23.4.

[25] Ibid., III, 23.7.

[26] *Westminster Confession*, 3.1.

[27] I should add that Augustine and Luther make the same point equally strongly and that Luther in *On the Bondage of the Will* explicitly denies human freedom in his refutation of Erasmus. One is not tilting at windmills in opposing a view that is so solidly rooted.

Sources of Controversy

Roger Olson was prescient in an early review of *The Openness of God* to ask

> How do American evangelical Christians handle theological diversity? Have we come of age enough to avoid heresy charges and breast-beating jeremiads in response to a new doctrinal proposal that is so conscientiously based on biblical reflection rather than on rebellious accommodation to modern thought? This may be the test.[28]

At first it seemed as if we had failed the test. Immediately following the review there appeared four responses which signaled deep hostility and which would set the tone for other reactions which would identify the openness model as heretical. Douglas Kelly charged us with denying the infinity of God and judged the book 'one of the saddest intellectual and spiritual retrogressions I have ever seen outside openly heterodox thinking;' Timothy George concluded that we had devised a 'user-friendly God who bears an uncanny resemblance to a late twentieth-century seeker.'[29]

There have been a lot of negative reviews in the ensuing years, complaining about various features of the model: e.g. too much immanence, too little transcendence; too great a polarization between sovereignty and freedom; a misunderstanding of traditional theism; too close to process theology; and the denial of exhaustive divine foreknowledge.[30] Only a few have expressed what C. Stephen Evans has written, 'The open God position is motivated by a desire to be faithful to the Bible and is consistent with both classical Christian orthodoxy and evangelical distinctives.'[31] At least in some quarters the call has gone out for a proper dialogue between open and conventional theists, a dialogue that is

---

[28] *Christianity Today* (9 January 1995), 30–4. The editors, having a sympathetic review in hand and anticipating fallout, invited four respondents with little tolerance for the position to comment, rendering Olson's hope for a charitable discussion unlikely from the start.

[29] Since 1995 *Christianity Today* has kept the issue alive, most recently in a dialogue between John Sanders and Chris Hall (January, 2001).

[30] T.L. Cross catalogues the criticisms contained in the reviews: 'The Rich Feast of Theology: Can Pentecostals Bring the Main Course or Only the Relish?', *Journal of Pentecostal Theology* 16 (2000), 30–1.

[31] Taken from the cover of G.A. Boyd, *God of the Possible: A Biblical Introduction to the Open View of God.* P. Yancey is himself an open theist, see 'Chess Master', *Christianity Today* (22 May 2000), 112.

beginning to take place.[32] In Terrance Tiessen's capable critique from a Calvinist standpoint there is no acrimony at all, even though he rejects the open view forcefully. This may be due, however, to the fact that Tiessen is a theologian whose work it is to consider options carefully he does not pretend to be a gatekeeper for the evangelical movement nor seek to stir up the emotional juices.[33]

Good relations ought to be possible since conventional and open theists both hold to what one might call 'basic biblical theism.' All of us hold to the fundamentals of orthodox theism, e.g. the immanent Trinity, the God-world distinction, God's actions in history, the goodness, unchangeableness, omnipotence, and omniscience of God, and the atoning death and resurrection of Jesus Christ. Our differences, which are real, are not new either but derive from an ancient debate between two streams of interpretation. On the one hand, there have always been 'free will theists,' beginning with the early fathers and developing into various Arminianisms. On the other hand, there has always been 'conventional', now called classical, theism, beginning with Augustine and opening out, for example, into Thomism and Calvinism. Openness theology is a form of free will theism and, therefore, receives a more positive reading within that tradition, while attracting the censure of the conventional, or immobility, theists. What we have here is a continuation of an age-old debate that should not stop now just because we have introduced some new interpretations into the discussion.[34] In fact, by doing

---

[32] An editorial in *Christianity Today* (7 February 2000) calls for dialogue and a cessation of hostilities. See 'God vs. God: Two competing theologies vie for the future of evangelicalism', 34–5. A joint article is planned for the near future to be written by Chris Hall and John Sanders. The conciliatory editorial evoked, however, an ominous letter to the editors (3 April) from Roger Nicole of Reformed Theological Seminary, Orlando which put *Christianity Today* itself on notice: 'It is unfortunate if the holders of the heretical (sic) view of the 'openness of God' could now boast about the 'openness of *Christianity Today*.' David F. Wells also deplores the openness of *Christianity Today* to a discussion of these issues; see *Modern Reformation* 9 (July 2000), 10–2. Discussions are, however, taking place even in the staunchly conservative circles of the Evangelical Theological Society (USA) and other academic settings and hopefully will not be stopped by the fearful gatekeepers.

[33] Tiessen, *Providence and Prayer.*

[34] John Sanders points to the fact that the early Greek fathers affirmed God's dynamic, responsive relationships with creatures and allowed himself to be affected by them in a way that Augustine could not admit in *God Who Risks*, 142–51. The Orthodox Churches have always rejected any doctrine of grace that infringes upon human freedom: T. (now Kallistos) Ware, *The Orthodox Church*, 226–7.

so, we have made Arminian thinking sharper and clearer and the only and obvious alternative to the conventional options. Our Calvinist critics call it 'consistent' Arminianism, a judgment I am not inclined to reject.

The openness model is not seen as a strange innovation outside the evangelical subculture. It is not alone in positing libertarian freedom or divine self-limitation of power to make room for the creature. It is not unusual for contemporary theologians to speak of the divine self-limitation or kenosis whereby God freely chooses to allow the world to impact him without, however, losing his lordship over it. It is not unheard of for people to think of God, having created the world and given it freedom, to be actively working within the world without dominating it. Indeed the openness model echoes many themes of the theology of hope, which recognizes a God who limits himself in creating a world which has the capacity to affect him without his losing his lordship over it. It thinks of a God who is not swallowed up by his relationship with the world but, having created a significant reality outside of himself, now works within it as the power of love without overpowering it. It sees evils happening because the world is not yet God's kingdom but where in the end God will cancel the chaos and make the world his home. Many today adopt an interactive view of God based on the divine choice. God voluntarily commits himself to the welfare of creation.[35]

In terms of reaction to the openness model from within the evangelical coalition, it ranges from warm but not uncritical appreciation on the Arminian side to profound dismay on the Calvinist side. Beginning with the more appreciative hearers, they are mostly found in Wesleyan, Arminian and Pentecostal circles of evangelicalism that affirm human freedom and deny absolute divine control. There is a natural affinity there.[36] The openness model belongs to the free will theistic traditions

---

[35] Jürgen Moltmann, in particular, affirms the main points of the openness model, including present divine knowledge. See R. Bauckham, *The Theology of Jürgen Moltmann*, 15–7. N. Murphy and G.F.R. Ellis refer to kenotic concepts of God like their own, *On the Moral Nature of the Universe: Theology, Cosmology, and Ethics*, ch. 8. In the same vein, K. Ward, *Religion and Creation*, 284. It is safe to say that Karl Barth would not have approved of any trend toward synergism; Tiessen, *Providence and Prayer*, ch. 10.

[36] It is not an accident that the memoir on my work was written by a Wesleyan, B.L. Callen, and was published in cooperation with The Wesleyan Theological Society, *Clark H. Pinnock: Journey Toward Renewal. An Intellectual Biography*. The openness model has intellectual roots in Wesleyan-Arminian thinking prior to the rise of process thought in the work of biblical theologian A. Clarke (d.1832) and of philosopher L.D. McCabe (d.1897). See L.D. McCabe, *Divine*

that are commonly called, not altogether accurately, Arminianism, harking back to the work of Jacob Arminius. His was a theology that had its setting in the Reformed debates of seventeenth-century Holland and which has developed from there. It is a position that holds to God's creation, for the sake of loving relations, of genuinely free humans, his universal love for all humanity and his desire to save all. It opposes a predestination from which conditionality is removed and rejects restricted redemption. Arminius broke with the classical view of the nature of God in holding that what God foreknows is conditioned by what creatures decide to do and that God genuinely responds to them as significantly free beings.[37]

The open view differs from the classical Arminians', however, in its understanding of certain of the divine attributes. Wesley and Arminius, for example, held to the traditional definitions of unchangeability, eternity and omniscience, which openness theists think jeopardize genuinely real divine/human relationships. Thus, openness theism calls for a more radical modification of the tradition than classical Arminianism does.[38] According to openness theism, for example, the future is partly settled and partly unsettled, partly determined and partly undetermined and, therefore, partly unknown even to God and it holds that God himself has a temporal aspect. Thus, the Arminian initiative, itself already an important revision in the conventional doctrine of God, is taken a step further by openness theism, in the direction, we think, of greater coherence. Calvinist critics who see us making a bad theology worse use this against us and it remains to be seen whether the traditional Arminians, and Molinists, will like being grouped with open theism in this way. We agree about libertarian freedom and the real interactions of God with humankind, but are they willing to overlook a significant difference like

---

Footnote 36 (*Continued*) *Nescience of Future Contingencies a Necessity.* Less favorable to my work is T. Gray and C. Sinkinson (eds.), *Reconstructing Theology: A Critical Assessment of the Theology of Clark Pinnock.*
[37] On the Arminian moves, see R.E. Olson, *The Story of Christian Theology: Twenty Centuries of Tradition and Reform*, ch. 28; R.A. Muller, *God, Creation, and Providence in the Thought of Jacob Arminius*; and J.I. Packer, 'Arminianisms' in W.R. Godfrey and J.L. Boyd III (eds.), *Through Christ's Word*, ch. 9. Jack Cottrell has written a classically Arminian rendition of 'The Nature of the Divine Sovereignty' in Pinnock (ed.), *Grace of God*, 97–119. See also R.E. Olson, 'Don't Hate Me Because I'm Arminian', *Christianity Today* (6 September 1999), 87–94.
[38] In recognition of this fact, perhaps I should have entitled my essay: 'From Augustine to Arminius and Beyond' in Pinnock (ed.), *Grace of God*, ch. 1. See also Ware, *God's Lesser Glory*, ch. 2.

the one concerning divine foreknowledge? On that detail the Arminians may not receive the open view. Indeed, Thomas Oden has dubbed it heretical because of that very point.[39] They may still prefer a C.S. Lewis who affirms libertarian freedom but relies on God's timelessness and exhaustive foreknowledge in his system to help God stay in control. He too would have grumbled, not at the open view as a form of free will theism, but at the other adjustments.[40] It may be that the Arminians were slow off the mark to criticize the open view of God because they felt a great affinity with it and did not want to add to the pain that the Calvinists were quick to inflict upon it. I suspect that a wave of Arminian criticism is yet to come.[41] This outcome also concerns me because, if the Arminian evangelicals decide to line with the Calvinistic evangelicals in opposition, there is little future for the open view in evangelicalism.

The real opposition to the open view of God, however, comes from certain Calvinists within evangelicalism, whom Karl Barth called neo-Calvinists when discussing the work of one of them, namely, the American Presbyterian, Loraine Boettner.[42] Barth, a European theologian himself, was part of the developing Reformed tradition that had moved itself beyond certain features of Calvinist thought such as double predestination. Boettner was the type of Calvinist who I term paleo-Calvinist because he had not moved beyond the *Westminster Confession*. His name symbolizes the scholastic Reformed roots of fundamentalist evangelicalism that lie deep within the orthodoxy of the old Princeton Seminary. It is characterized by a tight system of ideas held to be essential to the faith. At its most extreme its proponents equate true Christianity with Calvinist orthodoxy and exclude from the faith, not only openness of God thinkers, but the whole free will theistic tradition. To them, Arminians are tolerable only because they are confused, and openness theologians are not tolerated because they are clear in their rejection of theological determinism.[43]

---

[39] T. Oden, *Christianity Today* (9 February 1998), 46. W.L. Craig (an Arminian and a Molinist) is also displeased with this move; see *The Only Wise God: The Compatibility of Divine Foreknowledge and Human Freedom*.

[40] B. Worden thinks that John Wesley would turn over in his grave if he knew he had a follower like me, *Christian News* (4 July 2000), 10.

[41] Consider R.E. Picirilli, 'Foreknowledge, Freedom, and the Future', *Journal of the Evangelical Theological Society* 43 (2000), 259–71. Typically J.T. Murphree agrees with much of the open view except for its critique of divine timelessness and exhaustive foreknowledge: *Divine Paradoxes: A Finite View of an Infinite God*.

[42] K. Barth, *Church Dogmatics*, II/2, 36.

[43] See G. Dorrien, *The Remaking of Evangelical Theology*, ch. 1.

To understand the force of this reaction to openness theism, one must realize that twentieth-century North American evangelicalism has been dominated by the Presbyterian paradigm and that the debate, therefore, concerns political power as well as theological truth. This party has grown accustomed to dealing with Arminians in their midst and have ceased to regard them as much of a threat. After all, the latter hold to a number of items in the conventional package of divine attributes that ought to lead them back to traditional theism. But the openness model, a more radical version of free will theism, is a different kettle of fish. Being a more coherent alternative to Calvinism, it is a nightmare for them. It pulls threads of the old model more effectively and threatens to unravel the whole garment. Openness theology must be opposed more radically because it poses much more of threat. (I actually agree with the paleo-Calvinists about that.) As in politics, where winning however you do it is the only goal, so in this context the gatekeepers of orthodoxy will resort to anything. Apart from scare tactics and lying, the usual tactic is to put openness theology down by creating a sense of outrage. The trick is to identify your own version of traditional theism, be it Geisler's Thomism or Sproul's Calvinism, with orthodoxy and proceed to associate open-ness thinking either with semi-heretical Arminianism or, better still, with process theology, a recognized heresy.[44]

The rhetoric has been shrill. Don Carson writes, 'I have to say, with regret, that this book is the most consistently inadequate treatment of Scripture and historical theology dealing with the doctrine of God that I have ever seen from the hands of serious evangelical writers.'[45] Norman Geisler speaks of it as a 'dangerous trend within evangelical circles' and 'a significant deviation from the God of the Bible and traditional Christian theology which has dangerous consequences for the historical faith.'[46] In a British review, Frederick Leahy wrote, 'We have before us a hybrid theology — ultra-Arminianism grafted onto a Socinian-root stock and planted in the barren soil of human autonomy.'[47] From others we hear about a coming evangelical crisis and how nothing less than the Bible and the gospel are at stake.[48] Robert Morey even speaks of 'the

---

[44] The animus is so strong that practically anything can be charged, e.g. the open view presents a user friendly God, an ignorant God, or a God unheard of by anyone before. See the editorial in *World* (June 12, 2000), 26f.
[45] D.A. Carson, *The Gagging of God: Christianity Confronts Pluralism*, 215.
[46] N.L. Geisler, *Creating God in the Image of Man? The New 'Open' View of God – Neotheism's Dangerous Drift*, 11–2.
[47] F.S. Leahy, 'God's Coming Identity Crisis', *Review NOW* (April 1997). See also J.H. Armstrong (ed.), *The Coming Evangelical Crisis*.
[48] Ibid.

finite god of evangelical processianism.'[49] The Southern Baptist Convention meeting in Atlanta, 1999, repudiated the open view and reaffirmed
its own belief in conventional theism. The title of a recent lectureship by
an able Baptist critic reads, 'God's Lesser Glory: Open Theism's Diminutive Conception of Divine Providence.'[50] Bruce Ware writes

> Nothing less than the uncontested deity of God, his absolute lordship over
> all space and time, his universal and inviolable sovereignty, his flawlessly
> wise and meticulous providence, his undiminished and infinite perfection,
> and his majestic and incomparable glory have been compromised by open
> theism. We have here a different God, not merely a different version of God.
> For the sake of the glory that is God's alone we have no choice but to reject
> the openness model.[51]

The attacks and hostility never seems to end.[52] It astonishes me that
people can defend the 'glory' of God so vehemently when that glory
includes God's sovereign authorship of every rape and murder, his
closing down the future to any meaningful creaturely contribution, and
his holding people accountable for deeds he predestined them to do and
they could not but do.

Getting closer to the bone, R.C. Sproul and John Piper, in a taped
discussion, state that they regard the open view of God to be pagan, anti-
Christian, and blasphemous. Sproul states, 'Clark Pinnock is
not a believer – I would not have fellowship with him.' He writes else-
where, 'This fascination with the openness of God is an assault, not
merely on Calvinism, or even on classical theism, but on Christianity

---

[49] R.A. Morey, *Battle of the Gods: The Gathering Storm in Modern Evangelicalism*, ch. 7.

[50] Ware, 'God's Lesser Glory' (The Bueermann-Champion Lectureship) was
followed by *God's Lesser Glory*. The book, he says, is unkind to open theism
but not unkind to open theists, 9. It begins ominously with 'Why You Should Be
Concerned' in ch. 1.
  Though his aim is to refute the open view of God as such, the book is mostly a
criticism of the open view's understanding of one particular item, God's knowledge. This is because Ware believes that the major features of the open view all
come up in relation to it, 65. Indeed, the issue makes the open view and his
paleo-Calvinism the only two real options with a coherent position, 41–2.

[51] Ibid., 41. Ware is engaging Sanders' study, *God Who Risks*. See also A.B.
Canaday, 'Putting God at Risk: A Critique of John Sander's View of Providence', *Trinity Journal* 20 (1999), 131–63.

[52] The *Southern Baptist Journal of Theology* 4 (summer, 2000) considers openness pernicious, dangerous and harmful, 4. Ware says it is 'contrary to Scripture
and detrimental to the health of the church' in *God's Lesser Glory*, 9.

itself.'[53] Stackhouse speaks of this group of extreme Calvinists as almost cultic in claiming infallibility for their own positions and presuming to speak on behalf of all evangelicals. He asks for less arrogance and energy devoted to sorting out who are the true evangelicals and who are the pretenders, deviants and apostates.[54] Packer speaks of entrenched intellectualists for whom orthodoxy is all. They show little warmth in the battle for mental correctness and relationally they are remote.[55] One of their number, Albert Mohler, writes, 'The question is whether evangelicals will affirm and worship the sovereign and purposeful God of the Bible, or shift their allegiance to the limited God of the modern megashift.'[56] McGregor Wright considers openness an attack on the faith.[57] Paul R. House and Gregory A. Thornbury say that 'American Christianity is currently engaged in a crucial debate over the doctrine of God' and that 'nothing less than the biblical, orthodox doctrines of God and of salvation are at stake.'[58] We are not the only victims of harshness at the hands of establishment evangelicals. F.F. Bruce reports how H.L. Ellison's life was ruined by the sharp criticisms he received for writing a thoughtful essay on biblical inspiration.[59]

Even more moderately Reformed theologians weigh in with severe criticisms. Donald G. Bloesch, while appreciating aspects of the model, believes that it goes too far in the direction of making the revealed mysteries too transparent.[60] Millard Erickson writes, 'All in all, although this is in many ways a creative theology, we conclude that the difficulties involved with it strongly outweigh its strengths.'[61] Gabriel Fackre

[53] R.C.Sproul, *Willing to Believe: The Controversy over Free Will*, 143. As I have sought a reason why such critics can be so unkind and unfair, I have wondered if theologians do not tend to become the picture of the God that they espouse.
[54] See, J.G. Stackhouse (ed.), *Evangelical Futures: A Conversation on Theological Method*, 49–50, 57.
[55] J.I. Packer, 'An Introduction to Systematic Spirituality', *CRUX* 26 (March, 1990), 2–8.
[56] A. Mohler, 'The Battle over the Doctrine of God', *The Southern Baptist Journal of Theology* 1 (1997), 15.
[57] R.K. McGregor, *No Place for Sovereignty: What's Wrong with Free Will Theism*.
[58] P.R. House and G.A. Thornbury (eds.), *Who Will Be Saved? Defending the Biblical Understanding of God, Salvation, and Evangelism*, 15.
[59] F.F. Bruce, *In Retrospect: Remembrance of Things Past*, 187–8.
[60] D.G. Bloesch, *God the Almighty*, 254–60.
[61] M. Erickson, *God the Father Almighty: A Contemporary Exploration of the Divine Attributes*, 88, 92; also, *The Evangelical Left: Encountering Postconservative Theology Today*, ch. 4.

speaks of the promise and peril of an open view of God.[62] Gerald Bray too is very unfavorable.[63] Tiessen, though complementary to openness and eminently fair, takes it to be extremely unsound.[64] Tony Gray says concerning it, 'God does not play dice.'[65]

To understand the heat of the criticism from this quarter, one must remember the tension which has long existed between scholastic Calvinism and the more pietistic elements of the evangelical coalition and the fact that the former have always felt they had the right to define the movement theologically. This means there can be peace so long as the Reformed party is allowed to set the standards intellectually. Viewed in this way, the challenge of the open view of God is intolerable and must be snuffed out. The ugliness, the rancor and the rage should not surprise us when a theological issue has become a political one too.[66]

Part of me understands why there is such a fuss. Theologically the issues run deep. I also accept that the burden of proof lies on the open view insofar as it puts forward new ideas. But part of me does not understand. Don't we all, as biblical Christians, live as if the open view were true? We have real relations with God, whatever theory we hold. Part of me wants to play defense because of the harsh attacks, but part of me wants to play offense because the open view of God offers the church such a treasure. It accentuates, not diminishes, how truly glorious God is.

Besides the older players in the debate, the classical Arminians who are cautiously positive and the paleo-Calvinists who are extremely negative, there is a whole new large group called 'Christians in renewal' who enjoy a very relational and intimate spirituality and who, when they hear of it, often resonate with the open view of God. Their presence on the scene may make this a truly new debate and more than a rehash of the old one. As an open theist, I hope that the Pentecostals will opt for this dynamic model of God.

---

[62] G. Fackre, 'An Evangelical Megashift? The promise and peril of an 'open' view of God', *Christian Century* (3 May 1995), 484–7. In most respects, however, Fackre adopts the open view of God himself. See *The Christian Story: A Narrative Interpretation of Basic Christian Doctrine*, 250–61.

[63] G. Bray, *The Personal God: Is the Classical Understanding of God Tenable?*

[64] Tiessen, *Providence and Prayer*, part 2.

[65] T. Gray, 'God Does Not Play Dice', *Themelios* 24 (1999), 21–34.

[66] On the dominance of the scholastic party in the movement, see G. Marsden, 'The Evangelical Denomination' in G. Marsden (ed.), *Evangelicalism in Modern America*, xvi.

Indicating the Method

My approach to theological method is bi-polar. I believe that theology ought to be faithful and timely and have a double thrust. I must state the truth of the Christian message on the one hand (chs. 1–2) and open up the truth to the present generation on the other (chs. 3–4). We want to capture the truth of the revelatory foundations, while at the same time being conscious of the situation of contemporary hearers. As Paul Tillich put it, theology ought to satisfy two basic needs: to state the truth of the Christian message and interpret the truth for every generation.[67] Theology, then, moves back and forth between two poles, between the eternal truth of the revelatory foundations and the temporal situation in which it is offered and received. It is not easy to balance the two demands. Some theologians sacrifice aspects of the truth, while others refuse to speak to the contemporary situation. Some even manage to fail on both counts at once because they do not get the truth right and cannot communicate it effectively either! In the case of the doctrine of God, it is common to confuse the truth of the message with a temporal expression of it and impose that framework on an uncomprehending generation. Opinions of some earlier time can be absolutized at the expense of biblical truth and the needs of effective mission. This is what the open view of God is up against, I fear.

The four chapters consult a quadrilateral of sources in the attempt to be bi-polar: the Bible (ch. 1), tradition (ch. 2), reason (ch. 3), and experience (ch. 4). To be more precise, I adhere to the rule of Scripture within a trilateral hermeneutic.[68] First, as an evangelical, my primary commitment is to Scripture not to tradition, reason, or experience because I believe that any authentically theological model must have biblical backing and resonance. I hold the Bible to be the primary norm for theology in the midst of the other sources.[69] As will be noted, the open view of God takes Scripture seriously and does not set aside important biblical metaphors just because they do not fit the traditional system. Everyone would like to have the Bible on their side, but it will become obvious how difficult it is to justify the traditional model biblically in certain

---

[67] P. Tillich, *Systematic Theology* I, 3.
[68] See W.S. Gunter, et al., *Wesley and the Quadrilateral: Renewing the Conversation*; and D. Thorsen, *The Wesleyan Quadrilateral: Scripture, Tradition, Reason and Experience as a Model of Evangelical Theology*. A. Dulles ably discusses the contribution of the sources to the work of theology from a Catholic standpoint; see *The Craft of Theology: From Symbol to System*.
[69] C.H. Pinnock, *The Scripture Principle*; and *Tracking the Maze: Finding our Way Through Modern Theology From An Evangelical Perspective*, part 3.

important respects. This is because, just as Mormons read the biblical teaching through the lens of Joseph Smith's revelations, so conventional theists read it with the help of the great Hellenic philosophers.[70]

In terms of biblical interpretation, I give particular weight to narrative and to the language of personal relationships in it. Biblical history is real history, not a charade. It describes genuine personal interactions, not manipulation. I seek to recover the dynamism of biblical revelation. The story involves real drama and is a unique vehicle of truth and a powerful witness to the interactivity of God. It lifts up God's self-involvement in history and, supremely, the decision to become incarnate in Jesus Christ. Too often we have privileged the non-historical and supposedly non-metaphorical propositional material. But we have to take it all into account. As McGrath puts it, returning to the narrative of Scripture 'offers an invaluable catalyst for the cathartic process of purging evangelicalism of the lingering influence of the Enlightenment and reaching behind the Enlightenment to recover more authentically evangelical approaches to the role of Scripture in Christian life and thought.'[71] The Bible offers a narrative that tells of Yahweh, the living God, who seeks loving relationships with creatures that are open, dynamic and personal. We must take seriously how God is depicted in these stories and resist reducing important metaphors to mere anthropomorphic or accommodated language. God's revelation is anthropomorphic through and through. We could not grasp any other kind. We must take it all seriously, if not always literally.

What I oppose is the proof-texting method of evangelical rationalism which disregards narrative but plucks texts out of context in support of traditional notions and a system already in hand.[72] Loraine Boettner declares it as his purpose to lift up the Calvinistic system and prove it biblical and rational. Can you imagine Calvin saying that? Surely he would have said that it is to Scripture alone that we must be responsible.[73] Were one to read the Bible as a depository of timeless truths in support of a system, it would be possible to find verses to show that the Bible teaches practically anything. The true meaning of a text is not discerned out of context and away from the development of its meaning within Scripture itself. Biblical language is often metaphorical and

---

[70] F.J. Beckwith and S.E. Parrish, *The Mormon Concept of God: A Philosophical Analysis*, 109–10.

[71] A. McGrath, *A Passion for Truth: The Intellectual Coherence of Evangelicalism*, 116. Also S.J. Grenz, *Revisioning Evangelical Theology: A Fresh Agenda for the 21ˢᵗ Century*, ch. 5.

[72] Ibid., ch. 3.

[73] Barth, *Church Dogmatics* II/2, 36–7.

poetic, and although the Bible contains propositional statements, too much concentration on this aspect can lead to distorted interpretations.[74]

Among other hermeneutical presuppositions, I accept diversity among the biblical witnesses and recognize the dialogical character of the Bible. Being open to its overall drift, I try to enter into the struggle for truth that is going on there. The Bible does not speak with a single voice; there is dialogue between the different voices. The writings contain a long and complex search for the mind of God and in this struggle various points of view compete and interact. In constructing a doctrinal model, therefore, it is important to remember that the Bible is a complex work by many authors whose views may vary and that the text is open to various plausible interpretations. We should listen to the Bible as we would listen to a conversation; we are not meant to quarry Scripture for proof texts. This means I cannot claim that the Bible teaches the open view of God or any other subject simply and straightforwardly such that there is no counter testimony which probes and questions and objects.[75] For this and other reasons I look to the Holy Spirit in approaching the treasures of Scripture, praying that God's breath will make it a living word and the source of fresh insight. Scripture is inexhaustibly rich and, when approached prayerfully with new questions, yields new insights.[76]

Moving to the second source, tradition is important (ch. 2) because theology ought not to be biblical in an isolated way. Scripture may be *prima* for theology but it is not *sola* because tradition plays a role in interpretation. Theology needs to maintain continuity with the historic faith of the church. Conclusions of the past are important and alert us to fundamentals, promising directions and possible pitfalls. God has revealed himself in human history and these encounters lead to further encounters with the community in other times and places. The Spirit has proceeded from Christ to continue interpreting his saving work worldwide, and the biblical revelation gives rise to an interpretive tradition

---

[74] Dulles, *Craft of Theology*, 71–2.

[75] W. Brueggemann speaks of Israel's counter-testimony cross examining Israel's core testimony in *Theology of the Old Testament: Testimony, Dispute, Advocacy*, part 2.

[76] On the dynamism of word and Spirit, see D.G. Bloesch, *Holy Scripture: Revelation, Inspiration and Interpretation*, ch. 6; R. Hays, *Echoes of Scripture in the Letters of Paul*, ch. 5; R.N. Longenecker, *New Wine into Fresh Wineskins*, ch. 7; G.D. Fee, *Listening to the Spirit in the Text*; C.H. Pinnock, 'Biblical Texts: Past and Future Meanings', *Journal of the Evangelical Theological Society* 43 (2000), 71–81, and *Flame of Love: A Theology of the Holy Spirit*, ch. 7.

without which the faith could become petrified. We need to be energetic in verbalizing God's salvation in such a way that it becomes intelligible in other times and places. We receive God's word from others but equally must pass it on ourselves.[77]

Of course, the process of interpretation is not infallible; there have been changes and reforms in understanding. From time to time, barnacles have had to be removed from tradition for the sake of tradition, if it is to be kept viable. The Reformation called for such changes. While traditions are important, so are fresh insights. Tradition does not give us all that we need; Scripture always has more to offer. Time and time again the Bible has acted as a guiding, correcting and liberating counter-authority to tradition, and thus stands above it. Scripture must always be our guide and tradition must be oriented and re-oriented to the gospel. That may mean taking a new interpretive step, even a step not taken before. Human traditions, while needed to render the word of God intelligible, must be continually scrutinized for soundness and relevance. They are subject to correction and updating. How the open view fits into the flow of tradition will be a subject for chapter two.

Third, reason also has a role to play in theology; and helping us formulate what we want to say (ch. 3). Serious theologians value coherence and intelligibility in their work. They want, as far as possible, a model of God that is not only biblical and traditional but also timely and compelling. They want the Christian message to be understood by people in the present day. They want their concepts to be internally consistent and coherent with other beliefs that they hold. We must try to make the truth understandable if we are to communicate effectively because what is contradictory is not meaningful. A theologian who does not make sense will be in no position to criticize other proposals when they do not make sense. I, therefore, value reason in my theology and the contributions that philosophy, ancient and modern, can make to it.

The title of Olson's early review of the openness model was 'Has God Been Held Hostage by Philosophy?' The title implied that philosophy might be doing more than just helping theology express itself; it might actually be calling the shots. Thomistic thinking has done so in Catholic theology until recently, as process thought does for some modern Protestant thinking. One must be careful when drawing upon a philosophical conceptuality in theology. It is one thing for philosophy to provide categories to help us say what we want to say on the basis of revelation, but quite another thing to adopt a worldview that has been developed apart from revelation and allow it to dominate us

---

[77] H. Berkhof, *Christian Faith*, 91–100.

hermeneutically. There has to be discernment about which philosophical resources serve the proclamation and which hinder it. At the same time, there is no need for pessimism. If philosophy can play a role getting theology off track, it can also play a role in getting things back on track. Indeed, many today say they get more help from Christian philosophers than they do from theologians because, I would say, the latter, if they are evangelicals, seem to be more nervous about the truth and more defensive than the former. Nevertheless, for purposes of theology, not all philosophical systems are equally valid, so let us enter with care into dialogue with philosophy, ancient and modern, and make the best use of it that we can.[78]

Fourth, with respect to experience, theology should be concerned about existential fit and the practical adequacy of a theological model to meet the demands of life (ch. 4). I think one of the strengths of the openness model is its high degree of relevance to real life situations, confirming as it does deep human intuitions that our choices are not predetermined and the future is not altogether settled. It releases people to meaningfully live their lives. As individuals we are significant in God's eyes, he loves us and the things we do and say, the decisions and choices we make, and our prayers all help shape the future. Ironically, the open view resonates even in the lives of those who do not believe in it. It is no small point in favor of the openness model that it is difficult to live life in any other way than the way it describes, which may help to explain why the model has a simple appeal and why the alternatives are threatened outside the area of abstract thought. Believers experience Christianity, and life itself, in dynamic free will and personal terms and will find attractive a model that affirms our human reality and imposes no existential drag. Paul asks a question of the Galatians, 'Doesn't your experience teach you anything?' (Gal. 3:4)

Given the interest surrounding the model and the continuing debates about it, I thought it opportune to revisit key issues and address some of the questions that have arisen. The plan is, having taken up personal dimensions in the preface and mapped out a theological setting in the introduction, to revisit the main points, re-assess the evidence and soundness of the arguments, and take up objections. Thus the task is fourfold and involves re-considering:

1. The biblical basis of the model.
2. The problem of the pagan/biblical synthesis.
3. The philosophical aspects.
4. The existential fit.

---

[78] W. Hasker makes the point that if philosophers can perform negatively they can also perform positively. Pinnock, et al., *Openness*, 126.

In this book I want to celebrate the self-revelation of God in Jesus Christ, introduce reform into Christian theology, communicate effectively in a more timely way, and present a God with whom people can relate because he upholds their own creaturely significance. In a nutshell, the open view of God proposes to give a more serious reading to biblical metaphors and lift up from them a more dynamic and relational model of God, which we believe is more intelligible and practical than conventional thinking.

Whether the open view will succeed in becoming widely accepted as a model is far from certain. After all, it is viewed as a serious threat among certain Calvinists because they see it as a more coherent alternative to their own view, while, at the same time, it is controversial among Arminians for sacrificing exhaustive divine foreknowledge, which they appeal to in order to secure greater divine control over history that they feel the need of. So I do not know what will happen. To be accepted, the open view would have to overcome both the Calvinistic charge that it is heretical and the Arminian suspicion that it has gone too far. Thus the odds are probably against wide acceptance. At least it makes for a good topic in the Didsbury series of lectures.

Chapter One

The Scriptural Foundations

Christian theology celebrates the God who has revealed himself in Jesus Christ as attested in Scripture. To be sound, theology (the open view of God or any view) must be true to the biblical witness as primary source. Some critics say that openness theologians do not care about biblical teaching but rely on philosophical ideas and contemporary experience.[1] Were it true, the position would be in ruins, but it is far from true. Tradition, philosophy and experience are important sources but of greatest importance is Holy Scripture and whether the model is consonant with it. Millard Erickson, a critic, admits concerning the open view of God that 'there is a genuine attempt to be biblical.'[2] Dramatic proof of this can be found in John Sanders' book *The God Who Risks*, where a hundred pages are dedicated to close exegesis, a fact often overlooked by his critics.[3]

In terms of the Bible, the open view of God lifts up the personal nature of God. It looks at Yahweh's desire for loving relationships and covenant partnerships. It seems God did not create the world in order to exercise total control over it. Rather, he wants to enjoy the loving relationships – mutual, reciprocal and give-and-take – that are possible if it is not controlled. Far from a totally unchanging and all-determining absolute Being, the Bible presents God as a personal agent who creates and acts, wills and plans, loves and values in relation to covenant partners. God is often presented as the husband of his people and father of children, who nurtures, raises, and calls them to participate with him

---

[1] R.A. Morey writes, 'Modern processians do not even bother to examine Scripture as we have done. Since the Bible is not authoritative to them, why should they bother? They pride themselves on not proof texting. Indeed, since they have no texts to prove their position, what else can they do?' *Battle of the Gods*, 297. D.F. Wells (in a letter dated 24 July 2000) says it is 'not even close to being biblical'.

[2] Erickson, *Father Almighty*, 84.

[3] Sanders, *God Who Risks*, chs. 3–4.

dynamically in an open future. This is not the picture of the domination of a creator over creatures but the picture of a longing for loving fellowship with created persons.

It may turn out that it is the conventional, not the openness model, which has trouble with the Bible. It is hard to avoid the impression that, whereas openness theists are comfortable with biblical terms such as love, patience, wisdom and repentance, traditional theists prefer abstract philosophical terms like aseity, simplicity, immutability and impassibility. I hope it will become apparent that the open view of God is at least as biblical as its competition, maybe more so.[4]

The Self-Disclosure of a Personal God

For Christians the knowledge of God comes through his self-disclosure in:

1. The history of Israel, e.g. in the promise to Abraham, the revelation of his name to Moses, the deliverance of Israel from bondage, the giving of the law, and the preaching of prophets.
2. And especially in the life, death and resurrection of Jesus Christ, who is God's Word incarnate in a human life and through whom, Christians believe, God has taken the initiative to freely make his identity and purposes known to all humankind.

This revelation takes the form of interpersonal communication and frees us to see the world as created and redeemed by God. We get to know God, as we get to know other persons because God voluntarily makes himself known by the things he does and the promises he makes. Thus, God's revelation comes to us through a narrative that discloses God as an agent who acts in the world, revealing his character and purposes. This is the root metaphor. God is a person with a name. God acts and interacts, engages and suffers.[5]

Karl Barth captures the importance of this when he writes

---

[4] By way of comparison, consider N.L. Geisler's struggle to defend a Thomistic reading of the Bible on the doctrine of God in *Creating God*, ch. 4.

[5] On the gospel as 'eucatastrophe' and best story ever told, see Pinnock, *Tracking the Maze*, part 3. Personalists like H.H. Farmer see the essence of religion as a response to the ultimate as personal. On personalism in theology, see C. Partridge, *H.H. Farmer's Theological Interpretation of Religion: Towards a Personalistic Theology of Religions*.

Who God is and what it is to be divine is something we have to learn where God has revealed Godself. We may believe that God can and must only be absolute in contrast to all that is relative, exalted in contrast to all that is lowly, active in contrast to all suffering, inviolable in contrast to all temptation, transcendent in contrast to all immanence, and therefore divine in contrast to everything human, in short that God can and must be only the Wholly Other. But such beliefs are shown to be quite untenable, corrupt, and pagan, by the fact that God does in fact be and do this in Jesus Christ.[6]

The gospel commits us to a new way of understanding God. It requires a metaphysical revolution because in Jesus Christ we encounter a God who changes for our sake and suffers on our behalf. We are led to speak of God as one who humbles himself and proves to be perfect in his changing as well as in his not-changing. In the Greek world, perfection was associated with transcendence of time, change, and suffering, but in the gospel God acts in events and identifies with temporal history.

The God of the gospel is not the god of philosophy, at least not of Hellenic philosophy. The God and Father of Jesus Christ is compassionate, suffering, and victorious love. The god of philosophy is immutable, timeless and apathetic. We must speak boldly for the sake of the gospel: Augustine was wrong to have said that God does not grieve over the suffering of the world; Anselm was wrong to have said that God does not experience compassion; Calvin was wrong to have said that biblical figures that convey such things are mere accommodations to finite understanding. For too long pagan assumptions about God's nature have influenced theological reflection. Our thinking needs to be reformed in the light of the self-revelation of God in the gospel and we must stop attributing to God qualities that undermine God's own self-disclosure. Let us not treat the attributes of God independently of the Bible but view the biblical metaphors as reality-depicting descriptions of the living God, whose very being is self-giving love. When we do so, God's unity will not be viewed as a mathematical oneness but as a unity that includes diversity; God's steadfastness will not be seen as a deadening immutability but constancy of character that includes change; God's power will not be seen as raw omnipotence but as the sovereignty of love whose strength is revealed in weakness; and God's omniscience will not be seen as know-it-all but as a wisdom which shapes the future in dialogue with creatures.[7]

---

[6] Barth, *Church Dogmatics* IV/1, 186.
[7] See what may be the finest section in Barth's *Church Dogmatics*, 'The Reality of God' II/1, ch. 6.

The Church receives the picture of a triune personal God seeking relationships of love with significant creatures through the biblical narrative and divine self-disclosure. It is a revelation of unheard of relatedness and intimacy. It leads us into knowledge of God as threefold in nature and as a triune community of love. This is the picture revealed in Jesus Christ, the Father's Son and bearer of the Spirit. We see the Son in relation to his, *Abba*, Father and ministering in the power of the Spirit. We see God to be a communion of divine persons, each fully conscious and existing in the closest possible relationship of love. His name is Father, Son and Holy Spirit. Salvation is communion with God through Jesus Christ by the Spirit and is fundamentally relational.[8]

The Trinity is not an abstract formula but a summary description of the witness of Scripture to God's love incarnate in Jesus Christ through the Spirit in which God is self-revealed as a communion of Father, Son and Spirit. God is triune personal life in relationship – faithful Father, servant Son, and enlivening Spirit. These are three distinct ways of God's being present in the world; three ways that are grounded in God's eternal being. God is the one who lives in love and wills community with creatures; he is not a supreme monad that exists in eternal solitude. To speak metaphysically, the gospel alludes to a relational ontology of persons in communion.[9] The Trinity speaks to us of relationality and is not tied to substance philosophy.[10] The tri-personal God is the very model of love, a community where each gives and receives love, which is the antithesis of aloofness and indifference. Paradoxically, although the doctrine uses the language of Hellenic reflection, in confessing the Trinity we affirm a God who is nearly everything that the Greeks denied.[11] In trinitarian metaphysics, God freely enters into personal relationships with his creatures, not because he needs to (he already consists of a tri-personal community in which each gives and receives love), but because he wants to since relationality is an essential aspect of God. God did not need to create in order to love. He chose to create in order to share love. Creation results from the openness of God to make others

---

[8] M. Volf, *After Our Likeness: The Church as the Image of the Trinity*, ch. 5; S.M. Heim, *The Depth of the Riches: A Trinitarian Theology of Religious Ends*, ch. 2; T.V. Morris, *Our Idea of God: An Introduction to Philosophical Theology*, 174–84.

[9] J.J. O'Donnell, *The Mystery of the Triune God*; C.M. LaCugna, *God for Us: The Trinity and the Christian Life*, 243–317; R.W. Jenson, *The Triune Identity*.

[10] T. Peters, *God as Trinity: Relationality and Temporality in Divine Life*, 30–4.

[11] R.W. Jenson, *Unbaptised God: The Basic Flaw in Ecumenical Theology*, 119. At the same time, Jenson notes how incomplete our appropriation of trinitarian dynamism has been, 137–8.

who could enter into loving relationships with him. Personhood, relationality and community are more central to our understanding of God than independence and control. The type of relationship that God seeks to have with us is not manipulative, which is basically impersonal. It is I-thou not I-it. The lover does not seek to enslave the beloved. Were this to happen the lover would still be alone. In God we see a surprising omnipotence that creates, not to dominate, but to have creatures independent of it and capable of loving relationships.[12]

As triune, God is antecedently and internally relational and more than self-sufficient. God has no need of an external world to supply experiences of relationality because God experiences it within himself apart from any world.[13] But a world, if not necessary to God, is nonetheless a possibility and a desideratum. God is able, should he so choose, to become involved in the processes of a world and to enjoy the relative goodness of a world as he participates in it. A world would provide for God an external expression of his own perfect goodness. God is free in his benevolence to create a world to share his glory and to lead such a world, even at cost to himself, to the place where it can, in its own non-divine way, reflect the goodness which God eternally enjoys. Creation is a gift of grace; it is not something God needs but something he wants. In contrast to process theology, God creates unnecessarily out of his love and out of his desire to share life with creatures. God does not need a world in order to love, because his very nature is social and relational. He chooses to create and in creating displays the self-communicating love that God is and always has been. As such, without being necessary, the world has profound significance for the life of God.[14]

God seeks fellowship with us, even though he does not have to. Barth writes

> God is One who, without having to do so, seeks and creates fellowship between himself and us. He does not have to do it, because in himself and

---

[12] C.E. Gunton assesses the harmful impact on Western thought of a neglect of trinitarian relationality in God; see *The One, The Three, and The Many: God, Creation and the Culture of Modernity*. Also Pinnock, *Flame*, ch. 1.
[13] The God of the gospel is not a lonely God but a tri-personal loving communion: Sanders, *God Who Risks*, 184.
[14] G.A Boyd, 'The Self-Sufficient Sociality of God: A Trinitarian Revision of Hartshorne's Metaphysics' in J.A. Bracken and M. Suchocki (eds.), *Trinity in Process: A Relational Theology of God*, 73–94; and R. Rice, 'Process Theism and the Open View of God: The Crucial Difference' in J.B. Cobb and C.H. Pinnock (eds.), *Searching for an Adequate God: A Dialogue Between Process and Free Will Theists*, 195–200.

without us, he has that which he seeks. It implies so to speak an overflow of his essence that he turns to us but an overflow which is not demanded or presupposed by any necessity, constraint, or obligation, least of all from outside, from our side, or by any law by which God himself is bound and obliged. It is rooted in himself alone. God wills to belong to us and wills that we should belong to him.[15]

In a sense God needs our love because he has freely chosen to be a lover and needs us because he has chosen to have reciprocal love, not because it was foisted on him from without.

The creation matters to God, not only as an expression of artistry, but even more so as an expression of love. Here God freely chooses to actualize his potential to be the creator of a non-divine world and decides to have a world which would become part of God's own experience. God enjoys the world; it means something to him as an expression, but it is not an essential element of his self. The world provides an occasion for God's beauty to be expressed in new ways. God, though self-content in his triune sociality, is willing to be involved in a world, even in a world of suffering which love so often leads to. He has the willingness to be 'weak' in order to reveal how strong he is in himself. God has the disposition to communicate and share the wealth of divine life. The Trinity chooses to express itself by creating new partners for the eternal dance. Out of the ceaselessly spontaneous life of the Trinity, God takes on the risky adventure of creating a non-divine order and immersing himself in it. In effect, God says: 'I will no longer be God without humanity – I will be God with humanity.'[16] Thus when we speak of the Trinity we express our belief in the one God who is not a solitary being but a communion in love characterized by overflowing life. The Trinity is not a model that imparts secret information about the inner life of God, but a symbol that points to a three-folded relationality in God. It speaks of shared life at the heart of the universe and establishes mutual relationship as the paradigm for personal and social life.[17]

In creating, the triune God exercises freedom. He creates and redeems freely, not because of any necessity, but sovereignly. God freely loves us and wants us to love him in return. God had choices about what kind of world to create and whether to create it. In turn, we have been given

---

[15] Barth, *Church Dogmatics* II/1, 273–4.
[16] G.A. Boyd, *Trinity and Process: A Critical Evaluation and Reconstruction of Hartshorne's Di-Polar Theism Towards a Trinitarian Metaphysics*, 374–95.
[17] E.A. Johnson, *She Who Is: The Mystery of God in Feminist Theological Discourse*, 222–3.

freedom whether to love God or not. We must choose to participate in God's everlasting goodness.[18] It could be that sometime in the future our probation will come to an end and we will be able to love reliably and unchangeably. But, in this present life, we are free to enter into union with God or not. It may be that in heaven, the purpose of our probation having been fulfilled, freedom may be withdrawn. Perhaps we will not sin there because we will have been conformed fully to the image of Christ. In our earthly experience we see that character becomes more predictable over time. The longer we persist in a chosen path, the more that path becomes part of who we are. We become what we choose and the range of viable options diminishes over time. One may envisage a process of transformation that results in such a confirmation of character in which we will be able not to sin. But right now, in order to participate in the triune love, we have to choose it.[19]

God and the World

God's passion according to Kierkegaard is to love and to be loved. God's nature is loving communion, and creation and providence express his love. Often we stress creation as a power move, which it surely was. But, in a sense, creation was also an act of self-limitation, not of self-expansion. Creating human beings who have true freedom is a self-restraining, self-humbling and self-sacrificing act on God's part.[20] He gives us room to flourish because he wants freely chosen relationships of love with us. We are able to set purposes for ourselves and shape the future. We are capable of self-determination and responsible conduct, we can choose between loving obedience and rebellious disobedience, and can transform ourselves in the historical process.[21]

As far as God's relation to the world, Scripture presents God as a creator who is not remote but closely integrated, by choice, with the world. Ontologically, God transcends the world but at the same time enjoys a very close relationship to it. The world is dependent on God but God has also, voluntarily, made himself dependent on it in some important respects. God affects the world, but God is also affected by the world. God is sovereign,

---

[18] Morris, *Idea*, ch. 3; Sanders, *God Who Risks*, 316–8.
[19] Boyd, *God of the Possible*, 136–7; Sanders, *God Who Risks*, 336–7.
[20] G. MacGregor, *He Who Lets Us Be: A Theology of Love*, ch. 6.
[21] Our freedom is not unrestricted, of course. We did not create ourselves *ex nihilo* and we do not act in isolation but in communities. We emerge out of a past, are shaped by the decisions of others, but we also experience moving into an open future which will be shaped, in part, by the decisions that we make.

but he has also given power to creatures. Though Lord of time and history, God has also chosen to be bound up with time and history. Though God knows all there is to know about the world, there are aspects about the future that even God does not know. Though unchangeable with respect to his character and the steadfastness of his purposes, God changes in the light of what happens by interacting with the world. In short, the world is a dynamic project and God is very much involved in it. Over against traditional theism, the open view regards world process as more closely integrated with God than theology has ordinarily been willing to admit.[22] This is the reason we can receive revelation, because God stoops down and shares our context. He understands the conditions of our existence – our language, history and world – and relates to them. God has bound himself to having an intimate relationship with the world. God relates to us from within space and time.

As regards space, the Bible speaks of God having living space in the heavens: 'The heavens are the LORD's heavens' (Ps. 115:16). God has stretched 'out the heavens like a tent' to dwell in (Ps. 104:2), and from heaven he looks down on the earth (Deut. 26:15). It speaks of God freely moving within the world and not just working from the outside. God states in Jeremiah 23:24 that he has taken up residence in the world, 'Do I not fill heaven and earth?' Paul says that God is 'above all and through all and in all' (Eph. 4:6). The church was created to be 'a dwelling place for God' (Eph. 2:22). The prophet John declares: 'See, the home [tabernacle] of God is among mortals. He will dwell with them as their God; they will be his peoples, and God himself will be with them; he will wipe away every tear from their eyes' (Rev. 21:3–4).[23] Let's not tilt overly to transcendence lest we miss the truth that God is with us in space.

As regards time, God's relation is temporal and not totally different from ours. He too operates from within time. Of course, God existed before the world, endures in a way that the world does not and is everlasting, but he still relates to us from within the structures of time. God is described as making plans and carrying them out (Jer. 18:11; 29:11). There is temporal succession in God's thinking; he remembers the past, interacts with the present and anticipates the future. There are temporal gaps between what God plans and when he achieves the goal. The past is past and God remembers it; the future is future and God anticipates it. God is not thought of in terms of timelessness, whatever that means. At least since creation, the divine life has been temporally ordered. God is inside not outside time. He is involved in the thick of, and is not above,

---

[22] T.E. Fretheim, *The Suffering of God: An Old Testament Perspective*, 35.
[23] Ibid., 37–9.

the flow of history. How indeed could God be our redeemer if he were timeless? How could he even know what time it is and plan a sequence of actions? Oscar Cullmann says bluntly: 'Primitive Christianity knows nothing of a timeless God.'[24]
Fretheim writes

> The Old Testament witnesses to a God who shares in our human history as past, present, and future, and in such a way that we may even speak of a history of God. God has so bound himself in relationship to the world that we move through time and space together. Though God is the uncreated member of the community, he too can cry out: 'How long?' (Jer. 4:14; 13:27; Hos. 8:5)[25]

God's relationship with the world has real integrity. God binds himself to us and is with us where we are and when we are. Creation is his living space and history the realm of his activity. This does not make God dependent on the world necessarily. Rather it means that God, through grace, has decided to be independent of the world in some respects and dependent on it in other respects. God does not have to avoid every form of dependency in order to be great. On the contrary, God's greatness consists precisely in his loving willingness to be there for us.[26]

There is an issue that has not been raised yet in the discussion around the open view of God. If he is with us in the world, if we are to take biblical metaphors seriously, is God in some way embodied? Critics will be quick to say that, although there are expressions of this idea in the Bible, they are not to be taken literally. But I do not believe that the idea is as foreign to the Bible's view of God as we have assumed. In tradition, God is thought to function primarily as a disembodied spirit but this is scarcely a biblical idea. For example, Israel is called to hear God's word and gaze on his glory and beauty.[27] Human beings are said to be embodied creatures created in the image of God. Is there perhaps something in God that corresponds with embodiment? Having a body is certainly not

---

[24] O. Cullmann, *Christ and Time: The Primitive Christian Conception of Time and History*, 63. So also N.P. Wolterstorff, 'God Everlasting' in C. Orlebeke and L. Smedes (eds.), *God and the Good: Essays in Honor of Henry Stobb*, 181–203; Fretheim, *Suffering of God*, 39–44. Tiessen too rejects the notion of God as timeless: how can we conceive of a tripersonal God existing everlastingly in loving relations as timeless? *Providence and Prayer*, 322–5.
[25] Fretheim, *Suffering of God*, 44.
[26] F.G. Kirkpatrick, *Together Bound: God, History, and the Religious Community*.
[27] Brueggemann, *Theology*, 425–30.

a negative thing because it makes it possible for us to be agents. Perhaps God's agency would be easier to envisage if he were in some way corporeal. Add to that the fact that in the theophanies of the Old Testament God encounters humans in the form of a man.[28] They indicate that God shares our life in the world in a most intense and personal manner.[29] For example, look at the following texts. In Exodus 24:10–11 Moses, Aaron, Nadab, Abidu and seventy of the elders of Israel went up Mount Sinai and beheld God, as they ate and drank. Exodus 33:11 tells us that 'the LORD used to speak to Moses face to face, as one speaks to a friend.' Moses saw 'God's back' but not his face (Exod. 33:23). When God chose to reveal his glory. Isaiah saw the Lord, high and lifted up (Is. 6:1). Ezekiel saw 'the appearance of the likeness of the glory of the LORD' (Ezek. 1:28). John saw visions of one seated upon the throne (Rev. 4:2) and of the Son of Man in his glory (Rev. 1:12–16). Add to that the fact that God took on a body in the incarnation and Christ has taken that body with him into glory. It seems to me that the Bible does not think of God as formless. Rather, it thinks of him as possessing a form that these divine appearances reflect. At the very least, God chooses to share in the human condition, participate in human history; an intensely and remarkably involved participant.

The fact is that God loves to draw near to us through nature, theophany and incarnation. God loves to take on form and make himself accessible. Most people, I suspect, think that God chooses to be associated with a body, while being himself formless. That may be so, but it is also possible that God has a body in some way we cannot imagine and, therefore, that it is natural for God to seek out forms of embodiment.[30] I do not feel obliged to assume that God is a purely spiritual being when his self-revelation does not suggest it. It is true that from a Platonic standpoint, the idea is absurd, but this is not a biblical standpoint. And how unreasonable is it anyway? The only persons we encounter are embodied persons and, if God is not embodied, it may prove difficult to understand how God is a person. What kind of actions could a disembodied God perform? Embodiment may be the way in which the transcendent God is able to be immanent and why God is presented in such terms. I would say that God transcends the world, while being able to

---

[28] Fretheim, *Suffering of God*, ch. 6.
[29] C. Barth, *God With Us: A Theological Introduction to the Old Testament*. God is also embodied in the world itself in tangible ways such as in clouds, pillars of fire, thunder, lightning, smoke and the tabernacle presence. Fretheim, *Suffering of God*, 89–92.
[30] Ibid., 101–6.

indwell it. Perhaps God uses the created order as a kind of body and exercises top-down causation upon it.[31]

Whether God is or is not embodied, and in what sense, is certainly a mystery. But it is a fact that God loves to take on forms to facilitate his self-revelation and redeeming agency. As human subjectivity expresses itself in, with, and through bodies, so the transcendent subjectivity of God is somehow immanent in the patterns, processes, and events of the world. The evangelical narrative is unintelligible apart from the assumption of God's presence in nature and history and especially in Jesus Christ. Immanence is much too abstract a label for these involvements. Warm currents of grace flow through the cosmos, holding it together and bringing it to new levels of creativity in the service of the divine vision.[32]

Scripture presents a nice balance between the transcendence and the condescendence of God. God reveals himself to be 'the Holy One in your midst' (Hos. 11:9). He dwells 'in the high and holy place, and also with those who are contrite and humble in spirit' (Is. 57:15). We have too often favored God's remoteness in contrast to God's intimate presence. It is time to overcome the one-sidedness and give God's immanence its due.[33]

God's Partners

1. Creation

As a God in relationship with the world not isolated from it, Yahweh also takes on partners who affect him and agents who go face-to-face with him in dynamic not controlled relationships. God in freedom made such interaction possible and is passionately committed to it. God initiates in sovereign freedom and then engages partners in real give and take relationships. God's power is incomparable and he employs it for the good of the partner and not self-enhancement. Biased toward belief in meticulous sovereignty, theology has not done justice to these dynamic relationships. God's sovereignty is anything but serene. History is a drama with profound risks and enormous dynamics. God goes in for partnerships where the junior partners make a real contribution. It is a covenantal-historical way of understanding based on mutual vows and

---

[31] I.G. Barbour discusses top down causation in nature; see *When Science Meets Religion*, 172–4. Also see G. Jantzen, *God's World, God's Body*; D. Paulsen (Mormon), 'Must God be Incorporeal?', *Faith and Philosophy* 6 (1989), 76–87.

[32] G. Fackre, *The Christian Story: A Narrative Interpretation of Basic Christian Doctrine*, 254.

[33] H. Berkhof sees this clearly; see *Christian Faith*, 105–18.

obligations. It is not the situation of omnicausalism where even the input of the creature is predetermined. The open view of God celebrates the real relationships that obtain between God and his people. Real drama, real interactions and real learning are possible because history is not scripted and freedom is not illusory.[34]

On the grandest scale, creation as a whole is itself God's partner. It is a world blessed and fruitful, and home for human community. As such, it needs to be wisely managed by God's vice-regents. But it is also a world in jeopardy with forces at work that resist God and a power of chaos that hinders the blessing of God. The acts of creation as recorded in Genesis chapter 1 brought chaos under control and reintroduced God's order, but they did not eliminate the threat of this mysterious 'formless void' factor (v. 2). It is a situation where, although God has the upper hand, he is not now totally in control. Scripture presents God as engaged in conflict with powers of darkness. The tradition has presented an all too serene picture of the situation, where God does not have to struggle with any opposing power. Creation is God's partner not just a passive product.

How this situation came about is mysterious. I suppose that it stems from the fact that God delegated sovereignty to creatures, in this case the angels, and it has led to open warfare. The angels left their first estate before the appearance of humankind (Jude 6). This means that God is not now in complete control of the world and that genuine evil, which God does not want, exists. It means that things happen which God has not willed and that God's plans at this point in history are not always fulfilled. God confronts rebellious agents who are able to thwart his desires at least for a time and in a measure.[35]

Helmut Thielicke writes

> What we hear in the Bible again and again is that the powers of sin and suffering and death are hostile powers, enemies of God. God did not will that they should exist. They are disorderly and unnatural powers which broke into God's plan of creation. They are the dark henchmen of original sin, our own sin. In the healing of the paralytic, Jesus again makes it very plain that the sickness that he healed is only the other side of the same derangement and disorder which sin brought into the world. All these things are signs of the disorder, the rift that runs through the midst of creation.[36]

---

[34] Brueggemann, *Theology*. Cf. Tiessen, *Providence and Prayer*, 243–8, 309–15.

[35] G.A. Boyd, *God at War: The Bible and Spiritual Conflict*. A second volume on the history of theodicy is expected.

[36] H. Thielicke, *The Prayer That Spans the World: Sermons on the Lord's Prayer*, 25.

The situation of conflict will not, however, be permanent. Creation, which was blessed and fruitful but now is in jeopardy, will be restored with a victory over evil in the end. It will be taken beyond nullification to blessing again. God will judge the world but will not bring about a full end (Jer. 4:27). The world will become fruitful again. We await the new creation that God has promised and a fresh enactment of order and well-being (Is. 65:17).[37]

2. Israel

The people of Israel were, and are, God's partner. God's free and passionate commitment to Israel is a central theme in the Old Testament. He called her into being to be a people for his name's sake and a covenant partner. Being a bilateral covenant, expectations were attached and Israel was expected to be a responsive people. There were covenantal obligations in relation to peace and justice, and Israel was given a role in the well-being of the world, but she jeopardized her own existence by not responding to God's goodness. She resisted her own calling and became a partner under judgment leading to exile. God was willing to let Israel choose, e.g. whether to have a king or not (1 Sam. 8) because he knew that they hungered for the security the monarchy could bring them. God did not give up on Israel, even though they rejected his rule over them and sought to be like the other nations, but they had to reap what they had sowed. And even though the man God chose to rule them – Saul, a man God himself later rejected – failed miserably, God continued to deal with his people. Indeed the whole nation of Israel failed in its covenant relationship with God according to the prophets. This required a new initiative on God's part and led to the unique role of Jesus.[38]

Though God provided Israel with everything, the prophets claimed that they acted presumptuously and stiffened their necks. Even when God was gracious and merciful, they were disobedient (Neh. 9:16). God complains, 'I reared children and brought them up, but they have rebelled against me' (Is. 1:2). God planted a vineyard and did everything he could. He expected grapes and got only wild grapes (Is. 5:1–7). God says through Jeremiah (2:5), 'What wrong did your ancestors find in me that they went far from me?' God says through Ezekiel, 'I am sending you to the people of Israel, to a nation of rebels who have rebelled against me' (Ezek. 2:3). The prophets exposed the sins of the people relentlessly and warned of a failure in the covenant which God had

---

[37] Brueggemann, *Theology*, 528–51.
[38] Berkhof, *Christian Faith*, 225–49.

established with them.[39] Evidently God did not have control over his bride nor will he in future, but he does not give up on his people. God who scattered Israel will gather her (Jer. 31:10).[40] He says, 'For a brief moment I abandoned you ... in overflowing wrath for a moment I hid my face from you, but with everlasting love I will have compassion on you' (Is. 54:7–8).[41]

3. The Nations

Although the big story in the Old Testament is Israel as God's partner, he considers the nations to be his partners too.[42] They also exist under the rule of God and within the horizon of God's governance. God made a covenant with them all, through Noah, and they too have obligations. Their relationship with God was partly mediated through Israel but in part also stood independently of it. As Paul puts it, 'From one ancestor [God] made all nations to inhabit the whole earth, and he allotted the times of their existence and the boundaries of the places where they would live, so that they would search for God and perhaps grope for him and find him – though indeed he is not far from any one of us' (Acts 17:26–27). Among the nations too the Lord is king (Ps. 96:10). They fall under harsh judgment but the goal is to include them too. On that future day God will declare, 'Blessed be Egypt my people and Assyria the work of my hands and Israel my heritage' (Is. 19:25). God is not totally preoccupied with Israel and intends to bless the nations as well. He may have brought Israel out of Egypt but he also brought the Philistines out of Caphtor and the Arameans out of Kir (Amos 9:7). The nations are summoned to be God's servants too – they are punished for their arrogance but also promised new life.

---

[39] A. König, *Here Am I! A Christian Reflection on God*, 127–32. It was much the same situation when it came to God's dealings with the early church. How hard it was for God to convince Jewish believers to accept Gentiles and how hard for the Gentiles to figure where Israel stood with God, having rejected Jesus. But God keeps working with his people, warts and all, and proves resourceful at turning evil into something good. God is expert at working with real people in real history.

[40] Even the writing of the law on our hearts is still relational and not coercive. Knowing Jesus and experiencing the Spirit, however novel and incredibly wonderful, is still a relationship that we enter into freely. Nevertheless, in the depth of suffering, God turns from wrath and restores the relationship.

[41] Brueggemann, *Theology*, 413–49.

[42] Ibid., 492–527; J. Dupuis, *Toward a Christian Theology of Religious Pluralism*, ch. 1.

4. Individuals

Though the Bible's approach to the human persons is less individualistic than our own, nevertheless it too sees individuals as formed by love and summoned to obedience. Created as male and female in the image of God they are entrusted as God's regents with dominion over the earth. Created for fellowship and partnership with God they are given space in which to live wisely and obediently. It is assumed that the person is capable of choosing wisely and acting responsibly.[43] Facing judgment as a result of disobedience they are also invited to call on God in the midst of trouble and experience restoration and salvation.[44]

With the creation of humans (and angels), God found himself in a new situation, having to work out his purposes alongside creatures with liberty of their own, able to project their own intentions. In other words, God took a risk. Risk is a function of the fact that God has limited the degree of his control over the world in granting the creature genuine freedom, and this is not without pain to himself.[45] So long as human purposes coincided with God's plans, no problem would arise. The course of history could express God's will in harmony with humanity's own. However if, by a misuse of freedom, the creature should deviate from the divine purpose, tensions would begin to arise within history and forces at cross-purposes with the divine will would begin to reduce the harmonious situation into a chaotic warfare of purposes.

The Fall of Adam was a point in history when, just as human freedom was becoming a reality, humans began to act in ways contrary to the will of God and disruptive of the historical process. The Fall was a historical event which, antedating recorded history, determined its idolatrous character. It was the time when humans began to work against God's purposes and in a manner destructive of their own well-being. In a tragic and irrational act of rebellion, our first parents released into the world negative forces which have not yet been quelled and which continue to threaten humankind. At some point, we vetoed God's will, disobeyed his commandments and

---

[43] In contrast to the Protestant traditions see W. Brueggemann, *In Man We Trust: The Neglected Side of Biblical Faith* on the wisdom literature of Scripture.

[44] Brueggemann, *Theology*, 450–92.

[45] G.D. Kaufman, *Systematic Theology: A Historicist Perspective*, chs. 24–25. P. Little spoke of 'the risky gift of free will' in *Know Why You Believe*, 115–7. P. Helm contends that providence is risk free *The Providence of God*, while Sanders sees God as a risk taker, *God Who Risks*.

rejected his plans.[46] I take it that the Fall into sin went contrary to the will of God (it resulted in his judgment) and sheds light on the nature of God's sovereignty. The will of God is not something that is always done but something that can be followed or resisted. Contrary to God's will, history can become the scene of a struggle of purposes between God and created agents. The conflict does not seem to be one in appearance only, one in which God is acting on both sides, but a genuine struggle of contrary wills because his will can be defied by the creature who chooses to move against what God had planned. The Fall seems to have been a disaster that unleashed a cycle of cumulative degeneration into history. God's own creatures, taking advantage of the fact that God gave them room to trust or not trust him, succumbed to the temptation to distance themselves from their maker.[47]

The situation from the human standpoint is now utterly hopeless, because history has become a scene where humans work at cross-purposes with God. There is hope only if the power of God's love breaks into history to heal it, a power that could not arise from the corrupted body of humanity itself. With the call of Abram, God set to work in history to turn back the effects of sin and restore humankind. A man was called through whom a people could be prepared for the coming of God's kingdom, in whose midst a right relationship with God could be re-established, and through whom healing could spill over into the world. What was praiseworthy about Abram was his faith, i.e. his open responsiveness to the will of God (Heb. 11:8). His salvation was by grace but conditioned on an obedient response. Abram became the father of a new people because he heeded the call and, although his descendants have not always been as responsive as he was, nevertheless a right response to God still exists within this community. Thus a new possibility for the race has emerged, the possibility of entering into a right relationship with God and our fellows, which is the goal of our being created. Though human history since the Fall has been racing downwards toward perdition, God has entered history with a word of healing. Beginning with Abraham and after long historical preparation culminating in Jesus Christ, there has come to pass a new human

---

[46] Had the Bible not pointed to a primeval Fall, we would have had to postulate it to account for what has ensued. 'It will not do to consider these characteristics of human history to be simply man's heritage from the animal nature for the problem is precisely the *self-conscious* hatred, distrust, and perversity with which man acts which is something quite unknown from anything on the animal level.' Kaufman, *Systematic Theology*, 353.

[47] Sanders, *God Who Risks*, 46–9.

community made up of people from all nations, the first fruits of the community of love, which God has always intended humankind to be.

In the biblical narrative, one does not find a predestinarian decree operating behind the scenes, to ensure that God's will is always done. Rather, one sees God's response to a created partner. We see him weaving into his own plans the significant choices that creatures make. History is not a printout of pre-programmed events, all videotaped and decided. It is not a piece of theatre in which God, as it were, puts himself on the stage and the creatures are only what is performed. It is rather a situation where the creature is co-performer in a divine-human drama. There is a divinely willed two-sidedness to the relationship so that God's dealings with us are a real dialogue and not a kind of monologue that God conducts by himself. History is taken seriously and contains both a working together and a working against.

In his dealings with us, God is not a cosmic stuffed shirt,who is always thinking of himself. Rather he is open to the world and responsive to developments in history. He remembers the past, savors the present and anticipates the future. He is open to new experiences, has a capacity for novelty and is open to reality, which itself is open to change. God interacts with us in our narrated, storied lives in a real reciprocal relationship. Not only are we as persons affected by God, he is affected by us, or to put it another way, God is unchangeable with respect to his character but always changing in relation to us.

Scripture, like human experience itself, assumes libertarian freedom, i.e. the freedom to perform an action or refrain from it. With such freedom, people usually have alternatives in any situation. It is a gift that makes loving relationships that imply free response possible. It explains why God would hold people accountable for what they do and how sin could enter when God did not want it to. It explains why God is grieved when people do what he did not want them to and not what he did intend. It seems that God, in deciding to create humankind, placed higher value on freedom leading to love than on guaranteed conformity to his will. His plans for humankind included making room for beings who were themselves free and who possessed the power to shape the course of history for good or ill. God's strategy did not include manipulation.

This basic pattern is visible in the lives of individuals in relation to God. Adam was a creature endowed with the ability to respond to God's word and destined for loving reciprocal relationships with God. He was given freedom for the sake of such a relationship. In making such a creature with the ability to move freely into the open future, God limited his own freedom. He made room for a partner and accepted a degree of risk with the possibility, not certainty, of sin and evil occurring. In creating Adam, God showed himself willing to share power. He does not insist on being the only power. God created a significant 'other' in the person of Adam and gave him, together with Eve, space to live and operate. For the sake of loving relations, God chose not to exercise total sovereignty and took the risk that things might not turn out the way he wanted them to. The prohibition in the garden not to eat the fruit of a certain tree reveals that the situation was one of moral freedom and implies that the divine purpose for humankind may fail, at least in the short term. Humans are creative and morally responsible beings whom God created and placed in a world whose future is not definite and fixed. God sovereignly decided to enter into dynamic relations with the creature, and when things went badly he did not let the world fall into chaos but opted for a new beginning. God began with Adam and begins again with Noah. God displayed judgment, but in the context of the goal of bringing humankind back to himself. God shows that he is not prepared to give up on the creation project, whatever humans do.[48]

God called Abram and he freely responded. His faith in God was reckoned as righteousness and a dialogue began between them. A relationship occurred which developed throughout his life. In the stories about Abraham, we see a man's faith in God mature and God's confidence in a man grow. In one incident, God gave him the promise of an heir and Abraham trusted God for it. He had questions about how the promise would be fulfilled but God responded to his concerns. God was committed to the patriarch and to his promise to bless the world through him. Abraham was an ordinary man but God was committed to work with the material at hand. Wanting to deepen the relationship, God subjected him to a test on Mount Moriah. He asked Abram to surrender his son Isaac, who personified the divine promise. It was a wrenching experience and both partners, God and Abraham, learned from it: Abraham learned to trust God more deeply and God learned what Abraham would do under these circumstances (Gen. 22:12). In another incident, Abraham prayed for the city of Sodom. He spoke with God about the fate of the city and they decided together what should be done because its destiny had, apparently, not yet been sealed (Gen. 18:22). From this incident we see that God does not will to rule the world alone but wants to bring the creature into his decisions. Prayer highlights the fact that God does not chose to rule the world without our input. It also suggests that the future has not been exhaustively settled.

---

[48] T.E. Fretheim, *Creation, Fall and Flood: Studies in Genesis 1–11*, 105–21.

To take another example, God's relationship with Moses began in the context of Israel's oppression in the land of Egypt. God heard their cries and, moved by their sufferings, called Moses to be a deliverer. Moses, however, was not convinced and presented God with a number of objections. Amazingly, God did not become angry with Moses but respected him and dealt patiently with his concerns. God was able to do this because he had the freedom to move his plan forward in more than one way. He had goals but they were goals with open routes. Even Pharaoh was not a puppet; he was a person in a position to contribute one way or another to shaping the future.[49] Later on, when the people made a golden calf, God became exasperated and threatened to give up on Israel altogether. He thought of putting them aside and beginning again with Moses, but Moses interceded in prayer and God 'changed his mind' (Exod. 32:11–14).[50]

Divine repentance is an important biblical theme. At the time of the great flood God said that he was sorry that he had made human-kind and decided to judge the whole world and start over again (Gen. 6:8). It happened when God regretted Saul being king after he forsook God's ways (1 Sam. 15:35). Not that interpreting such texts is simple and undialectical. The context of the passage says, 'God is not a mortal that he should change his mind.' God was sorry that he made Saul king. However, the writer of Samuel wants us to think carefully about what it means to say God repents. Nevertheless, it appears that God is willing to change course, especially where judgment is concerned, because he loves to be merciful and to relent from punishing (Joel 2:13; Jon. 4:2).

How history will go is not a foregone conclusion, even to God because he is free to strike in new directions as may be appropriate. If we take divine repentance language seriously, it suggests that God does not work with a plan fixed in every detail but with general goals that can be fulfilled in different ways. God is faithful to these goals but flexible as to how to fulfill them.[51] Although repentance is a metaphor, which should not be pressed too far, it is revelatory of the way God exercises sovereignty. It depicts God as free to adjust plans in response to changing

---

[49] T.E. Fretheim, *Exodus*, 96–103; R.T. Forster and V.P. Marston, *God's Strategy in Human History*, ch. 11.

[50] Job was another one of these difficult covenant partners whom God took seriously. Their interaction was marked by honesty and respect on both sides and in the end they reached an understanding.

[51] Not all texts that mention God repenting are exactly the same, there are some where God had set conditions and, upon their fulfillment, 'changes' to be faithful to his own promises. It is easier to interpret them in a less dynamic fashion.

situations. It does not imply that God is fickle or untrustworthy but that he is flexible in faithfulness. He can take things into account when acting and be creative in pursuing his plans. We should not regard this metaphor as a mere accommodation but as indicative of how God works. God is able to remain faithful to his purposes even while altering plans to fit in with changing circumstances.[52]

Jonah was called by God to preach doom to Nineveh. Not wanting to do it, the prophet headed off in the opposite direction. God had to deal with his stubborn prophet and put him back on thee road to Nineveh. When Jonah delivered the message, the Ninevites repented. Their king reasoned that God, known to be merciful, would respond if they repented and alter his plan to send judgment. It is the very character of God 'to relent from punishing' (Jon. 4:2).[53]

Mercy may have been implicit in the original call and Jonah knew it. This may have been the reason he did not to want to go to Nineveh: he knew that God might not judge Nineveh if it repented and this disgusted him. He knew that God was free in relation to his decree and despised the idea of God showing mercy to Assyrians. But even when Jonah begrudged God's generosity, God did not give up on him but reached out to rebuild the relationship. The same dynamic patterns occur in the New Testament, even in the stories about Jesus. Though he proclaimed the kingdom of God faithfully, he met with rejection. He did not, however, give up but became obedient unto death. Though he asked that the cup be removed, he accepted that it was God's will that he should die, as expressed in the servant songs of Isaiah. He gave himself up to his enemies believing that redemption would come through his suffering. It is a dynamic story, not cut and dried, and illustrates the way God is free to carry out his plans.[54]

The biblical narrative reveals the nature of God's sovereignty. God in freedom placed himself in a position of relatedness with creation. He has respect for the integrity of his creatures and has made humans for give and take relationships. Though he has his own plans, God is open to input from creatures. Though he has goals, God is flexible in the working out of details. What God wants to happen does not always

---

[52] Sanders, *God Who Risks*, 66–75. Dispensational theology recognizes the flexibility of God: God offered Israel the kingdom in Jesus and his plan was thwarted, which led to a fresh initiative.

[53] Also Joel 2:13. It is not naive literalism to suppose that God repents – it is basic to his nature not to want to carry through, even on a judgment that he had announced.

[54] E.F. Tupper, *A Scandalous Providence: The Jesus Story of the Compassion of God*.

come to pass on account of human freedom. There are disasters and set-backs and God can even suffer humiliation because love makes him vulnerable. God is willing to humiliate himself by taking back a disreputable woman, Israel, as his wife (Hosea). Like the father of the prodigal son, he welcomes his son home gladly even though the lad had wished him dead. Through wisdom and resourcefulness, God tries different paths to bring his purposes to successful conclusions. There is no blueprint that governs everything that happens, it is a real historical project that does not proceed smoothly but goes through twists and turns. The type of relationship God displays toward us is not one of control but one of love, which opens God himself up to rejection. There is no unconditional guarantee of success because there are risks for God and the creature.

God does not go in for tactics of manipulation because he values personal relationships in which parties are voluntarily involved. God wants the love of real persons not automatons. For this reason, though God initiates the relationships, he cannot control them. The love he seeks is reciprocal; he loves us but does not try to make us love him in return. He is dependent on human beings for these loving relations. In creating human beings to love them, God assumed a position of vulnerability in relation to them. In fact, God made himself more vulnerable than we are because, though we can count on his steadfast love, he cannot count on ours. Had God not granted us significant freedom, including the freedom to disappoint him, we would not be creatures capable of entering into loving relationships with him. Love, not freedom, is the central issue. Freedom was given to make loving relations possible. In order to have personal relationships, God gives us freedom and limits his own almightiness to give us room to respond. The biblical story presupposes what we call libertarian freedom. This is plain in the ways God invites us to love him and in the ways in which he holds us responsible for what we decide.[55]

God sovereignly created human beings in his image in order to enter into personal relations with them. God can choose what kind of sovereignty to exercise and he has chosen to exercise an open and flexible sovereignty. There are different kinds of sovereignty: there is the kind that controls everything and there is the kind that makes love possible. Robots cannot enter into loving relationships. The open view of God has

---

[55] Human freedom is, of course, finite freedom and we should not exaggerate it. Though we contribute to making history, we are also made by history. In freedom we work with what we have been given. Kaufman, *Systematic Theology*, 332–9.

a dynamic concept of providence in which God interacts with the world and responds to events as they happen. It is the outworking of a historical project, not a divine blueprint. God depends on wisdom and resourcefulness and not coercion to get his way. The goal of the project is to produce people who love in all their relationships. God's commitment does not change, but the paths God takes to achieve it can change according to what his wisdom deems best at any given time.[56]

Prayer indicates the dialogical nature of the divine-human relationship. It speaks of a dialogue of faith in which God and humanity work in partnership to maintain the covenant relationship. Prayer is an activity that brings new possibilities into existence for God and us. It does not suggest a fixed world and prescribed calm, relationships. It indicates a relationship of reciprocity in which God speaks, acts and listens, while believers speak, act and listen in response to God. In prayer, God is revealed as willing, purposeful and above all personal. Prayer involves the mutual participation of divine and human partners in the tasks of living. In prayer humanity's status is lifted to the high level of partnership with God. Both have voice and the two are bound together in relationship.[57]

Creating such creatures, however, introduced risk into the situation, because the outcomes are not controlled. Though we can count on God, God cannot count on us. We are even able to hurt God by refusing his offer and by working at cross-purposes to him. Affected by this, God may show anger but mostly sets about restoring the relationship and rebuilding the trust. Paradoxically, relationships of love give God the greatest pleasure and the deepest sorrow, just as they do in human affairs. They are unspeakably wonderful but can also go terribly wrong. 'Sovereignty' does not have to mean that everything is decided in advance a foregone conclusion. God is engaged in a historical project and is not following a script.

Such a perspective on the dynamism of God's sovereignty offers an intelligent way to respond to the problem of evil. If God were all-controlling he would be the author of evil, which is a blasphemous thought. The reality of creaturely freedom allows us to say that evil originates, not with God, but with creatures and is the misuse of their God-given freedom. This enables us to think of sin as an intruder

---

[56] Some like R.K.M. Wright equate sovereignty with total control and conclude that open sovereignty is no sovereignty at all, hence the title of his book, *No Place for Sovereignty: What's Wrong with Free Will Theism?*

[57] S.E. Balentine, *Prayer in the Hebrew Bible: The Drama of Divine-Human Dialogue*, 37, 142, 262, 265, 271.

which does not belong, and understand that certain natural evils are the result of the Fall of humankind and angels. God sovereignly decided to create a world containing morally free beings who had the possibility of serving God or not. This was something for them to decide such that sin was a possibility, though not a certainty, at the time of creation. God knew the creature and is, therefore, responsible for the possibility of evil but not for its actuality. It is a good thing for us to have the freedom to choose between good and evil, even though it entails the possibility of making wrong choices.[58]

Some evils like the disasters of war are pointless. God did not want them to happen even though, having happened, God can often accomplish something good through them. Rapes and murders, for example, are tragedies that make God weep. God did not send them and thus God can be 'a very present help in time of trouble.' Not everything that happens in the world happens for some reason, for example, to teach us something. Some things are genuine evils: things that should not have happened, things that God did not want to happen. They occur because God goes in for real relationships and real partnerships.

A Partly Settled Future

God's relation to the future also sheds light on the nature of the world and his relationship with it. The way in which God knows the future reinforces the conviction that history is dynamic and not pre-programmed. Scripture makes a distinction with respect to the future; God is certain about some aspects of it and uncertain about other aspects. He is certain about what he has decided to do and what will inevitably happen but less certain about what creatures may freely do. In reference to the coming captivity of Judah, God says through Ezekiel, '*Perhaps* they will understand, though they are a rebellious house' (Ezek. 12:3). Commenting on Israel's unfaithfulness, God says through Jeremiah, 'I *thought*, "After she has done all this she will return to me"; but she did not return' (Jer. 3:7). Later on, God admits how he had thought the people would respond but that they did not (Jer. 3:19). In another place, God orders Jeremiah to proclaim his word and says, 'It *may be* that they will listen' (Jer. 26:3). Such references are often swept under the rug because the tradition has assumed that they cannot mean what they seem to say but the witness stands – God faces a partly unsettled future. God knows

---

[58] R. Swinburne, *Providence and the Problem of Evil*, 35, 127.

some things as certain and other things as only possible. God's fore-knowledge, it seems, is not exhaustive in detail.[59]

These texts occur in a broader context that supports taking them seriously. Why, unless the future was somewhat unsettled, would God be said to regret things that happen when they happen? Why, unless the future was somewhat open, would God be pictured as delighted and/or surprised by something? Why, unless the future was somewhat open, would God test people to discover things about them? Why, unless the future was somewhat open, would God speak of the future in conditional terms? How, unless the future was somewhat open, could God be said to change his mind? Many considerations point in the same direction. The future is not entirely settled.[60]

There is a story in 2 Kings 20 that illustrates this dramatically. It describes God's interaction with king Hezekiah on the matter of the timing of his death. God had announced that the king would soon die but the king prayed and the Lord added fifteen years to his life. (Evidently the initial prediction had been conditional without the point being stated.) Thus the time of the king's death was shifted to a date more remote in time. This shows that the exact time of death was not forever settled in God's mind but was something flexible, depending on the circumstances. Jeremiah captures these dynamics in his portrayal of God as a potter who, if a pot turns out to be unsatisfactory, will go back to the drawing board and try something else (Jer. 18:7–10). The future is not something fixed in God's mind in meticulous detail, some things can go one way or another. The future is still in the making and open to as yet unrealized possibilities. One implication of this is that God is free to shape the future, as are we. He is not subject to an iron law of his own making but free to act flexibly as required. The fact that God knows some things in the future as certain and others things as possible establishes the fact that the creation project has an unquestionably dynamic character.[61]

---

[59] Ware strives mightily, chiefly against G.A. Boyd, to demonstrate that the biblical texts which appear to show that God's knowledge of the future is non-exhaustive do not do so, indeed cannot do so, because of other texts which are thought to settle the matter beyond reasonable doubt; see *God's Lesser Glory*, chs. 4–5. Both men are worthy protagonists and this is something that Bible readers are going to have to decide on over time. For my part, I see Ware denying the implications of certain texts in order to proceed with what he takes to be the meaning of another set of texts, and I see Boyd offering a coherent explanation of them all.

[60] Fretheim, *Suffering of God*, ch. 4. Resistance to such texts and their meaning is very strong among traditionalists.

[61] Boyd, *God of the Possible*.

Resistance to this notion is profound and it is not surprising that critics of the open view of God focus on this facet of the model.[62] One reason is that belief in a divine omniscience that is less than exhaustive is surprising relative to our traditions. Another is that we are not used to thinking of God as taking risks, which such a belief entails. The fact that the traditional view is tightly bound to a strong doctrine of predestination is another. Nevertheless, for God to create a world with an open future would be a noble action, and to have a creation over which he rules with wisdom and flexibility would be breathtakingly wonderful and a sign of strength, not of weakness. Is it not a beautiful thing that God can adjust to changing circumstances as a responsive personal being? How can it be dishonoring to suggest that God does not know the future exhaustively when it was God himself who decided that the future would be partly settled and partly unsettled? God knows absolutely everything, including the possible as possible and the indefinite as indefinite. What would dishonor God would be to say that God knew something as definite which was not yet definite. Now that would be a defect.

Resistance is also due to the belief that there are texts that establish exhaustive divine foreknowledge. But are there? Psalm 139 is often cited, for example, but what it describes in a poetic way is God's thorough knowledge of the psalmist even to the point of knowing his inner thoughts. This is indeed a marvelous text. The divine foreknowledge is not at all meager in my view! A very great deal can be known about the future by knowing the past and the present, including what people are likely, though not certain, to do in given situations. But the psalm does not prove God's knowledge of the future is limitless. To take another example, God can speak of a person like Jeremiah in terms of a purpose for him before he was born (Jer. 1:5). The subsequent story however does not suggest it was a fait accompli. Jeremiah had to decide whether and how to respond to the calling. The fact that one is called does not guarantee anything. We would never have heard of Jeremiah's call had he not responded. Biblical teaching on the divine knowledge is magnificent but does not require us to posit exhaustive foreknowledge. On the

---

[62] E.g. J. Piper, *The Pleasures of God*, 70–4; and Ware, *God's Lesser Glory*, part 2. Strategically it makes a lot of sense to zero in on it. Exhaustive divine omniscience is almost universally held in the traditions and denying it can be made to sound heretical, though the charge is surely rash. But the real motivator is the fact that exhaustive divine omniscience needs strong predestination to explain how it works (the open view agrees with the Calvinists that it does, in contrast to classical Arminian thinking and the doctrine of middle knowledge). In this way they hope to isolate the open view and argue for the greater coherence of their own version of theological determinism.

contrary, Scripture leaves the impression that the future is somewhat open and the story is still unfolding; what a wonderful truth it is when you consider its bearing on our significance as God's covenant partners.[63]

Is the argument not trumped, however, by predictive biblical prophecy? Some claim that certain predictions entail exhaustive divine foreknowledge and prevent us from appealing to the evidence that suggests limited prescience.[64] Biblical prophecy is a complex phenomenon, but does not entail any such thing.[65]

First, some prophecies announce what God is planning to do and what he will bring to pass (e.g. Is. 46:11, 48:3). Of course God knows aspects of the future that he has predetermined. Second, some prophecies are conditional, leaving the future open, and, presumably, God's knowledge of it. God explains, 'I may declare concerning a nation or a kingdom that I will build and plant it, but if it does evil in my sight, not listening to my voice, then I will change my mind about the good that I had intended to do to it' (Jer. 18:9–10). As with Moses, 'the LORD changed his mind about the disaster he planned to bring on his people' (Exod. 32:14). Such texts suggest an open future – it could go one way or the other. What happens rests with the response of the people and what God will do is yet to be decided. Third, there are imprecise prophetic forecasts based on present situations, as when Jesus predicts the fall of Jerusalem. Such prophecies are rooted in present situations, for example when God says through Isaiah that Egypt and Assyria will become his people in the future. It is a promise in general terms and a blessed hope more than it is a precise prediction. It is often claimed that Ezekiel's prophecy of the destruction of Tyre was fulfilled in detail (Ezek. 26:1–21), but that is not so according to Ezekiel 29:17–20. The city continued to be inhabited right up until Jesus' own day. Nebuchadnezzer did not do to Tyre exactly what Ezekiel had predicted. We have no right to make a

---

[63] M. Carasik, 'The Limits of Omniscience', *Journal of Biblical Literature* 119 (2000), 221–32. Boyd deals extensively with the complex biblical data in *God of the Possible*, chs. 1–2. Fackre agrees with this interpretation in *Christian Story*, 256–8.
[64] Cf. M. Erickson, *God in Three Persons: A Contemporary Interpretation of the Trinity*, 219; and Geisler, *Creating God*, 130.
[65] Concerning biblical prophecy, Sanders writes, 'God can predict the future as something he intends to do regardless of human response, or God may utter a conditional statement that is dependent on human response, or God may give a forecast of what he thinks will occur based on his exhaustive knowledge of past and present factors.' *God Who Risks*, 137.

prophecy more precise than it is.[66] Fourth, the fulfillment of a prophecy may differ from what the prophet had in mind. Ezekiel predicts a new temple (Ezek. 40–48) but according to the New Testament its fulfillment transcends any earthly building (Jn. 2:19–22). It was fulfilled in the appearance of the church, which is God's temple of the last days. Often when Jesus says that Scripture is being fulfilled, he is not referring to some precise prediction but to his understanding of how God is leading in salvation history. Fulfillments can transcend the original terms of the prophecy because God is free to fulfill them as he decides. In a certain type of apologetics people emphasize precise fulfillments, but the fact is that prophecies are often vague as to the nature and timing of their fulfillment and do not require us to assume exhaustive foreknowledge. Long-range forecasts are often symbolic and vague in matters of detail (e.g. Daniel and the Revelation). Few biblical prophecies allow us to assume exhaustive fore-

---

[66] We may not want to admit it, but prophecies can be fulfilled in surprising ways. For example, in Joseph's dream, his family bowed to him (Gen. 37:9–10), but not necessarily every single member did so. (His mother, having died earlier, was not able to bow.) To take another example, Jerusalem was destroyed by the Babylonians in the sixth century, not by the Assyrians in the eighth century, as it might appear from Micah's oracle (Mic. 3:9–12); the oracle was fulfilled nonetheless because it was the destruction – not the timing of it – that was Micah's burden. Isaiah looked forward to a return of the exiles and to a golden age (Is. 41:14–20). His hope was initially fulfilled, though on a smaller scale than he might have wished; it was the foretaste of a greater fulfillment to come. Ezekiel predicted the destruction of Tyre (Ezek. 26) but also noted that the fulfillment fell a little short of his prediction (Ezek. 29:18). Although John the Baptiser seemed to expect divine judgment to be the main theme of the coming Messiah, Jesus spoke more of mercy. (John's darker theme did surface later on.) According to Paul, the second coming seemed to be just around the corner (1 Thess. 4:17), even though we know today that it still has not come. His word was, however, perfectly appropriate, given the fact that Paul thought the coming could happen at any time. We see an example of hyperbolic speech in Jesus' prediction of the fall of Jerusalem, how not a stone would rest upon another. As a hyperbolic oracle, it was fulfilled just as God intended. I see God as free in the fulfilling of his own prophecies and not bound to a tight (i.e., overly literal or precise) script; the world is God's project, and he works creatively with it. He is free to do new things and free to strike out in new directions – within his overall plans, of course. We cannot pin the free God down. We ought to celebrate the creativity of our loving and relational God, always mindful of the fact that God is free and that God always works in continuity with his own eternal plans and affirmations.

knowledge. No one is required to read them in such a way and cancel out the texts of hesitation.[67]

It is very meaningful to think of the future as partly settled and partly unsettled because it tells us that not everything has been decided at this point in time. It means that the future is a realm of possibilities not just of actualities. This is true even for God, though his awareness of the future possibilities and his anticipation of the future actualities is hugely greater than our own. Nevertheless, the future is open for God as well because everything is not yet settled. This was the kind of creation project he freely entered into. Think of what it would mean for God's freedom if everything were settled. God himself would not be free to act except in predetermined ways. He would have to consult his own fore-knowledge to know what to do next.

This truth certainly summons us to rely on God's faithfulness and resourcefulness to work things out and not on a divine crystal ball. We have to trust God and not an abstract omniscience as our guarantee. No one now knows how God, pursuing an open route strategy, will win the final victory over sin, for example. Even God knows that the scenario is partly settled and partly unsettled. But we have God's promises to rely on. We can be sure that God, as a kind of master chess player, will win, but we cannot be sure exactly how the end game will play itself out. It is two millennia after the resurrection of Jesus; it is taking God a long time to bring his kingdom in. Peter suggests that God is waiting for more people to repent and that is what is affecting the schedule of last things (2 Pet. 3:9). We have to trust that God knows what he is doing and depend on his promises, even though he will undoubtedly surprise us with unexpected moves – consider the unexpected ways in which he brought the Old Testament prophesies to fulfillment in the New Testament.

Thinking of the future as partly settled and partly unsettled forces us to concentrate our attention on the wisdom of God. Many decisions about the future rest in human hands; people have been given the choice between life and death and what they decide is not a foregone conclusion because their responses are not scripted. God issues genuine calls for real responses. It is the wisdom of God that we marvel at, not abstract omni-science. Our focus should be on the promises of God, not on his access to a videotaped future. Of course we wonder how God can, apart from exhaustive foreknowledge and in the light of libertarian freedom, bring about the victory. The answer is that God has promised a new creation. It is not necessary to win every single skirmish and know every single

---

[67] The appeal to prophecy as supernatural has been an apologetic mainstay for centuries and has distorted the interpretation of prophecy. See S. Travis, *I Believe in the Second Coming of Jesus*, 135–43.

detail ahead of time in order to deliver on his promise. God is capable of acting unilaterally and has not placed everything under the control of the creature. He is wise, resourceful and can cope with all contingencies. Our assurance is based, not on a rational system, but on God's promise and on his track record. God does not promise things he cannot deliver. He is not an insecure deity who needs to control everything and fore-know everything in order to accomplish anything!

God is in the business of remaking persons, and achieving that takes time and requires patience. God does not risk for risk's sake, but for love's sake. Love is a pilgrimage into the unknown because it does not know the outcome of every detail in advance. There is an element of the unknown because love abandons securities and goes on a journey. It cannot altogether control what happens but it is worth the price. God takes risks but not unlimited risks. His project is a sound one. He knows that he will accomplish everything, even though he faces opposition on the way to victory.

Though limited in knowing the future in exhaustive detail, owing to the nature of the future, God knows the future in very important ways. He knows the past and the present. He knows all the possibilities. He knows the power of his love to influence the creature. 'When he roars, his children shall come' (Hos. 11:10). God knows what he can do and we trust him. God is the God of hope and we share in his hopefulness. The end is in view, though the precise route to it is open and subject to circumstances.[68]

Divine Sovereignty

Divine sovereignty can be understood in a way similar to omniscience. Just as Scripture imagines the future as partly settled and partly unset-tled and allows a coherent reading of the whole Bible without resorting to contradictions, so too it presents God's sovereignty as partly unilat-eral and partly bilateral. God is not the only power in the universe; he created other powers. Not only does God have to rule with them in mind, he may even have to contend with them. The point is that God is not viewed as being completely in control and exercising exhaustive sov-ereignty. Though no other power can match God's power, each has a degree of influence that it can exercise. The situation is pluralistic: there is no single and all-determining divine will that calls all the shots.[69]

---

[68] P. Fiddes, *The Creative Suffering of God*, 100–9; Sanders, '*God Who Risks*, 170–3.
[69] Cf. Tiessen who takes the view that God is comprehensively in control of everything that happens; see *Providence and Prayer*, 289–98.

God controls some things, but not everything. He conducts a 'general' rather than a 'meticulous' sovereignty. Sanders writes, 'God has sovereignly decided to enter into a project in which he desires reciprocal loving relationships and so does not control everything that happens.'[70] God does not manipulate the creature and does not micromanage the universe. The term 'sovereignty' is not synonymous with 'all-controlling.' God is under no obligation to exercise all-controlling sovereignty if that is not what he wants to do. What sense does it make to claim that God is all-controlling when the Bible describes him responding to changing circumstances and resorting to alternative plans? Why does the Bible describe him grieving, repenting and being responsive? Is this not the reason why we can say that God is not the author of evil and that it comes from somewhere else? God does not get everything that he wants in every given situation. That is the plight of a lover. God's sovereignty is general sovereignty because he has set up a world order in which creatures have input into what happens. This creates a situation of risk, but it is also the context where love can flourish.

Are there not, however, texts that require one to think that God controls everything? There are certainly texts which, when lifted out of context, can sound like that.[71] One can quote Romans 9, which says that God hardened Pharaoh's heart and crushes pots as it pleases him to make it seem like his sovereignty is all-controlling. But to do so it is necessary to ignore factors like judicial hardening, Jeremiah's free-will orientation to his pot-making image, and the unfolding meaning of Romans 9–11.[72] The overall drift of Scripture presents something very different. It speaks about the Lord who denies the power hungry entry into the kingdom of God. Rather, he loves his enemies and takes the form of a servant, allowing himself to be pushed out of the world so that he can redeem it. According to the gospel, God exercises his power in

---

[70] Sanders, *God Who Risks*, 208.

[71] In constructing his antinomy (contradiction) involving divine sovereignty and human freedom, J.I. Packer refers to eight verses in *Evangelism and the Sovereignty of God*, 22 n.1. None of these texts require such a conclusion, and if any did the weight of the evidence implying libertarian freedom would be nullified See Sanders, *God Who Risks*, 34–7. Curiously, since it is likely that Packer views freedom as compatibilist (determinist), there is no antinomy anyway.

[72] J. Calvin, *Concerning the Eternal Predestination of God*; B.B. Warfield, 'Predestination', *Biblical and Theological Studies*, 270–333; L. Boettner, *The Reformed Doctrine of Predestination*, section one; J. Feinberg, 'God Ordains All Things' in Basinger and Basinger (eds.), *Predestination and Free Will*, 19–43; J. Piper, *The Justification of God*.

distinctive ways. It is a power of love, not compulsion, and he triumphs through weakness.

Certain passages in Scripture appear to teach determinism, but a closer examination of their contexts shows that such interpretations are mistaken. For example, Calvin says of the wind in Jonah 1: 'I infer that no wind ever arises or increases except by God's express command.' This is a possible but by no means a necessary inference from the text.[73] One can construe the potter and clay language in Romans 9 as deterministic only if you disregard Jeremiah's original image, which was that God is free to change his plans and start over again, if he wants to. Similarly, when God says through Isaiah, 'I form light and create darkness,' he is not claiming to be the author of evil but is instead referring to the light of Israel's deliverance from Babylon and to the darkness which was God's judgment on the Babylonians. When God asks through Amos, 'Does disaster befall a city unless the Lord has done it?' the reference is to divine judgment on sins, not to disasters in general. When we read in Lamentations 3:38, 'Is it not from the mouth of the Most High that good and bad come?' the exile is under consideration, not evils in general. God sends blessings and curses. When it says in Proverbs, 'The human mind plans the way but the Lord directs the steps' (Prov. 16:9), it should not be over-generalized. It is not telling us that, for example, every bad king of Israel and Judah was ordained to be bad and do what they did. When God says, 'Who makes the mute or deaf, seeing or blind? Is it not I the Lord?' (Exod. 4:11), he is not saying that he causes their disablement but that he can use a poor speaker like Moses. God doesn't need perfect specimens but uses weak people. We must not base awesome conclusions on flimsy evidence. The Bible does not teach that God exercises all-controlling sovereignty.[74]

There is no antinomy here. God rules the world in such a way as to allow for creaturely input. There are not two sets of texts – one affirming exhaustive sovereignty and the other affirming human freedom. That

---

[73] Calvin, *Institutes* I.16.7.

[74] F. Lindstrom, *God and the Origin of Evil: A Contextual Analysis of Alleged Monistic Evidence in the Old Testament*; and T. Inbody, *The Transforming God: An Interpretation of Suffering and Evil*, 80–4. The evidence adduced by Packer in *Evangelism* to support the determinist pole of his alleged antinomy/contradiction is weak. D.A. Carson, in a long book entitled *Divine Sovereignty and Human Responsibility: Biblical Perspectives in Tension* devotes only seventeen pages to establishing the determinist pole in John's Gospel and even in them he includes alternative readings; see181–98. He does not wrestle with the problem he has created for the dynamic nature of the unfolding story of redemption.

would create a contradiction. We are not asked to believe that God exercises all-controlling sovereignty and still holds human beings morally responsible. The Bible is coherent and the contradiction is imaginary. All-controlling sovereignty is not taught in Scripture. There may be mysteries that go beyond human intelligence but this is not one of them. One can hold both to divine sovereignty and human freedom because sovereignty is not all-controlling. The Bible, not rationalism, leads to this solution.[75]

God's Passion

In Scripture, God is revealed as transcendent but also as involved in the world most intimately. God does not simply rule over creation, he is moved and affected by what happens in history. Events arouse joy or sorrow, pleasure or wrath in him. Our deeds move, grieve, gladden, or please him. His nature is not characterized merely by intelligence but is also characterized by pathos. Abraham Heschel writes

> The God of the [Greek] philosophers is unknown and indifferent to man; he thinks but does not speak; he is conscious of himself but oblivious of the world; while the God of Israel is a God who loves, a God who is known to man and concerned with man.[76]

Whereas traditional theology balked at this dimension, the open view of God celebrates the interactivity.

God first created the world and then bound himself to it. This involved a self-limitation on God's part and an act of self-sacrifice. Creation marked the beginning of the passion of God who decided to relate to the world intensely and let himself be affected by it. God wants to share in our history and participate in our life. He wants to communicate with us in as personal a way as possible, even, if need be, as a suffering God.[77]

---

[75] Sanders, *God Who Risks*, 34–7.
[76] A.J. Heschel, *The Prophets*, 224.
[77] The impassibility of God was an axiom of Platonic theology, God being incapable of suffering from an external or internal cause. Hence God cannot experience sorrow, sadness, or pain. This is the most questionable aspect of conventional theism and, when denied, it can bring the model down. Owen, *Concepts*, 23–5; Heschel, *Prophets*, ch. 12; König, *Here Am I!*, 91–102; W. McWilliams, *The Passion of God: Divine Suffering in Contemporary Protestant Theology*; W.J. Harrington, *The Tears of God: Our Benevolent Creator and Human Suffering*; Bauckham, *Moltmann*, ch. 3.

The Old Testament speaks of God's suffering in many ways (as explored below). God speaks through Hosea:

> When Israel was a child, I loved him and out Egypt I called my son. But the more I called them, the more they went from me. Yet it was I who taught Ephraim to walk, I took him up in my arms; but they did not know that I healed them. I led them with cords of human kindness, with bands of love, I was to them like those who lift infants to their cheeks. I bent down to them and fed them. But they will return to the land of Egypt and Assyria shall be their king because they have refused to return to me. How can I give you up, Ephraim? How can I hand you over, O Israel? My heart recoils within me; my compassion grows warm and tender. I will not exercise my fierce anger; I will not again destroy Ephraim; for I am God and no mortal, the Holy One in your midst and I will not come in wrath (Hos. 11:1–9, selected verses).

1. God suffers because of his people

God seeks a covenantal relationship with his people and can be wounded when it is broken. God is anything but coolly unaffected by what the partners do. God even asks himself in effect, what did I do to deserve this? (Jer. 2:5) What more could I have done? (Is. 5:4) God accepts partners with complete seriousness, allowing them the opportunity to participate in the shaping of their own future. Their destiny is generated by God's ongoing interaction with his people and is not something he imposes on them. His relationship with them is emotional and intellectual. God actually internalizes the relationship.[78]

2. God suffers with his people

God hears the cries of his people and mourns over their suffering (Exod. 3:7–8). He even laments over them (Amos 5:1–2). He weeps and wails and mourns. God is deeply involved and not at all removed and detached. In anguish, he visits them with judgment, only to suffer with them. God works in death to bring about life. Judgment becomes a prerequisite of salvation. 'For a brief moment I abandoned you, but with great compassion I will gather you. In overflowing wrath for a moment I hid my face from you, but with everlasting love I will have compassion on you, says the LORD, your Redeemer' (Is. 54:7–8).

3. God suffers for his people

God bears the sin and accepts the cost. He bears the brunt of his people's rejection. God immerses himself in the depths of their sufferings and

---

[78] Fretheim, *Suffering of God*, chs. 7–9.

thereby overcomes the powers of death. God gives himself and expends his life for the sake of his people. God is burdened by their sins. God gasps and pants like a pregnant woman (Is. 42:14). Something has to be done. God's own suffering precedes the birth of a new order. Redemption involves the suffering of God as he bears the cost of human sin and the brunt of rejection. By entering the vale of death, God deals with the powers of death.

God suffers in the context of the covenant relationship, which is viewed as a marriage (often a bad marriage) in which God is anything but apathetic. The experience often leaves God hurt and frustrated and wondering what to do. The husband cannot control the bride. He could punish her but cannot bring himself even to do it. After all, Israel is his firstborn son (Exod. 4:22). He gave birth to her and nursed her like a mother (Is. 49:15). He carried Israel like a father carries a son (Deut. 1:31). God remembers the honeymoon they had but suffers the humiliation of having to be the husband of an adulterous wife (Jer. 2:2). Nevertheless, despite the humiliation, God works to restore the relationship. How deeply the divine lover is affected by what happens! How profoundly the relationship matters to God![79]

This trajectory of the divine passion culminates in the New Testament where, in the incarnation, we observe that God, far from being unchangeable in every respect, changes for our sakes because of his love for us. The God of the gospel becomes involved in the sufferings of Jesus Christ. Father, Son and Spirit both suffer, though in different ways. The Father suffers the death of his Son and the Spirit feels both the Father's pain and the Son's self-surrender. A God who cannot suffer, as tradition has had it, is less than man and far from the God of the gospel. The Hellenes thought that change was a mark of inferior being, whereas the gospel presents us with perfection of a very different kind. It presents a God who is perfect in his changing and perfect in his relating to the world. This is a God who gives himself sacrificially to us and does not remain in splendid isolation. It is in this act of becoming that Jesus is most, not least, like God. What a contrast to the metaphysical absolute that has difficulty being personal much less incarnate. If change and suffering can be ascribed to God, the mystery of the incarnation is much more comprehensible. Divine perfection is perfection in change. This is a God who changes and suffers while remaining perfect. In this unique understanding humanity does not need to ascend to God because God has already graciously descended to us.[80]

---

[79] Sanders, *God Who Risks*, 87–8. Tiessen also picks up on the divine suffering, *Prayer and Providence*, 325–30.

[80] J.M. Hallman, *The Descent of God: Divine Suffering in History and Theology*; and Fiddes, *Creative Suffering*.

In the cross of Christ, we see more than self-emptying, even self-sacrificing. We see the 'weakness' of God by which he saves people. He does not overpower them, but woos them. We see God saving the world by loving his enemies and by suffering. We see God become weak and powerless in order to save. Paradoxically, when God's absence was most apparent, on the cross, God's presence was most profoundly revealed. God became most present when he shared the experience of absence with Jesus. The kenosis of Christ is often mentioned, how he humbled himself and became a slave, but this self-emptying was what he had seen his kenotic Father do.

The cross of Jesus is God's true glory (Jn. 12:23). Taking up the towel is the paradigm of God's power (Jn. 13:4). Instead of using his power to enforce compliance, God travels the path of vulnerable love. He only takes steps to redeem the world when it goes wrong and makes himself vulnerable, because he cares so much. Even his wrath shows how much he cares! He cannot stand idly by and watch the beloved ruin herself.[81] God loves so much that he cries out in pain: 'O that my people would listen' (Ps. 81:13). Jesus too cries out, 'Jerusalem, Jerusalem, the city that kills the prophets and stones those that are sent to it! How often have I desired to gather your children as a hen gathers her brood under her wings, and you were not willing' (Mt. 23:37). How vulnerable God makes himself; even when we work at cross-purposes he does not give up on us.[82]

God is sensitive and responsive in his loving. He relates to the world in dynamic not static terms and truly interacts with creatures. He influences them and they influence him. History is not the product of divine action alone and God's will is not the sole explanation for everything that happens. Human decisions and actions make contributions too. History is the combined result of what God and creatures do. Even God's knowledge is dynamic rather than static. Instead of viewing the whole course of history in a timeless instant, God knows events as they take place and takes note of what transpires. God is receptive to new experiences and flexible in the way in which he works toward his objectives in the world. God is the living God, wide-awake and not asleep. The counsel of God is not timeless and fixed. He did not make all the

---

[81] Heschel, *Prophets*, ch. 16; König, *Here Am I!*, 93–6.
[82] Ibid., 72–5, 91–102. This is a crucial issue. Many of our critics accept the passibility of God seemingly unaware of the effect of doing so on the conventional package of divine attributes. They do not seem to grasp that accepting passibility may require the kind of doctrinal revisions which the open view is engaged in. If God is passible, then he is not, for example, unconditioned, immutable and atemporal.

decisions once and for all apart from the world but is even now making them as he works out the details of the final restoration. History is being fashioned 'according to his counsel', but the question is: what we will do with his counsel? Will we reject it, as the lawyers did, or embrace God's salvation (Eph. 1:11; Lk. 7:30)?[83]

Interpreting Scripture

On 7 February 2000, an editorial in *Christianity Today* asked for both sides in the debate over the open view of God to take Scripture more seriously. This is important for us because the Bible is the place where one finds a revelation of the living God and the personal metaphors that support the open view of God and make an implied critique of the abstract categories that so often predominate in conventional theism. Reform in the doctrine of God is needed precisely because of the Bible, which authorizes the open view in significant ways.

There are different ways of reading the text – for example, biblical theology, existential hermeneutics and narrative theology – but there is also the way of searching out doctrinal truth in the Bible, which is favored by evangelicals. Granted, texts can be imprecise and admit a variety of interpretations because exegesis is not an exact science, owing to the historical situatedness of text and reader. But there is freedom to choose between meanings, both at the macro and micro levels, and one may be influenced by one's own control beliefs and press texts in direc-tions favored by them. For this reason, we cannot expect one model to triumph over the others. A decision will have to be made as to which reading seems more probable and plausible. At the very least, the open view appeals to an impressive array of biblical support.[84]

What we find in Scripture is a range of images designed to disclose something of God's nature. They seem to tell us that creation is a dynamic project and that God is personal and relational. Unfortunately, theologians have not often read the Bible in this way. The dynamic meta-phors have often been viewed as accommodation to the human mind and not taken with full seriousness. They were given for the benefit, as

---

[83] It is a mistake to view God's counsel as an all-inclusive decree and detailed plan, completed before time and executed after creation. In reality, God's plan in Christ is to save a lost world and is even now being worked out: ibid., 132–5.

[84] When he presents Christian theism, Geisler cites only one human authority: St Thomas Aquinas. Who, one wonders, is creating God in whose image? See *Creating God*, ch. 2. T.G. Weinandy, on the other hand, supports the Thomist position with rich scriptural testimony in *Does God Suffer?*, ch. 3.

Philo said, of those whose natural wit is dense and dull. Texts are taken for their psychological effect but not for their theological significance. Offense has been taken from the fact that they involve language drawn from the human sphere, but what other language is there? (How ironical that we who celebrate the incarnation of the Word should balk at concrete images and that those who believe humankind is created in the image of God should balk at anthropomorphisms!) In many ways God is incomparable to the creature but in other ways he is comparable, for example when he acts and suffers, changes and cries out. We ought not to say that these are 'only' human ways of talking about God, while the 'serious' language is provided by our natural reason. It is fitting to speak of God in human terms because humans have been created in God's image and because the best self-revelation of God has been in human form. The human way of speaking of God is the divine way and we must heed it![85]

The open view of God proposes to take biblical metaphors more seriously and thereby recover the dynamic and relational God of the gospel, but in doing so it runs the risk of being too literal in its interpretation. Although being literalistic may appeal to ordinary Christians who like to read the Bible in a matter of fact way, it appeals less to theologians and philosophers who feels loss in the area of intelligibility. It can even make faith in God impossible. It could give the impression that God fumbles the ball just like we do or that God is limited as to place and knowledge (cf. Gen. 18:16–33, where God says he has to go over to Sodom to find out just how wicked these people are). We must avoid presumption in the matter of our speech about God whose reality transcends whatever we say about him. Purely affirmative theology, without the check of negative theology, may make God the creature of our intellect as the Eastern traditions have always reminded us. Interpreting metaphors seriously may not mean interpreting them literally, but it does require us to weigh all the evidence with care.[86]

---

[85] In König, *Here Am I!*, there is a chapter on the 'incomparableness' of God followed by a chapter on the 'comparableness' of God, chs. 1–2. Ware, in contrast, leaves me with the impression that he is not open to certain neglected biblical testimony and is unwilling to integrate it into his model, because it cannot fit. As a tactic, he tries to make open theists look foolish when they do try to take it seriously; see *God's Lesser Glory*, chs. 4, 6, 7.

[86] In this case, there are other texts which tell us that God did not need to travel to Sodom to find out about it (Jer. 23:24), but none that tell us God knows everything before it happens (Amos 5:15). Cf. Fretheim, *Suffering of God*, ch. 4. Though often cited in this connection, Isaiah 41:21–25 does not teach exhaustive omniscience but God's power to affect the future by what he plans to do. Cf. Boyd, *God of the Possible*, 29–31.

Admittedly it is not always easy to interpret these metaphors but we should respect the fact that they are metaphors of revelation and, as such, deserve high respect. On no account should they be negotiated away under the pressure of alien assumptions. It is so easy, for example, to use terms such as perfection, infinity and transcendence to smuggle human ideas about God into theology and not listen to Scripture. How often have we heard reasoning like this: the Bible may say that God repents but, being infinite, he doesn't really. Or, the Bible speaks of 'before and after' with God but, since we know there is no before and after with God, it cannot be so. What is it that prevents us taking seriously the imagery about God changing his mind and/or acting in time? Why can't we allow such passages to speak? Basic to God's character is the fact that that he 'relents from punishing' (Joel 2:13; Jon. 4:2). What disqualifies such texts from being hermeneutically significant like other passages are? Why do we downgrade them as accommodated language and, in effect, silence them?[87]

Conventional theists need to explain why the scriptural portrait of God, which is replete with drama and risk, is read in ways that rule them out. Why does it seem as if they are suppressing these dimensions of the text or, at best, making the story sound dynamic when it really isn't?[88] And on the other hand, where is the biblical support for key features of conventional theism, for example the dogma of divine unchangeableness, or the assumption of timelessness and impassibility, or the doctrine of all-controling sovereignty, or the notion of exhaustive foreknowledge? I think that it would be easier to object to the open view of God on grounds that it is not sufficiently traditional rather than that it is not sufficiently biblical. The model takes Scripture very seriously, especially the dynamic, personal metaphors, while our critics seem to consider it beneath them. Embarrassed by biblical anthropomorphisms, they are inclined to demythologize and/or deliteralize them.[89]

At the same time, there is a Scylla and Charybdis to be negotiated. On the one hand, there is the danger of missing the truth of the metaphors.

---

[87] Compare the reviews of Sanders' *God Who Risks* by S.N. Williams, *Books and Culture*, November 1999, 16–8, and P. Helm, *Modern Reformation*, November 1999, 49.

[88] P. Helm denies it is dyamic, see *Providence*, 51–4. Meanwhile, Tiessen insists that it is dynamic though comprehensively predestined: *Providence and* Prayer, ch. 13.

[89] The hermeneutical trick is to locate 'exact' texts which supposedly establish God's metaphysical attributes like infinite, timeless, impassible, etc. and then dismiss a large body of other texts as 'anthropomorphic' or 'anthropopathic'. In my view, all texts are human language and metaphorical and must be heard; when one listens to them, one has to call into question how the metaphysical

What are the texts of divine repentance telling us? What is it that God's suffering implies? On the other hand, we do not have to be crassly literal. There is not always a one-for-one correspondence in texts that tell us important things. In any analogy there is something literal about reality that we don't want to miss and, at the same time, something different. We need to avoid both literalism and agnosticism. The way forward is to work with the diversity of metaphors and follow the grain of them. For example, God repents, but not as humans do; God suffers, but not exactly as we do; God works out his purposes in time, but not subject to the ravages of time as we are. I do not take every biblical metaphor literally but I do try to take them all seriously. I especially do not want to diminish the reality of God's involvement in time and space and the intimacy of his relationship with us.[90]

One avoids literalism by denying a one-to-one correspondence between metaphors and God's being and agnosticism by affirming a real correspondence between them. One looks for the implications of the metaphors and appropriates the insights they offer into divine reality. All language is anthropomorphic and metaphorical, it is all we have to work with. God reveals himself in the medium of such language, albeit partially. If we lose the metaphors, we lose the self-disclosure. We would end up saying nothing at all. An 'infinite' God beyond metaphor is not a God we can know anything about. We know God because God has participated in our history and makes use of anthropomorphic language in his self-presentation. God shares the context of our spatio-temporal world and makes himself known as a being in relation with us. The truth about God arises from God's use of metaphor and God's coming to us in embodied ways.[91]

We take such expressions as God being a father, a king, a rock, etc. not literally but appropriately and seriously. The problem with the tradition is not that it takes the biblical language metaphorically rather than literally but that it bypasses truths conveyed by it. For example, even though the Bible says repeatedly that God changes his mind and alters his course of action, conventional theists reject the metaphor and deny that such things are possible for God. How could a God, assumed to be exhaustively sovereign and omniscient according to conventional definitions, shift from Plan A to Plan B? The Bible must be misleading us

---

Footnote 89 (*continued*) attributes are being defined. Geisler attempts to deal with biblical material that seems to fit the open view somewhat better than his own decidedly philosophical model; see *Creating God*, ch. 4.

[90] Sanders, *God Who Risks*, 19–23; and Fretheim, *Suffering of God*, ch. 1.

[91] Philosophy itself is metaphorical according to G. Lakoff and M. Johnson, *Philosophy in the Flesh: The Embodied Mind and Its Challenge to Western Thought*.

when it suggests such things! Why can we not agree that, since God is said to repent, it follows that God is free to alter his course of action where appropriate and follow a plan different from the one previously announced? What from a biblical standpoint is the problem here?

Metaphors have meaning and traditionalists owe an explanation as to what they think the meaning is. For example, what does it mean for God to grieve, to interact, to weep, to cry out, to respond to prayer? Let us be done with this 'higher criticism' that sweeps away what the Bible says. The Bible states that God was sorry that he made humanity but conventional theists insist that he could not possibly have been sorry. That would imply that God did not intend things to work out that way. The Bible presents God suffering with his people, but God cannot possibly be feeling grief if he is in control. The gospel presents the Son suffering for us, but that can only refer to his human nature not his divine nature, if God lacks pathos. How long do theologians intend to permit the Hellenic-biblical synthesis to influence exegesis? It is not the open view of God that suffers from a lack of biblical support. The problem lies in the conventional view that treats the Bible loosely and forces it onto a Procrustian bed and pre-established system. We do not have the right to dispose of inconvenient metaphors that do not fit our presuppositions. We must not use alien categories to critically re-interpret and eliminate what the Bible itself says. How ironic it is to find conservatives devoting such an inordinate amount of effort to establishing the authority of the Bible only to depart significantly from it when they come to something that challenges the dogmatic tradition.

We must let Scripture speak to our definitions of the attributes of God. The Bible's representation of God's changeable faithfulness speaks to the issue of immutability. The sufferings of God and the cross of Christ speak to the issue of impassibility. God's saving activities in time speak to the issue of his eternity. God's vulnerability and the reality of human freedom speak to the issue of sovereignty. God's hesitancy about unsettled aspects of the future speaks to the issue of omniscience. Our definitions should flow from an integrated reading of the Bible and not be established on other grounds. This does not mean we take everything literally and do not weigh issues. God is not a lion because he roars, but yet there is truth in the metaphor which needs to be received. Granted, as the apophatic tradition tells us, there are limits to our knowledge of God. Only God knows God truly. Any creature must accept that creatureliness imposes limitations on what we grasp about him. Nevertheless, we gladly receive the positive witness that we have and do our best to understand it.

Chapter Two

Overcoming a Pagan Inheritance

Reform in the doctrine of God is required on the basis of the scriptural foundations. Influences that have distorted our understanding must be confronted so that we can achieve greater theological soundness. We need to identify the type of divine perfection envisaged by the biblical witnesses and consider how better to conceptualize certain of the attributes of God based upon that witness. The main direction is already clear – we need to be more affirming of God as a living person involved in history and less as a remote absolute principle. In one sense, there is nothing new about this: ordinary believers have always relied upon God's dynamic interactivity in the life of faith. But the situation in theology has been less positive: from early times, under the influence of alien ideals of perfection, theology has lost somewhat the biblical focus. A package of divine attributes has been constructed which leans in the direction of immobility and hyper-transcendence, particularly because of the influence of the Hellenistic category of unchangeableness.[1]

Every theology interacts with its environment. It seeks to conceptualize and it creates a kind of synthesis. We have a responsibility to pay attention to the insights of the surrounding culture so that we can communicate the gospel more effectively. Greek thinkers offered the early Christian theologians a worldview in which the divine could be seen as the unifying principle. This was no small gift, though it exacted a considerable price. It set up a tension between Greek and biblical ideals of perfection, requiring theologians to reconcile the incomparable God of the Bible, ever responding to changing circumstances and passionately

---

[1] E. Brunner, *The Christian Doctrine of God*, 152–6; R.B. Edwards, 'The Pagan Dogma of the Absolute Unchangeableness of God', *Religious Studies* 14 (1978), 305–13. The pagan neo-Platonic influence was alive, for example, in Augustine's work from first to last. See P. Brown, *Augustine of Hippo: A Biography*, 307; O.W. Heick, *A History of Christian Thought* I, 24–30.

involved in history, with something like the Unmoved Mover of Aristotle, a God completely sufficient unto himself. The exact relation between ancient Greek philosophy and conventional theism is certainly complex, but one does not have to be an expert to sense the significant struggle to align these two orientations.[2]

Later on we will ask how far the open view of God has accommodated faith to the modern/postmodern world, but the issue here is an alien influence stemming from ancient sources.[3] Our goal is to achieve a sounder theological expression of our faith. We are somewhat in Blaise Pascal's position when he realized how different the God of the philosophers was from the God of Abraham, Isaac and Jacob. Pascal recognized that there was a pagan legacy, which needed to be overcome. The tendency was to present God as one-sidedly transcendent – completely separate from and above the world – and not as the living God. It is a tendency embedded in our own thinking and leads us to suppose it is biblical when it is not. It is what allows conservative dogmatics to entertain definitions of God's attributes that are more philosophical than biblical, without seeming even to be aware of it.[4]

What is happening, I think, is that theologians are trusting their intuitions concerning what God must be like, intuitions shaped by the intellectual environment as much as by Scripture. We are allowing culture to

---

[2] Olson writes, 'The story of Christian theology was deeply influenced by philosophy – especially Greek (Hellenistic) philosophy'. See *Story*, 54; and 'North African Thinkers Examine Philosophy,' 84–98. The 'Hellenization' of doctrine, however, is too strong a description of what happened. Certainly, a correlation took place between scripture and Greek thought but that was inevitable and right. However, there was as much dehellenization as there was Hellenization. The fathers stood up to pagan influences more often than they succumbed to them; see J. Pelikan, *The Emergence of the Catholic Tradition (100–600)*, 45–55.

[3] W. Pannenberg balances an appreciation of the Greek input with critical discernment: 'The Appropriation of the Philosophical Concept of God as a Dogmatic Problem of Early Christian Theology' in *Basic Questions in Theology* II, 119–83. Küng also understands the issue in a commanding way: *Does God Exist?*, 184–8. Also see O'Donnell, *Trinity and Temporality*, 44–52. Sanders also traces the development of theism in the early church in Pinnock, et al., *Openness*, ch. 2; and *God Who Risks*, ch. 5.

[4] One thinks, for example, of C. Hodge, *Systematic Theology* I, ch. 5; and L. Berkhof, *Systematic Theology*, ch. 6. Though each author wants to be biblical, one senses another world of thought. For other examples, see H. Schmid, *Doctrinal Theology of the Evangelical Lutheran Church*; H. Heppe, *Reformed Dogmatics: Set Out and Illustrated from the Sources*; J. Macquarrie, *In Search of Deity: An Essay in Dialectical Theism*, ch. 3.

have a larger influence than it should. We are gravitating toward accepted ideas about God and not to what he is disclosing about himself, which is ironically a liberal theological method. Barth pointed this out in relation to Melanchthon who, when he took up the doctrine of God, seemed to shape it from a source other than God's revelation, i.e. from an independently formed and general idea of God.[5] John Sanders explains, 'Sometimes the attributes of God are derived on the basis of the *dignum deo* (what it is dignified for God to be according to natural theology) instead of looking at the particular sort of project God is seeking to accomplish in history.'[6]

It is tempting to think of God abstractly as a perfect being and then smuggle in assumptions of what 'perfect' entails. Does a perfect being suffer or not? Is a perfect being timeless or not? We may ascribe to God attributes of greatness as we conceive them and miss what God is actually telling us in his word. We may resist the truth that God responds to what is happening in history because we think it might jeopardize God's unchangeability as we imagine it. We might think it unworthy of God to respond to contingencies since this implies that God changes in some way. We could even reason that it would be better for God to know the future exhaustively than for God to know the future as partly settled and partly unsettled, even though the Bible seems to take the latter view. What we are doing, in effect, is seeking to correct the Bible; to derive truth about God not from biblical metaphors but from our own intuitions of what is 'fitting' for God to be. In this way God's nature is made to conform to our notions of what deity should be like and, if the Bible does not measure up to this standard in its speech about God, we invoke our own subjective criteria to correct it.[7] However, our intuitions about God, and this goes for everyone, have to be tempered and even corrected by the biblical revelation.[8]

When Calvin met items in the Bible that did not fit into his system, he would say that God is 'lisping' like a nursemaid lisps to a child. Granted, there is some of this going on, but it is easy to use this idea to correct the Bible by one's own way of thinking. Calvin knew, or thought he knew, that God cannot repent or be surprised, hence if such a thing is said it must be a case of God lisping. He knew the truth about God independently of the Bible and could judge when the Bible spoke in childish ways. If, for example, the Bible presented God operating in time, he knew from

---

[5] Barth, *Church Dogmatics* II/1, 259.
[6] Sanders, *God Who Risks*, 13.
[7] MacGregor, *He Who Lets Us Be*, ch. 2.
[8] Morris, *Idea*, 35–45.

his system that it could not be so. He knew, or thought he knew, that it is 'better' for God to be timeless and possess his being all at once rather than to be temporal, even if it threatens the biblical concept of God as personal agent, as it surely does.[9]

The Pagan Legacy

Jesus spoke Aramaic, not Greek, and the Bible was written in Jerusalem, not Athens. The Christian doctrine of God was, however, shaped in an atmosphere influenced by Greek thought. It is not difficult to imagine possible effects of this. What if Plato's assumption that God cannot change was current at the time of the rise of Christianity? He had argued in the *Republic* that deity, being perfect, cannot change or be changed because any change in a 'perfect' being could only be change for the worse. Whatever Plato meant by this, the power of this idea on Christian thinking has been enormous. It pressured early theologians into supposing that the relations God has with this world must be unchangeable and non-temporal relations, which puts a terrific strain on the biblical witness. What if Aristotle's belief that God is an Unmoved Mover, which moves other things without moving itself, was a respected idea in the culture in which Christianity developed?[10] It is not going to be easy to square the dynamic biblical portrait of a God who is involved in the world and affected by it with Greek axioms like these that are fundamentally static. Yet that is exactly what has been attempted. It may also not prove easy to square the biblical concept of the transcendent creator with modern presuppositions (ch. 3).

The fact is that the conventional doctrine of God has a double origin, in the Bible and in Greek thinking.[11] Bloesch states, 'A compelling case can be made that the history of Christian thought shows the unmistakable imprint

---

[9] Radical feminists today are putting together a new biblical/pagan synthesis. They are combining the values of the world-transcending Yahweh with those of the world-renewing Ba'als. This is a topic for another time; see L. Wilkinson, 'Post Christian Feminism and the Fatherhood of God', *CRUX* 36 (2000), 16–30.
[10] Plato, *Physics* VIII, 5.
[11] Hanlon, *Immutability*, 1; Owen, *Concepts*, 1; L. Sweeney, *The Divine Infinity*; G.L. Prestige, *God in Patristic Thought*; T. Boman, *Hebrew Thought Compared With Greek*. Mormon scholar S.E. Robinson, in a dialogue with C.L. Blomberg, highlights the influences of Greek philosophy on developments in Christian doctrine; see S.E. Robinson and C.L. Blomberg, *How Wide the Divide? A Mormon and an Evangelical in Dialogue*. R.N. Ostling and J.K. Ostling question Robinson and Blomberg's reading of the developments in doctrine; see *Mormon America: The Power and the Promise*, 309–10, 422.

of a biblical-classical synthesis in which the ontological categories of Greco-Roman philosophy have been united with the personal-dramatic categories of biblical faith.'[12] Tertullian asked a famous question: 'What has Athens to do with Jerusalem?' His query implied it had nothing to do with it, but the answer as concerns the doctrine of God is actually 'much in every way!'[13]

1. Philo of Alexandria

Philo defined the divine essence as 'that which is'. This is a non-relational term that displaces the personal God of the biblical revelation and causes God's attributes to acquire meanings they would not otherwise have had.[14]

2. Augustine

Augustine, though quoting the Bible extensively, allowed neo-Platonic ideas to influence his interpretations. The influence was deep and lasting and put God in a kind of box. It preferred stability to change and being to becoming.[15] It meant that immutability and impassibility took precedence over God's suffering love. It spelled God's immunity to time, change, and real relations with creatures. It required that God's knowledge and will be unchangeable. As Aquinas would later put it so memorably,

> Since God is outside the whole order of creation and all creatures are ordered to him and not conversely, it is manifest that creatures are really related to God himself, whereas *in God there is no real relation to creatures, but a relation only in idea*, inasmuch as creatures are referred to him.[16]

---

[12] Bloesch, *God the Almighty*, 205. For details, see J.D. McLelland, *God the Anonymous: A Study in Alexandrian Philosophical Theology*; R.A. Norris, *God and World in Early Christian Theology: A Study in Justin Martyr, Irenaeus, Tertullian, and Origen*; H. Chadwick, *Early Christian Thought and the Classical Tradition*.

[13] J.L. Gonzalez sees it as a kind of idolatry, *Manana: Christian Theology from a Hispanic Perspective*, ch. 6. But not all agree; Prestige writes, 'I must make clear my fundamental outlook. I do not believe that the importation of hellenistic rationalism, to expound and explain the facts of Christian history, was illegitimate.' See *Patristic Thought*, xiii.

[14] McLelland, *God the Anonymous*, 25–44.

[15] R.T. Wallis, *Neo-Platonism*, 160–78. Also H.J. Blumenthal and R.A. Markus (eds.), *Neo-Platonism and Early Christian Thought*; and T. Finan and V. Twomey (eds.), *The Relationship Between Neo-Platonism and Christianity*.

[16] Aquinas, *Summa Theologica* I, 1a 13.7. Is it not astonishing that this is what so many have the temerity to call the 'orthodox' view?

3. Thomas Aquinas

In his *Summa Theologica,* Aquinas presents arguments for the existence of God based on the philosophy of Aristotle and concludes at the end of each proof, 'This is what everyone calls God.' But is it God and ought it to be? Do we really want to assume that God is an unmoved mover or something approximating it? Surely the gospel does not view God in terms of changeless thought and timeless being but in reference to historical events. It testifies to a God who became temporal in a man, Jesus of Nazareth, with whose sufferings and death God identified himself. We cannot assume that God is what people think God is because, very often, that is not the God revealed in Jesus. Richard Lovelace remarks, 'A good many non-biblical and anti-biblical presuppositions from Aristotle slipped through into the system without being filtered out by biblical understanding.'[17]

This is the danger I also see in 'perfect being' (or Anselmian) theology today that also starts from an intuition of perfection and goes to a discussion of the divine attributes by way of deduction. It says, if an infinitely perfect Being exists, we can conclude, for example, that God is thoroughly benevolent, necessarily existent, and a conscious agent with unlimited knowledge and power, who is the ontologically independent source of everything. While I appreciate the clarity it can introduce into the discussion of God's attributes once they are known, I sense in it a continuation of the human speculation that has led us astray. Whether a perfect Being exists and what such a Being is like is not, I submit, intuitively obvious. If it were, we would have known about it much earlier.[18]

Though Aquinas was a marvelous Christian thinker in so many ways; this is an illustration of how not to proceed. Thomas derives divine attributes from reason rather than revelation. He proceeds from a demonstration of God's existence to his explanation of what God's nature *must be.* If God is the unmoved mover and the first cause of everything, he must be pure actuality without potentiality – otherwise, he would require a mover and a cause for himself. To say otherwise, Thomas thought, would be to suggest there is some lack in God that would make it impossible for him to be first cause. Because of God's complete actuality of being, God must not be really related to creatures because to be really related would imply a kind of imperfection in God. Even the fact that there are creatures makes

---

[17] R.F. Lovelace, *Dynamics of Spiritual Life: An Evangelical Theology of Renewal,* 176.
[18] P. Clayton, *The Problem of God in Modern Thought,* 132–6.

no real difference to God. Aquinas allowed natural theology to determine the doctrine of God to some extent.[19]

These brief examples show that there has been a Christianization of Greek, and a Hellenization of Christian, thought. There was a tension between the ideals of an immutable perfection beyond the world and a creative sovereignty over and in the world. As a result, pressure was exerted on theology toward monopolarity and one-sidedness, toward conceiving of a Reality in every respect absolute and whose relations to the world are nominal and external.[20]

Theologians have to particularly face up to the influence of the pagan dogma of the absolute unchangeableness of God, which has placed severe limits upon how certain of his attributes are understood. It has created unnecessary difficulties and skewed our thinking. It forces us to think of God knowing a changing world in an unchanging way, as acting in a temporally changing world in an atemporal way, as experiencing time as simultaneous whole and not successively. Such tensions originate in the syncretism of biblical and Greek thought and arise out of the tension between Hellenistic and biblical ideals of divine perfection.[21] African theologian A.G. Nnamani identifies the problem:

> The attempt to merge Hellenistic and Semitic conceptions of God into one acceptable notion of God has been a basic preoccupation of theology since the onset of Christianity. It has been a challenge for theologians to harmonize two apparently contradictory understandings of the divine reality. In practical terms, this has always meant mediating between the immutable and impassible God of the Greek philosophers and the dynamic and passionate God of the Semite biblical experience. The difficulties with such an endeavor are all too obvious in the history of Christian theology. In view of the differences between the Semitic and the Hellenistic perception of the God-world relationship, the task of evolving a feasible mediation between their various conceptions of the divine reality is wearisome. In fact, it does at times seem impossible. Yet it is indispensable for any theological inquiry that is truly Christian.[22]

---

[19] See Olson, *Story*, 340–2. The same pattern holds for the reasoning of Anselm; ibid., 322.

[20] The influence of Philo, the Alexandrian Jewish philosopher, on the early patristic tradition was immense. He showed them how to interpret the Bible in the manner of middle Platonism. Weinandy, *Does God Suffer?*, 74–82.

[21] Edwards, 'Pagan Dogma', 5–13; and E. Hatch, *The Influence of Greek Ideas and Usages Upon the Christian Church*.

[22] A.G. Nnamani, *The Paradox of a Suffering God: On the Classical, Modern-Western and Third World Struggles to Harmonise the Incompatible Attributes of the Trinitarian God*, 263.

At issue is whether it is proper to use an extra-biblical idea of deity to interpret the Bible and whether we should require Scripture to speak through a filter. Should an axiom of what God 'must be like' intellectually be allowed to determine interpretation? Shall we continue flattering God with epithets like absolute being instead of honoring God's self-revelation in the crucified Jesus? Certainly not!

In Hellenistic thinking God is essentially what the world is not. Divine reality begins where the world leaves off and is defined in terms of opposition. This leads to formulating a concept of God by denying characteristics of the world to God, the *via negativa*. It leads to using negative abstractions such as atemporality, unchangeability, simplicity and apathy. In the case of the latter, it was thought that if God could be made to suffer by another, he would be vulnerable to that other being. It would be exercising influence over him and God would not then be unlimited and unconditioned. For God to be God in this way of thinking, he must be incapable of being changed or moved to suffer. Although nowadays few theists defend the notion of the apathy of God, they seldom reflect on the implications of not doing so. In rejecting divine apathy, one is: acknowledging Hellenistic influences on theology; agreeing about the need of reform in the doctrine of God; and questioning several of the related attributes, e.g. if God suffers, he changes, is conditioned, has temporal experience and limited sovereignty. The conventional attributes rise and fall together. If God is personal and enters into relationships, God cannot be immutable in every respect, timelessly eternal, impassible, or meticulously sovereign. Piecemeal reform will not do the job; we need some thorough rethinking.

Please notice that I am not leveling a crude charge of the Hellenization of Christian doctrine. There are aspects of the synthesis that I think are positive. The Greek ideal of perfection emerged against the background of the fickle gods of the pantheon and was a lofty concept of God relative to that context. Syncretism is not always a bad thing but there are always dangers. We must let the divine self-disclosure speak. Room has to be made for the freedom of God. The Hellenistic assumptions place God so far away from us and as high above us as possible. They lead us to a one-sidedly transcendent deity. The side of God that is turned away from us predominates and the side of God that has turned toward us is diminished. It is not wrong to exalt God's otherness, except at the expense of divine relatedness.[23]

---

[23] W. Pannenberg, [*Systematic Theology?*] 'The Appropriation of the Philosophical Concept of God as a Dogmatic Problem of Early Christian Theology', 119–183 See also G. Watson, *Greek Philosophy and the Christian Notion of God*; H.A. Wolfson, *The Philosophy of the Church Fathers.*

The fathers, because of their belief in impassibility, had great difficulty handling Jesus' suffering. Richard Bauckham writes, 'Here the shift to categories of divine nature and the Platonic definition of the divine nature which the fathers took for granted proved serious impediments to anything more than a formal inclusion of human humiliation, suffering and death in the identity of God.'[24] They could handle exaltation better than humiliation and needed a theology of the cross. They needed to be able to see God as revealed in the passion of Jesus, as glorified in his degradation. The gospel brought something new to light: God is a radically self-giving God and descends to the lowest condition. The fathers, with their presuppositions, had trouble handling it.[25]

Again, this is not a criticism of the historic faith of the church. My faith too is in the triune God. I maintain that God and the world are ontologically distinct, that God interacts with the world, and that God is omnipotent, omniscient and wholly good. I am a standard Christian theist but I oppose a version of basic theism that incorporates certain Greek categories causing distortions in doctrine. I oppose the tendencies shaped by Greek assumptions about the divine.

To a degree, we have allowed the doctrine of God to be accommodated to aspects of the ancient philosophical horizon that has introduced nuances, which do not serve the biblical witness, into the definitions of God's attributes.

Tertullian, who could be zealous in rejecting Greek ideas that he found incompatible with the biblical faith, failed to free himself from the Greek concept of static perfection. Although Tertullian often defined God's eternity as everlasting not timeless, and saw that divine repentance implied God changing a prior purpose, he also insisted on the Greek view that there was no change or temporality in God. Though he rejected a number of pagan assumptions, he accepted the most damaging – the concept of the absolute unchangeableness of God. If only he had asked, 'What does Elea have to do with Jerusalem?' and not, 'What does Athens have to do with Jerusalem?'(It was Parmenides of Elea who introduced the idea of exaggerated immutability that resulted in the mixed message we still hear today.)[26]

Karl Barth deserves credit for blazing a fresh trail in his treatment of the perfections of God. He gave God's attributes a Christological

---

[24] R. Bauckham, *God Crucified: Monotheism and Christology in the New Testament*, 79.

[25] Hallman, *Descent of God*; Moltmann, *Crucified God*, ch. 6.

[26] Edwards, 'Pagan Dogma', 311–3. Also Brunner, *Christian Doctrine of God*, 151–6, 241–7, 293–302.

foundation that enabled him to break with abstract categories. His exposition revolves around the truth that God chooses to love us out of his own freedom and he identifies God as the living God encountered in the history of the divine self-disclosure. Barth does not appeal to general principles or static concepts but focuses on God as revealed in the history that climaxes in Jesus Christ, and puts great emphasis on the dynamic character of the divine being. A revision of what it means to be God will have to be given if Jesus is God-with-us. The gospel does not invite us to think of God in abstract ways and then seek the presence of this deity in Jesus. Instead, it presents the coming of God's Word in a servant who humbles himself and becomes obedient unto death. Besides redefining what humanity means, the revelation redefines what divinity means.[27]

Nicolas Berdiaev writes

> The static conception of God as *actus purus*, having no potentiality and completely self-sufficient is a philosophical, Aristotelian, and not a biblical conception. The God of the Bible, the God of the revelation, is by no means an *actus purus*. He has affective and emotional states, dramatic develop-ments in his inner life, inward movement.[28]

Is it not extraordinary how limited is the conventional conception of God? What a gulf between how people often view God and how God is self-revealed! Self-satisfaction, self-sufficiency, stony immobility and the demand for continual submission are qualities that Christianity con-siders sinful in people, yet often ascribes to God. What in humanity we consider sins are, nevertheless, posited as God's attributes! The conven-tional doctrine of God needs to be Christianized. We need to think through our doctrine in the light of Jesus Christ. We should take the self-revelation of God more seriously; not bring a ready-made doctrine and fit revelation into it. In this way we might even reduce the force of objec-tions to faith in God: how beautiful is the God who goes out from himself and gets involved in people's affairs?[29]

Evangelical Theology

James Oliver Buswell Jr, a conservative presbyterian theologian, ques-tions, in his treatment of the doctrine of God, divine immutability, time-lessness, impassibility and pure actuality. He admonishes us: 'We should

---

[27] Barth, *Church Dogmatics* II/1, ch. 6.
[28] N. Berdiaev, *The Destiny of Man*, 28.
[29] O'Donnell, *Trinity and Temporality*, 23–5.

shake off the static ideology which has come into Christian theology from non-biblical sources.'[30] Michael Horton admits that, 'It is true that the church has sometimes strayed beyond the biblical story to borrow from Greek philosophy in its defense of a God who does not suffer.'[31] Many evangelicals share this concern about pagan borrowing: including Nicholas Wolterstorff, Hendrikus Berkhof, Donald G. Bloesch, Harry Boer, Vincent Brummer, Adrio König, Stephen T. Davis, H.D. McDonald, Richard J. Foster, Philip Yancey and Dallas Willard.[32] Stephen T. Davis, for example, holds to God's temporal not timeless eternity. Davis insists that there are ways in which God changes and denies that God causes human free choices.[33] The open view of God is not alone in seeing a need of reform; its 'sin' was to take it into other areas, such as divine sovereignity and foreknowledge.

Of special interest is the way in which conservative Calvinist authors now want to say that God responds to us and is unhappy when things go badly. They are trying to work such themes into their work. They know that evangelicals believe these truths and try to co-opt them, even though divine changeableness is incompatible with theological determinism. Many are taking advantage of the rhetoric of the open view of God, which Bible readers find compelling, and are trying to work it into their own language.

Ronald Nash, for example, expresses unhappiness with both Thomism and process theism. He speaks about the need to modify conventional theism and sees that the concept of immutability must be changed[34] Nash does not defend divine timelessness, though he holds to exhaustive foreknowledge.[35] In short, he seeks 'a mediating concept of God.'[36]

Terrance Tiessen defends God's having temporal experiences and rejects the view that God is timeless. Tiessen defends God's passibility in order to be clear about God's involvement in the world. He does not dismiss, as many Calvinists do, such expressions as God's repenting and grieving as mere anthropomorphisms.[37]

---

[30] J.O. Buswell Jr, *A Systematic Theology of the Christian Religion* I, 56.
[31] M. Horton, *We Believe: Recovering the Essentials of the Apostles' Creed*, 243.
[32] Sanders, *God Who Risks*, 161–4.
[33] S.T. Davis, *Logic and the Nature of God*, chs. 1, 3 and 5.
[34] R.H. Nash, *The Concept of God*, 105, 114.
[35] Ibid., 83 and 66 respectively.
[36] Ibid., 36, 113–115.
[37] Tiessen, *Providence and Prayer*, ch. 13.

Millard Erickson notes such flexibility too and seems to accept it.[38] Impassibility is undoubtedly the Achilles heel of conventional thinking. It was as self-evident to our ancestors as it is out of question to us, but as soon as one tinkers with it the edifice trembles.[39] To our ancestors God was either perfect or passible; to us God is both perfect and passible. To them God was perfect or changeable; to us he is both perfect and changeable.

Most evangelical theists, however, either do not acknowledge a problem or, if they do, respond to it with half measures.[40] Like Arminius himself, they know modifications have to be made but draw back from making them – at least, coherently. Typically, Calvinists reject impassibility and, therefore, modify immutability but hold onto timelessness, all-controlling sovereignty and exhaustive foreknowledge. Tiessen denies timelessness and impassibility but sticks to all-controlling sovereignty – but why would God grieve if he were meticulously sovereign? McLeod upholds divine passibility and redefines immutability in terms of faithfulness but continues to defend all-controlling sovereignty, which makes nonsense of these moves.[41] Geisler thinks that God responds to prayer without it affecting his immutability.[42] Packer defends libertarian freedom and then maintains that all-controlling sovereignty is simultaneously true. (A theologian is not obliged to be logically consistent but there is a price to pay for exempting oneself from the laws of rationality, it is intelligibility.)[43]

Millard Erickson is aware of the pagan roots of immutability and timelessness, and modifies the definitions, at least a little. On several attributes, he sees the problem of the Greek influence – e.g. immutability, timelessness, impassibility and simplicity – and moves cautiously toward theological reform. He nearly breaks free of the biblical/classical synthesis but then retains the category of all-controlling sovereignty in order to defend exhaustive divine foreknowledge. This move shuts down the very dynamism in God which Erickson sees the need to

---

[38] Erickson, *Father Almighty*, 88.

[39] M. Sarot, *God, Passibility and Corporeality*, ch. 1.

[40] Bray, ordinarily an astute evangelical theologian, does not seem to understand the problem; see *Personal God*.

[41] D. MacLeod, *Behold Your God*, chs. 4, 21. In his discussion of the current debate surrounding the doctrine of God, McLeod is clearly aware of the harm done to Christian doctrine through the influence of neo-Platonic ideas. He openly admits how unscriptural conventional theism has become and advocates courageous reforms, ch. 23.

[42] Geisler, *Creating God*, 85–7.

[43] Packer, *Evangelism*, ch. 1. Even Helm makes this point in *Providence*, 61–6.

recover. The conventional package of immobility attributes is very tight. If you retain one, you might as well retain them all. Retaining all-controlling sovereignty, for example, hinders reforms needed in other areas from doing any good.[44] Bruce Ware and Wayne Grudem are good examples of theologians who accept the need to reformulate immutability but refuse to surrender timelessness, all-controlling sovereignty and exhaustive omniscience. It remains a mystery how one can say that God acts and feels in response to different situations whilst saying that he causes everything and knows everything.[45]

On a positive note, this shows that conventional theism is not as monolithic as is sometimes suggested. Even those who complain about openness theism are revising their views along some of the same lines as the openness view. There is no single old model – it comes in various forms and every version of it is a revised version. When seen in this light, it becomes apparent that the open view belongs to the discussion and should not be sidelined.

Less positively, these developments show that many evangelicals are half-hearted about the need of reform, even though they see that it is necessary. They fiddle with details but lack the courage to challenge the conventional thinking head on. They are aware of a problem and take some measures to resolve it but do too little to make a real difference. One cannot just introduce dynamic and relational features into the doctrine of God without reconsidering undynamic and unrelational features of it like meticulous sovereignty and exhaustive foreknowledge.[46]

The conventional package of attributes is tightly woven. You cannot deny one, such as impassibility, without casting doubt cast on others, like immutability. It's like pulling on a thread and unraveling a sweater. A little boldness is required; tentative changes will not do. Wolterstorff comments

> Once you pull on the thread of impassibility, a lot of other threads come along with it. Aseity, for example – that is, unconditionedness. The biblical witness seems to me clearly to be that God allows himself to be affected by the doings of the creatures God created. What led the traditional theologians

---

[44] Erickson, *Father Almighty*, 203–9. Curiously he makes this move in the chapter on God's foreknowledge and not in the one on God's power.

[45] B.A. Ware, 'On Opening What's Closed and Closing What's Open: Rethinking the Doctrine of God in the Light of the Openness Proposal'; W. Grudem, *Systematic Theology: An Introduction to Biblical Doctrine*, chs. 11–13, 16.

[46] Similarly B.A. Demarest and G.R. Lewis, *Integrative Theology: Knowing Ultimate Reality – The Living God* I, 177, 215, 203, 321.

to affirm aseity was their philosophical argument that the world is such that it can only be explained if we postulate a being which is the condition of everything but itself, itself being conditioned by nothing. To give up aseity then is to give up an argument for God's existence – an argument which is questionable in any case. One also has to give up on immutability and eternity. If God really responds, God is not metaphysically immutable and, if not metaphysically immutable, not eternal.[47]

The conventional package of attributes is tightly drawn. Tinkering with one or two of them will not help much. The open view lays down the gauntlet and invites other theologians to take a firmer grip and submit more coherent alternatives. By the same token, the open view has to consider how far this unraveling can be allowed to go. We have ourselves resisted tossing out creation *ex nihilo*, which plays a major role in the classical package.

As conventional theists, Thomists and Calvinists have different agendas. Thomists care a lot about immutability and do not think of themselves as determinists. Calvinists care a lot about sovereignty and do not hold the line on immutability and unconditionality. Nevertheless, both tend to shut down biblical dynamism, even while placing the emphasis at a different point in the immobility package because the two themes do connect. God must be immutable and sovereign to be unconditioned, otherwise he would find himself in a risky situation, i.e. having to responding to a changing world. In reality, it is the Calvinists, not the Thomists, who dominate the evangelical context. It is, therefore, the issue of sovereignty and not immutability that predominates in the discussion.[48]

The open view and evangelical theology are generally moving toward a more dynamic position, and we can move forward together. I should not exaggerate my distaste for the conventional thinking. I do not regard it as merely a Hellenistic corruption of the Bible. Had the tradition

---

[47] N.P. Wolterstorff, 'Does God Suffer?', *Modern Reformation* 8.5 (1999), 47. Also see his 'Suffering Love' in T.V. Morris (ed.), *Philosophy and the Christian Faith*, 196–237. On the key category of the unconditionedness of God, see Sarot, *God, Passibility and Corporeality*, ch. 2.

[48] It is encouraging to see reforming tendencies at work too. Having noted such developments among Calvinists previously, the Thomists are working at redefining their central category: see W.N. Clarke, 'A New Look at the Immutability of God' in R. Roth (ed.), *God Knowable and Unknowable*, 43–72; O'Hanlon, *Immutability*; and 'Does God Change?', *Irish Theological Quarterly* 53 (1987), 161–83; T.G. Weinandy, *Does God Change?* Our own evangelical Thomist, Geisler, however, has few misgivings and thinks that the objections can be met without giving ground; see *Creating God*, ch. 5.

uncritically absorbed the motif of a totally unchangeable God and unmoved mover it could not have proclaimed the reality of the living God as it did. What I am saying is that it has been characterized by one-sidedness. The tendency developed to place God as far away from and as high over us as possible and to prefer abstract categories to biblical ones. I appreciate the magnificence of Thomist and Calvinst thought but want us to distance ourselves from the tendency to see God too much as a solitary, narcissistic being who suffers from his own completeness.

We need to let God's own self-revelation dominate our thinking rather than what natural reason and tradition tell us that God must be like. Preunderstandings, preconceptions and control beliefs that are part of the biblical-classical synthesis threaten to control our interpretation of the Bible. That grip must be broken. Recall Bloesch's judgment, 'A compelling case can be made that the history of Christian thought shows the unmistakable imprint of a biblical-classical synthesis in which the ontological categories of Greco-Roman philosophy have been united with the personal-dramatic categories of biblical faith.'[49] If he is right, reform in the doctrine of God is called for.

The Open Nature of God

Let us attend now to modifications to the definitions of attributes in the doctrine of God, which are needed on the basis of biblical revelation. Let us try and lessen results of the biblical-classical synthesis and achieve a better understanding of God as a triune, loving person, reliable and flexible, sensitive and resourceful, patient and wise, everlasting and all-knowing. It is not a question of diminishing the glory of God, which is so well captured in traditional thinking, but of recapturing God's true beauty so often obscured by it. So what do we get when we subtract the pagan influences?

1. The personal God
We ought to view God in personal not absolutist terms. The primary category in Christian theism is person not substance. God is a subject who relates to us and has purposes for history. He is a personal being who created the universe and rules over it. God is not a part of the world. He is ontologically distinct and has the power to act in relation to it, the world being a sphere of divine creativity and subject to his will. In the Old Testament, God even gives himself a personal name, Yahweh, and in the New Testament the Trinity is the model of interpersonal

---

[49] Bloesch, *God the Almighty*, 205.

relationships and created the world with a view to such relationships God makes decisions and acts on them. The divine/human relationship is often spoken of in terms of marriage, child rearing and adoption. None of this would be true of an impersonal entity. God created humanity in his image, as an analogy of God, and the very basis of speaking of God in human terms. God wants to be thought of as a person who relates with other persons, who loves and suffers, responds and plans.[50]

Regarding God's name, Northrop Frye writes

> In Exodus 3:14, though God gives himself a name, he defines himself as 'I am that I am', which scholars say is more accurately rendered 'I will be what I will be'. We might come closer to what is meant in the Bible by the word 'God' if we understood it as a verb, and not a verb of simple asserted existence but a verb implying a process accomplishing itself. This would involve trying to think our way back to a conception of language in which words were words of power, conveying primarily the sense of forces and energies rather than analogues of physical bodies. God may have lost his function as subject or object of a predicate, but may not be so much dead as entombed in a dead language.[51]

The various versions of conventional theism argue that God is personal but leave the impression of absolutism. As immutable and timeless, God is not free to act and interact as a person would. As absolute monarch, God is the author of a story in which he is really the sole performer and we are but names in the script. All this renders so many biblical metaphors almost meaningless.

God is a relational being who thinks and acts, loves and knows, but unlike human persons who possess bodies. God is not normally associated with a body, although he has the ability to become embodied, as happened when the Word became flesh. He can also choose to use the universe as a kind of body, as we saw in the Old Testament. He can ride on the clouds and inhabit the heavens. Scripture often imagines what God is like and projects a physical form for God in the theophanies. It also compares embodied personal agents to God, in whose 'image' they were made. Being in some way embodied is not as foreign to Scripture as it is to tradition, which prefers spirit to flesh. The fact is that Scripture does not insist on God being formless. Fretheim comments, 'Israel did not conceive of God in terms of formlessness but rather that the human form of the divine appearances

---

[50] An early essay of John Sanders is a classic, 'God as Personal' in Pinnock (ed.), *Grace of God*, ch. 8.
[51] N. Frye, *The Great Code: The Bible and Literature*, 17–8.

constituted an enfleshment which bore essential continuities with the form which God was believed to have.'[52]

The only personal agents we know about are embodied agents. It might help us to imagine divine agency if God were somehow, mysteriously, embodied. It might also explain the divine passibility and even divine omniscience if God could access feelings of ours and his own. It would also overcome the spirit-matter dualism that so impoverished our sense of God's sacramental presence in the church.[53] I would venture to say that corporeality is a subject that ought to be on the modern agenda and which has been neglected hitherto. We need to consider more carefully what form of corporeality would be appropriate to ascribe to God. The world is surely not God's body in the way we experience it. That would make it difficult to express the gracious, non-necessary and asymmetrical relationship of God to the world. But the idea is a subject for thought.[54]

2. God as a loving person

The open view of God emphasizes that he is a loving person; love is the very essence of his being. God created others so that he could enjoy them and they could experience his love and reciprocate it. God sovereignly chooses to love us and is conditioned by our willingness or unwillingness to receive or refuse love. Love is precarious and makes even God vulnerable because it may not be reciprocated. Jesus describes God as a father who is waiting for a son, whom he had not wanted to leave home in the first place, to return. It was not within his power to compel him to do so. In a word, lovers are vulnerable because love is precarious. On another level, giving birth to children and raising them is also a risky business because parents can influence, but not control, their children.[55]

Love is more than an attribute; it is God's very nature. How strange then that love appears so far down on the list of God's attributes in

---

[52] Fretheim, *Suffering of God*, 105. Also see ch. 6.

[53] Pinnock, *Flame*, 119–29.

[54] A rare scholar to take this seriously is Sarot, *God, Passibility and Corporeality*, ch. 7. Ascribing passibility to God may be acceptable but critics will certainly think that his suggestion that a form of corporeality might also be ascribed to God is heretical. As far as I know, no other openness theologian has suggested it so far. Jantzen has made an excellent beginning in *God's World*. Swinburne takes the traditional view and presents God as an omnipresent disembodied spirit; see *The Coherence of Theism*, ch. 7. Beckwith and Parrish discuss the Mormon view of God as embodied in *Mormon Concept of God*, 114–6.

[55] Sanders, *God Who Risks*, 175–81.

conventional theism – it comes after discussions of the metaphysical and under the category of ethical attributes. This arrangement itself shows the influence of Greek thought. Where is the fundamental insight that God is essentially self-communicating love? Even worse, what happens to loving relationships if God is immutable and all-controlling? Where is the intensity and reciprocity in God's loving?[56] Loving relationships cannot be thought of in static terms because they are intrinsically dynamic. God is affected by the objects of his love and made vulnerable by them. The loved one can make the lover happy or unhappy. Strangers do not affect us in this way, only those closest to us. The loved one can hurt the lover in ways the lover cannot prevent. Conventional theism has great difficulty thinking of God as loving, waiting, longing, repenting and even failing. Understanding love as only an attribute of God is a problem. If theologians would restore love to their thinking about God's nature, the road would be open to the open view of God, which is a theology of love.[57]

God, as essentially loving, relates to his creatures in loving ways. He does not stand back, aloof in isolation, and protect himself from being vulnerable. God is characterized by a glorious relativity and splendid sensitivity to creatures. This is seen dramatically when God shares human life in the incarnation of the Word. God has limitless power, but that power expresses itself in bringing others into existence and loving them.[58]

Making love central does not make wrath unreal. God also displays wrath. The risen Lord rides out on a white horse, putting down what is evil. Even to the church he says, 'I punish all whom I love' (Rev. 3:19). Wrath does not negate the fact that God loves and aims to give humanity a share in the divine life. Rather, wrath signals that God is not indifferent to our human responses. He is a jealous God and cares about what we do with what he gives. This is a 'holy' love, a love that claims us so seriously that it does not tolerate spiritual adultery. It is a love that wants to change us and not leave us the same. When we refuse love's offer, God

---

[56] Brunner, *Christian Doctrine of God*, ch. 15.
[57] There is another reason why love as an essential attribute of God is problematic for Augustinians. The doctrine of double soteriological predestination makes it impossible to say that love is an essential attribute of God, if, in fact, he rejects some without showing mercy. In that case, God must be love only in a volitional sense – God may decide to love but it is not his nature to love. See T. Talbott, 'The Love of God and the Heresy of Exclusivism', *Christian Scholars Review* (1997), 99–112. N.L. Geisler correctly speaks of the voluntarism of Calvinism in *Chosen But Free*, 235–42.
[58] P. Kreeft, *The God Who Loves You*.

manifests himself to us in another way – as wrath. God becomes wrathful because he loves us. God would not become angry if he was not loving. If he did not care about the creature, there would be neither love nor wrath. God's wrath burns against those with whom God has an interest. The prophets like Hosea and Jeremiah who proclaim God's love so profoundly are the very ones who also speak of wrath. Wrath does not belong to God's nature in the way that love does. It arises out of the pathos of love. God becomes angry because he is love. He does not become wrathful spontaneously out of his nature. Rather, he reacts to evil and it is in his dealings with faithless creatures that God becomes what he was not previously, i.e. angry. In the gospel God himself became a victim of human wrath and by his wisdom used it to overcome the powers of darkness, by letting the wrath fall on the whole old Adamic solidarity represented by Jesus.[59] Volf comments

> God will judge, not because God gives people what they deserve, but because some people refuse to receive what no one deserves; if evildoers experience God's terror, it will not be because they have done evil, but because they have resisted to the end the powerful lure of the open arms of the crucified Messiah.[60]

3. The communal God

God is more than a single loving person too – he is a loving community of persons in which each gives and receives love. This goes deeper into why we say that God is essentially loving and relational, not isolated and aloof (1 Jn. 4:7). Relationality, community and mutuality characterize his inner life. God was antecedently relational as triune creator and projected a world where personal relationships with creatures would be possible. God created significant others who could experience the divine love and reciprocate it both to God and to other co-creatures. Other monotheistic faiths have the problem of a 'lonely' God, but this is not true of Christianity. God enjoys loving communion. He did not have to create the world to experience relationships of love because he exists as Father, Son, and Spirit. This implies that creation was a free gift and not something that God needed to do.[61]

---

[59] See König, *Here Am I!*, 93–5; Berkhof, *Christian Faith*, 118–33; and Heschel, *Prophets*, ch. 16. Erickson says that openness theologians do not speak of God's wrath but we do: *Father Almighty*, 85. On wrath and atonement, see Pinnock, *Flame*, 93–111.
[60] M. Volf, *Exclusion and Embrace: A Theological Exploration of Identity, Otherness, and Reconciliation*, 298.
[61] Boyd, *Trinity and Process*, 374–404.

The loving relational essence of the Trinity – three persons in a caring, sensitive and responsive communion – is central to the open view of God. God's very being is an open and dynamic structure, a relational ontology of loving persons. God is the power of love and not just sheer almightiness. Relationality belongs to God's very essence because at the heart of reality is shared life, God's own life, characterized by spontaneity and giving. Such an essence implies dynamism, both internal and external to God. God's inner life is inexhaustibly expressive: out of the abundance of his own divine self-sufficiency flow contingent experiences of love with created reality external to God. It seems that God has chosen to express himself in creation such that creation would mirror God-self back to him.[62] Thomas Torrance remarks

> The indwelling of the Holy Spirit along with the Father and the Son in the Holy Trinity imports an openness on the part of God in which, by virtue of the inherent movement of his own eternal being, he is free to relate himself to what is not himself and become open to created realities beyond himself.[63]

Belief in the Trinity expresses faith in one God who is a communion of love. God is characterized by overflowing life – he is not solitary – and this lies at the heart of the universe.

God is to be thought of as movement, not simple, immutable substance. He is internally and externally dynamic and relational. 'Simplicity' is, along with impassibility, one of the most alien of the Greek-influenced attributes of God. It prevents us adopting a social model of the Trinity and appreciating the dynamism of it.[64] Tragically, Calvin had a doctrine of the Trinity that, if it had been allowed to operate fully, could have moved his thought away from causal and toward personal categories.[65] The same is true of Jonathan Edwards.[66] It seems as if the traditional attributes of God – infinity, immutability and impassibility – overtook the biblical presentation of God as someone who is essentially relational: who interacts with people and even suffers on their account.

---

[62] LaCugna, *God For Us*, ch. 8.

[63] T.F. Torrance, *The Christian Doctrine of God: One Being, Three Persons*, 153.

[64] L. Hodgson, *The Doctrine of the Trinity*, 144–57; C. Plantinga, *The Hodgson-Welch Debate and the Social Analogy of the Trinity*, 306. On simplicity, see Erickson, *Father Almighty*, ch. 10.

[65] P.W. Butin, *Revelation, Redemption, and Response: Calvin's Trinitarian Understanding of the Divine-Human Relationship*, 125, 127; Sanders, *God Who Risks*, 156–7.

[66] Boyd, *Trinity and Process*, 389–93.

4. Changeable faithfulness

As loving communion, God is characterized by changeable faithfulness, a better term for God's immutability. God is completely reliable and true to himself and, at the same time, flexible in his dealings and able to change course, as circumstances require. God is mobile and able to make moves but is not in any way capricious. He is unchanging amidst changing encounters. An analogy would be that of the steadfastness of a loyal friend who has bound himself to us in such a way that we can rely on him utterly. The old term immutability has the feeling of an alien philosophical climate with its emphasis on the immobile and the dispassionate. It does not express the responsive and vulnerable love of God that is central to the Christian story.[67]

The category needs be reformulated in ways that allow certain kinds of change. Although a personal agent must be able to change, Augustine defined God's immutability in Platonic terms and Thomas Aquinas restated it in terms of Aristotle's contrast between potentiality and act.[68] It was a changelessness entailed by God's timelessness and far from the sort of moral changelessness that the Bible attributes to God. Wolterstorff writes

> God's ontological immutability (the strong sense) is not part of the explicit teaching of the biblical writers. What the biblical writers teach is that God is faithful and without beginning or end, not that none of his aspects is temporal (the weak sense). The theological tradition of God's ontological immutability has no explicit biblical foundation.[69]

One way to express this is to say that God is necessary and changeless in some respects but free and changing in others, or that God is necessary and changeless in nature but that his nature is that of a temporal and personal agent. God changes in some respects but not in others, just as a human being relates in flexible ways with someone, while being annoyed with the same person. In God's case, we might say that *who God is* does not change but *what God experiences* changes. God's nature does not change but his activities and relationships are dynamic. God's character is stable but God is not static when it comes to associating with creation. I would say that God is

---

[67] Berkhof, *Christian Faith*, ch. 22; Sanders, *God Who Risks*, 184–8.
[68] Swinburne, *Coherence*, 219–23.
[69] Wolterstorff, 'God Everlasting', 202. Wolterstorff is the theologian more than any other that I place hope in as far as getting the open view of God established among evangelicals goes.

unchangeable in changeable ways, i.e. unchangeable in essence but ever changing in the relationships of love that he values.[70] God is characterized by changeable faithfulness and is not immutable in every respect, i.e. God is open to the world and interacts with it. Thus, there is contingency in God's experiences of the world. Biblical categories such as suffering, repentance and temporality bring this out by expressing the dynamism of God's interactions. In creating the world, for example, God experienced something new. He became the creator of this world and experiences novelty from it because of his decision to leave room for the contingencies that accompany freedom. In history, God realises his nature as the One who loves by loving creatures in particular settings and ways. God's experiences change, while God's essential nature remains the same. By choosing to be open to the world, God chooses at the same time to change in his experience. God is changeless in nature but ever changing in his experience of a changing world. God has to change in accessing the knowledge of a changing world.[71]

On the one hand, we should affirm strongly that in one important respect God does not change. God as revealed in Jesus Christ is unchangeably loving and triune – Father, Son, and Holy Spirit – and exists from everlasting to everlasting. Nothing at all can change his essential nature as the One who loves in freedom. Therefore, God is never fickle or capricious. He can always be relied upon to be faithful to his words of promise. As one of the psalmists says, 'though the works of God perish, God always remains the same' (Ps. 102:25–27). God himself says through the prophet, 'I the Lord do not change' (Mal. 3:6). God will always be the God of grace and glory which believers know him to be and absolutely depend on.

On the other hand, being a person and not an abstraction, God changes in relation to creatures. In the Christian story, God changed when he became creator of the world; God changed when he made human beings in his image and began to deal with them as free persons; God changed when he entered into a covenant with Israel; God changed when the Word became flesh and came close in the form

---

[70] Though a sharp critic of the open view of God, B.A. Ware often seems to grasp our burden: see 'An Evangelical Reformulation of the Doctrine of the Immutability of God', *Journal of the Evangelical Theological Society* 29 (1986), 431–46.

[71] Erickson seems to see this: *Father Almighty*, 112. However, Bray can only charge that the open view of God holds that God's being changes, which, of course, it does not; see *Personal God*, 74.

of a man; God changed when he felt the bitterness of the cross; God changes when dealing with his friends. God does not change when it comes to his nature but changes when it comes to associations with the world. That is why I say that God is characterized by changeable faithfulness and is not immutable in every respect.

Believers know that God is unchangeable in changeable ways as they relate to him, but the tradition, under the influence of Greek philosophy, has had difficulty admitting any kind of change in God. It has tended to exaggerate God's unchangeability at the expense of his ability to be changeable in personal relationships. Tradition has taken the truth of God's unchangeableness too far in the direction of immobility and inflexibility. God has been made to appear to be a solitary, narcissistic being, while the truth that God enters into real relationships is obscured and the biblical portrait of God distorted.

A God that cannot change at all is not the Lord presented by Scripture. If God cannot change at all, how does he act in certain places and at certain times? How could he grieve over something that has happened? How could he hear and respond to prayers? God is immutable in his essence but flexible in his dealings. He could have avoided change by not making a dynamic world and getting involved with it, but out of his love for us he has voluntarily subjected himself to change. In the book of Jonah, having told the prophet to declare Nineveh's destruction in forty days, God relented and called it off because the people repented (Jon. 3:10). When Nineveh repented, God's loving character required him to change direction. God's relational consciousness changed when Nineveh repented but his inner being of love remained the same. In another passage, God is presented as considering whether to fulfill his promise to Abraham through Israel or by raising up a new people from Moses instead (Exod. 32:10). In such cases, God is faithful to his goals but free to alter his plans to accommodate changing circumstances. God is unchanging in his nature but changes in his relations with us. In his nature God is perfectly reliable and can be depended upon completely because his concern for the creature is constant and unaffected by anything. But God can, at the same time, respond to the changing needs of his people and alter direction where necessary. God's nature is that of a creative person who interacts. His unchangeableness does not rule out the quality of responsiveness that enables God to deal with every new situation creatively.

It has often been objected that God cannot change because a being that does not change is superior to one that does. This was the standard objection in tradition to the picture I have painted but it is not convincing. A static and immobile God is not more perfect than our heavenly Father who knows us perfectly, appropriately responds and changes in relation to us. I love to think that God is like the partner in a dance. As we act out our steps God is always there, leaping at just the right moments, steadying at others, and keeping perfect balance with the living reality that we are. Let us celebrate both the faithfulness of God our true friend (stable and unchanging) and the responsiveness of God (sensitive and caring) who is at our side in every changing circumstance, responding to every need.

Immutability is about God's unchanging trinitarian nature and relational faithfulness. God's changing experiences are due to God's decision to make the kind of world he did. Because God is aware of what is changing in the world, his awareness undergoes the changes that are caused by the reality of which he is aware. The element of dynamism must be introduced into the category by distinguishing between God's unchanging essence and God's changeable relationships.

God is necessary and changeless in some respects, then, but free and changing in others. God is changeless in nature but his nature is that of a creative agent and personal God. God is changeless in the perfections he possesses but constantly changes in the ways in which he realizes them. God's immutability is personal, not static. God has an unchanging intention to love but that involves relational mutability; God can make the adaptations and responses necessary to carry it out. God's changing is central to the perfection of the biblical God. It means God is flexible and able to strike out in new directions as is required. It is God's nature to be able to relent (Joel 2:13–14).

5. God's intimate relationship with the world

God, as a loving person, is involved in the world and is affected by creatures. This challenges the traditional view of the impassibility of God. Far from being aloof or abstract, God maintains a personal and intimate relation to the world. He is moved by what happens and reacts accordingly. God is a subject and events arouse in him joy and sorrow, pleasure and anger. He experiences pathos, for example he loves, laughs, repents, can be delighted and become angry. It is said that when God was sorry that he made humankind, it grieved him to his heart (Gen. 6:6). Love leads to suffering. God feels the pain of rejection. He suffers because of his people and also with and for them. The world affects God emotionally and he is moved by the sufferings of his creatures. The fact that God is love rules out the doctrine of impassibility, which entails that God has no desires that can be thwarted; he cannot suffer or be in any way vulnerable. A.M. Fairbairn declared a century ago, 'Theology has no falser idea than that of the impassibility of God.'[72] Most theologians today agree with him and reject it.[73]

Scripture speaks of the suffering of God. God's heart can be close to breaking (Hos. 11). God knows his people's condition and feels their pain (Exod. 3:7f). God laments and mourns over them. Even for Moab God says, 'My heart cries out' (Is. 15:5). The issue for Christians is not whether God could suffer but how God could not suffer. God made a world with suffering in it and he would be less than God if he ignored it. He would be less than God if he lacked sympathy or refused to share in the suffering of creatures. Erickson concludes

> It seems indubitable, in the light of the number and variety of biblical texts attributing emotions of several kinds to God, that impassibility in the sense of God being utterly devoid of any feelings cannot be accepted. However these emotions are to be understood, God is simply not without them.[74]

It is astonishing, when you think about it, that impassibility could have become orthodox belief in the early centuries. Here perhaps more than anywhere else we find the bankruptcy of conventional theology. Divine suffering lies at the heart of the Christian faith. The

---

[72] A.M. Fairbairn, *The Place of Christ in Modern Theology*, 483.

[73] R. Goetz, 'The Suffering God', *Christian Century* 103 (1986), 385; see Sarot, *God, Passibility and Corporeality*. Not all reject impassibility however. Weinandy mounts a wonderful defense of it in *Does God Suffer?*; divine impassibility, he says, does not mean we cannot predicate grief and sorrow to God, 168.

[74] Erickson, *Father Almighty*, 161–64. Here certainly the Greek influence is plain. The fathers thought it absurd to suppose that God could in any way be dependent on his creatures. Pelikan, *Emergence*, 42.

[75] J.Y. Lee, *God Suffers For Us: A Systematic Inquiry into a Concept of Divine Passibility*; K. Kitamori, *Theology of the Pain of God*. At places in theologies like these, one senses the value of Third World thinking. Ironically in the early church it was the Arians not the orthodox who struggled with the suffering of God. At the heart of their thinking was a God who suffered. They wanted to make room for it by conceiving of the Son as a lesser deity. Though this is not a good idea, they should be credited at least with being aware of the scandal of the cross. Athanasius, on the other hand, showed no interest in the issue. Here surely we have some unfinished business from the early church; see R.P.C. Hanson, *The Search for the Christian Doctrine of God: The Arian Controversy*, 121–2.

participation of the divine pathos in our world is the very expression
of the divine nature.[75] Henri Nouwen writes

> On two occasions, Jesus invited his closest friends (Peter, James, and John)
> to share in his most intimate prayer. The first time he took them to the top of
> Mount Tabor, where they saw his face shining like the sun and his clothes
> white as light (Mt. 17:2). The second time he took them to the garden of
> Gethsemane, and there they saw his face in anguish and his sweat falling to
> the ground like great drops of blood (Lk. 22:44). The prayer of the heart
> bring us both to Tabor and Gethsemane. When we have seen God in glory,
> we will also see God in misery, and when we have felt the ugliness of God's
> humiliation, we will also experience the beauty of the transfiguration.[76]

Like Peter we need to learn that Christ could suffer, but even more that
the Father of Jesus bears the burdens of the world too. Nicholas
Wolterstorff writes:

> God is love. That is why he suffers. To love our suffering, sinful world is to
> suffer. God so suffered for the world that he gave up his only Son to suffer.
> The one who does not see God's suffering does not see his love. God is suffer-
> ing love. Suffering is down at the center of things, deep down where the
> meaning is. Suffering is the meaning of our world. The tears of God are the
> meaning of history.[77]

God opens himself to human opposition and suffers, even unto death.[78]

In conventional theism, impassibility was tied in with other attributes
like immutability and unconditionality. Though it was held to be axiom-
atic that God could not be changed by anything outside himself, it was,
as H.P. Owen says, 'the most questionable aspect of classical theism.'[79]
After all, how can God love us and experience nothing? How does God
avoid suffering if he is intimately involved with the world? How could
God become fully man and suffer death on the cross without experiencing any of the pain that Christ endured? Does God not bear our sins and
sorrows? Is it not in suffering that God is most god-like, not least god-
like?[80]

---

[76] H. Nouwen, *The Only Necessary Thing: Living a Prayerful Life*, 120. See
also Moltmann, *Crucified God*.
[77] N.P. Wolterstorff, *Lament for a Son*, 90.
[78] E. Jüngel, *The Doctrine of the Trinity: God's Being is in Becoming*, 83.
[79] Owen, *Concepts*, 24. Cf. P. Helm, 'The Impossibility of Divine Passibility' in
N.M. de S. Cameron (ed.), *The Power and Weakness of God: Impassibility and
Orthodoxy*, 125–37.
[80] Hallman, *Descent of God*; Wolterstorff, 'Does God Suffer?' 45–7.

It was the opinion of the medieval Jewish thinker Maimonides that God could not become incarnate, because of the suffering that would entail. But Michael Wyschogrod, a contemporary Jewish scholar, asks what became of the freedom of God to dwell with his people? Who is limiting God here?[81] Arius too rejected the incarnation because it posited change and suffering in God. And he was right; if God truly enters this world, he is not immutable. The incarnation requires relational metaphysics and makes sense only if God can change. The prejudice against mutability and passibility in God made it much more difficult to work out a doctrine of incarnation in the early church. It is the heart of the Christian message that God suffers for us and for his glory. His perfection is a perfection in changing. It is so much easier to appropriate the truth of incarnation if change and suffering can be attributed to God and be taken seriously at the philosophical level. Christian theology has always needed a different point of departure in order to express its radical claims about Jesus. To his great credit, Luther reached out for this idea even though he still held it in tension with his notion of the hidden God.[82]

In recent theology more attention has been paid to the divine pathos.[83] After all, the idea of divine suffering lies at the heart of the gospel. What kind of incarnation and what kind of atonement is it if God is impassible? Bonhoeffer said, 'The Bible directs man to God's powerlessness and suffering – only a suffering God can help.'[84]

At the same time, we need to distinguish, as in the case of immutability, ways in which God does and does not suffer. Surely God does not suffer in every way that we do as mortal, sentient creatures. Because God is involved in the world, God experiences pathos, but not in exactly the same way that we do. There are different ways in which God might be passible or even impassible. God certainly cannot lose control and

---

[81] M. Wyschogrod, 'A Jewish Perspective on Incarnation', *Modern Theology* (April 1996), 195–209.

[82] D. Ngien, *The Suffering of God According to Luther's 'Theologia Crucis'*, 8, 72, 178; Sanders, *God Who Risks*, 153. Also see D. Ngien, 'Abraham Heschel's Theology of Divine Pathos in Response to the 'Unmoved Mover' of Traditional Theism'.

[83] McWilliams, *Passion of God*.

[84] D. Bonhoeffer, *Letters and Papers from Prison*, 188. Cf. Fiddes, *Creative Suffering*, ch. 2; K.J. Clark, 'Hold not Thy Peace at my Tears: Methodological Reflections on Divine Impassibility' in K.J. Clark (ed.), *Our Knowledge of God: Essays in Natural and Philosophical Theology*, 167–93. Wolterstorff has come out in favor of divine passibility in part because of his own grief expressed in *Lament*. Also see 'Does God Suffer?', 45–7.

become distraught, but, as the loving person he is, he can be emotionally affected. God can be touched by joy and sorrow; he can care about us deeply and sympathize with our suffering; he can love mercy and hate injustice; and he can redeem us through suffering. Is it not this very vulnerability that makes us love God so?[85]

In the world, there is much suffering and, because God is good, he shares in it and does not ignore it. Yet God can be blissful and suffer at the same time because he can contemplate the values contained in his own being and the values being realized in the world. God's happiness is greater than the sufferings of the world. He can, therefore, share in them while transmuting suffering into forms of happiness. God shares in our sorrows and transmutes them into something better. God suffers on account of creation, but his joy cannot be destroyed.[86]

6. Sovereign Lord

As creator of the world God is the sovereign Lord. The world depends on God and God could, if he chose, make the arrangement that Warfield imagined: 'The governing hand of God working out his preconceived plan – a plan broad enough to embrace the whole universe of things, minute enough to concern itself with the smallest details and actualizing itself with inevitable certainty in every event which comes to pass.'[87] God could do that but has chosen not to do so. Instead, although the world depends on God, it has been given relative independence and derived autonomy. It was created with its own principles of operation that are intelligible in their own right (e.g. laws that govern physical objects) and with a measure of freedom. The fact that God is the creator does not require him to control every aspect of the world. Surely God can create such creatures as he wills and has chosen to create some beings with the capacity of freedom. We must not forget that God is 'sovereign over his sovereignty' and can make the kind of world he likes – in this case, a world with free creatures in it. This is, I think, the majority Christian position.[88]

---

[85] On the subtleties, see M.M. Adams, *Horrendous Evils and the Goodness of God*, 168–77; and R.E. Creel, *Divine Impassibility: An Essay in Philosophical Theology*.

[86] K. Ward, *Holding Fast to God*, 36–7.

[87] Quoted by D.F. Wells, *God in the Wasteland: The Reality of Truth in a World of Fading Dreams*, 164; see Warfield, 'Predestination', 270–333. Erickson writes, 'God knows what free human beings are going to do because he has foreordained their actions', *Father Almighty*, 203–4.

[88] Swinburne writes, 'All Christian theologians of the first four centuries believed in human free will in the libertarian sense, as did all subsequent Eastern

This means that God is a vulnerable, though superior, power.[89] God limits himself with regard to power. For example, he gives creatures room to decide things and binds himself to the promises he makes. After the deluge God promised not to send a universal flood again, and in saying so limited his actions in the future. With the fall into sin, a clash occurred between God and the creature, and God had to adjust to it. God exercises power in ways appropriate to the creation project.[90] Fackre writes

> Our inclination to make deity serve our own ends is such that we will not let the God of the Bible be who this God wills to be. So we smuggle into the story our own assumptions. In these, God becomes the projection of our conceptions of power. In the ancient world, the Oriental potentate furnished the model of omnipotence, and God became the one who by fiat and force exercises immediate sway. Assumed here as well, is a machismo image shaped by masculine self-projections. But the God of the biblical narrative is the God who is neither an autocratic regent nor a take-charge sheriff. This creator gives the world the space and time it needs to be what it will be. God does not normally act upon it by force or fiat but by vulnerable love.[91]

Thus God exercises sovereignty by sharing power, not by domination. But why exalt control as the heart of sovereignty when a more glorious concept is at hand biblically? The God of the gospel is a truly self-confident and sovereign God. But his sovereignty is kind and generous not manipulative: he ordained prayer, he relents, Jesus is born in a stable and dies God-forsaken on a cross. Paul says that this seems foolish to the carnal mind, yet that it is the very wisdom of God (1 Cor. 1:18). God is so sovereign that he saves the world by choosing weakness. This self-limitation of God coincides with the act of creation. It is a self-limitation that God himself established for the sake of a measured independence of the world and the possibility of genuine freedom in the world.[92]

Footnote 88 (*continued*) Orthodox theologians, and most Western Catholic theologians from Duns Scotus (in the fourteen century) onwards. The main Catholic declaration on this issue is that of the Council of Trent in the sixteenth century, which is firmly in favor of human free will, and in my view the context of that declaration positively implies libertarian free will,' *Providence*, 35. Also see Swinburne, *Coherence*, ch. 9.

[89] Berkhof uses striking language for the title of chapter 21 – 'The Defenceless Superior Power' – in *Christian Faith*. God is vulnerable but not, I think, defenseless.

[90] Fretheim, *Suffering of God*, 71–8.

[91] Fackre, *Christian Story*, 258–9.

[92] See Tupper, *Scandalous Providence*, 327. Also, G. Harkness, *The Providence of God*, 104–7; H.W. Robinson, *Suffering – Human and Divine*, 39.

God uses omnipotence to free and not enslave. God wants us to be free and, in a way, sovereign too. God's power is unlimited and he is free in the exercise of it. Thus he can, if he wishes, make creatures that he permits to control their own destinies. In a sense, God limits his own power in allowing us to be free. The power itself is unlimited but God chooses to actualize a particular world whose development he leaves largely in the hands of creatures. This leaves the future open and largely under our control. God does not predetermine it, though he could do so. Does this idea diminish omnipotence or enhance it? What other than omnipotence could create free creatures and still feel confident that its purposes will be realized? What is most admirable about God's power, I think, is not his ability to subjugate but his willingness to lift creatures up.

God is free and sovereign Lord but, at the same time, has decided not to be alone. He has willingly opened up the divine mystery and used his freedom to establish communion with us. God has elected to give himself away. This is the way in which God chooses to use his sovereignty. God is the one who surpasses everything yet stoops down and dwells with us. This surprising but coherent picture of God is the heart of the good news and must not be lost sight of owing to alien assumptions. God's sovereignty is interactive and general, not all-determining and meticulous. God's will is not unchangeably fixed like a blueprint, nor God's power manipulative. God has objectives and plans for the world and he has opened routes for their accomplishment. God's purposes are implemented in genuinely historical contexts in which his plans are dynamically worked out and can be modified in response to circumstances. God's plans are both comprehensive and flexible. Against the idea of omnicausality, the open view of God posits a dynamic situation where God is not all-controlling; other agents count for something. God's almightiness is not an abstract domineering power. It is essentially the power of love.[93] A God who loves cannot be conceived in a deterministic way, like the power of the puppeteer. His power is greater: it is the power to create finite agents who are creators in their own right. Kierkegaard captures the marvel of it: 'Omnipotence can not only bring forth the most imposing of things, the world in its visible totality, but can create the most delicate of all things, a creature independent of it.'[94]

God is the ultimate power but this does not mean that he has all the power there is. God has also, within limits, given self-determining power to the created reality. God's power means that he is omnicompetent and

---

[93] Sanders, *God Who Risks*, ch. 7.
[94] A theme of Placher's, *Narratives*, ch. 1.

can deal wisely with any circumstance that arises, not that he causes everything. It means that nothing can ultimately defeat him. God is an energetic, creative, and sovereign being who has created other beings whom he encourages to be energetic, creative, and sovereign too. God is a being powerful enough to ensure that creatures share in freedom. It takes omnipotence to create and manage freedom. God, in order to be powerful, does not have to be a despot. God is free to create any kind of world he chooses, including one in which interactive freedom pertains. God's power is such that it allows him to rule over creation even when the finite agents within it work against him. His power is also such that it can transform a wicked heart; no tyranny, however absolute, can accomplish that. God's power is displayed in the starry heavens above and in stooping down to our weakness.

How weak God would be if his sovereignty were threatened by any element of risk or uncertainty? Only a pathetic god would reign over the world in dictatorial ways. Imagine having to control everything in order to be able to achieve anything! Who admires such dictatorial power? One can submit to, but not love, such a despot. The God of the gospel doesn't need a blueprint to feel confident. He works out his purposes resourcefully and does not depend on manipulation. God can create such beings as he wills. He has chosen to create beings with the capacity for choice. In such a world, God does not exercise a sovereignty of total control. He resorts to a higher kind of power, one that requires more by way of competence. More wisdom is surely required to govern creatures that are in a personal relationship than those that are under all-determining control. God made himself vulnerable by creating the universe and took risks in wanting loving relationships. To work with a history where the outcomes are not predetermined and with creatures that are able to resist him is a challenge and, no doubt, a source of great delight even for God.

Let us not confuse God's lordship with the excessive omnipotence of tyranny that sets God's power in opposition to the very creatures he rules over. God wills the existence of creatures and does not set himself against them. God's power is the power of love and a power that gives us life and sustains us. It is not an omnicausality that excludes the autonomy of creatures. God governs with power but also with respect for the God-given freedom of creatures. Despite having the power to control everything, God voluntarily limits the exercise of that power. God is almighty, but what 'almighty' means has to be defined in terms of the kind of relationship involved. Almighty could mean all-determining control or it could mean a power that does not monopolize but delegates power. And, given the reality of evil in the world, God's delegation of power seems completely undeniable.[95]

God uses his power to foster loving relationships, not dominate. The open view of God has a place for sovereignty but recognizes different kinds of sovereignty that God can select and make actual. In the case of this world, he has chosen the kind that makes loving relationships possible. It is a worthy exercise of power. It requires great wisdom and patience. Robert Wright, in *No Place for Sovereignity*, denies God's right to choose to be sovereign without controlling everything. But this is to limit God. One needs to look at the cross of Jesus to understand the power of God. God voluntarily limits his power so that he can relate to the world in the self-sacrificing ways that he chooses and which reflect his own nature.[96]

God has chosen to be a vulnerable, superior power – he lets sinners challenge his rights and they seem to take the initiative away from him. This is because God wants to love and not overpower. It is the vulnerability manifested in Jesus, who renounced earthly power and let himself become a victim. This runs contrary to the way we naturally think about God – even the disciples could not grasp it. They wanted God to be irresistibly almighty. They succumbed to the very temptation that Jesus should seize levers of power. But that is not God's way. God is the father who lets the prodigal take his possessions and depart and still longs for him to return. Irresistible power can bring forth a world, but only a relational power can make the most delicate of things, a creature independent of it.

7. Temporal agent

God is a temporal agent. He is above time in the sense that he is above finite experience and measurement of time but he is not beyond 'before and after' or beyond sequence of events. Scripture presents God as temporally everlasting, not timelessly eternal. It depicts God planning and deliberating, acting and reacting within the temporal. God is presented as experiencing past, present, and future successively not timelessly. God is the one 'who was and is and is to come' (Rev. 1:4). As a person acting in the world God has temporal capacity. The psalmist writes, 'from everlasting to everlasting you are God' (Ps. 90:2). Clearly God is temporally related to creatures and projects himself and his actions

---

[95] See W. Pannenberg, *Systematic Theology* I, 415–22; II, 48.
[96] C.H. Pinnock, 'God's Sovereignty in Today's World', *Theology Today* (April 1997), 15–21; and A. Case-Winters, *God's Power: Traditional Understandings and Contemporary Challenges*. Cf. Wright, *No Place for Sovereignty*.

along a temporal path. However he may relate to other worlds, God relates to this world temporally. Indeed, if he did not do so, he could not be our savior. To act in time God must somehow be in time. Time must be a realm in which he can function. Time, in a certain sense, must be a property of God, a property he cannot fail to possess as a personal agent. Scripture is clear that God experiences temporal duration when he enters into give and take relations with us.[97]

According to Scripture, God moves with his people through time. He is even described as wondering what they are going to do next! God says 'I thought, after she has done all this, she will return to me, but she did not return' (Jer. 3:7). God had thought he could bless his people but they proved unfaithful (Jer. 3:19-20). God had planted a pleasant vineyard and put a lot of effort into it but it yielded only wild grapes, and in Isaiah 5:1–4 he asks why. He had hope for things to happen which did not happen and he was disappointed. God existed before creation and before creaturely time but since then has related to the world within the structures of time. God is not thought of in terms of timelessness. He makes plans and carries them out; he anticipates the future and remembers the past. Since creation, divine life has been temporally ordered. God is participant not onlooker; he enters the time of the world and is not just above the flow of history looking down, as it were, from some supra-temporal vantage point. God is inside not outside time, sharing in history – past, present, and future. Wolterstorff writes

> If God were eternal, he could not be aware, concerning any temporal event, whether it was occurring, nor aware that it will be occurring, nor could he remember that it had occurred, nor could he plan to bring it about. But all of such actions are presupposed by and are essential to, the biblical presentation of God as a redeeming God. Hence God as presented by the biblical writers as fundamentally in time.[98]

In another place Wolterstorff writes, 'I hold that God is everlasting rather than eternal. I hold that God is not outside time but that God exists at every time and that there is temporal succession and flow within God's own life.' He adds, 'What's decisive for me is Scripture. No one can deny that Scripture applies the terminology of time to God.' Though open to discussion as to what exactly time is, it is important not to lose hold on the fact that God works in time to rectify the conditions that the

---

[97] See N.P. Wolterstorff, 'God Everlasting'; Morris, *Idea*, ch. 7; A.G. Padgett, *God, Eternity and the Nature of Time*, 23–37.
[98] Wolterstorff, 'God Everlasting', 200. Also, surprisingly, Tiessen, a reformed theologian, in *Providence and Prayer*, 321–5.

rebelliousness of creatures have brought about. The history of salvation loses all its meaning if God only operates outside of time and not in time. We can only speculate what things would be like apart from the world and before it existed – perhaps then God experienced a kind of timelessness because there was nothing to measure temporally. The really important thing to say is that at least from the moment of creation, God enters into temporal relations with his creatures. One might speculate that God is timeless without creation and temporal subsequent to creation.[99]

Conventional theism took a wrong step when it claimed that God is outside the temporal order. If he were temporal, it was reasoned, God's present would be limited by the past and the future. It would imply that there are forms of being which God has lost and forms of being which God has not yet attained. Immutability and timelessness are tied together. To be immutable, God must be timeless because to be temporal is to experience change. So God must exist in a timeless present, and events that are sequential for us must be simultaneous for God. Thus the Platonic idea of timelessness became an attribute of the Christian God. It was held that God must exist in a timeless present, even though the Bible does not say that and even though we have no idea what it even means. This is wrongheaded. A timeless God could not create a temporal world and operate within it as our redeemer. It would place in jeopardy the notion of God as a person. A timeless God could not genuinely respond, deliberate, or do many of the things the Bible says God does. As Nelson Pike says, a timeless person would not be much of a person.[100] God must know what time it is now and thus not be outside time. What could it mean to say that Caesar crossing the Rubicon, Napoleon living in Paris, and Churchill being the prime minister of Britain are simultaneous? How can God be a person and deal with us if outside time? His thoughts would be one thought that somehow lasts forever.[101] If God is personal he is temporal, and if he is temporal then he is inside and not outside of time. Time is not a 'thing' that God may or may not have created. Time is the concomitant of God and personal life. It exists because of God's nature. Ultimate reality is personal and somehow an everlasting flow of loving interaction.[102]

---

[99] See N.P. Wolterstorff, 'God and Time', *Philosophia Christi* 2 (2000), 5–10. Essays by W.L. Craig, A.G. Padgett, P. Helm, and others, accompany Wolterstorff's article.
[100] N. Pike, *God and Timelessness*, 128–9. Erickson sees God as both transcending time and entering into it: *Father Almighty*, 139.
[101] C. Taliaferro, *Contemporary Philosophy of Religion*, 156–63.
[102] J.R. Lucas, *The Future: An Essay on God, Temporality, and Truth*, 213.

I admit that we cannot easily grasp how God's time relates to our human time. God's time cannot be the only measurement between God and created objects; it must refer to the everlasting relations of the Trinity as well. Whatever God's eternity is like, it includes the possibility of time and the capacity to relate to us within time. God demonstrates that he has the power to do so and that his existence is in a positive relation to time. One need not know the exact nature of time to know that God experiences successions of events in relation to creatures. God is from everlasting to everlasting and beyond the limitations of time as we experience them. God does not move from birth to death as we do and is not temporal in the way we are temporal. We cannot know how it is with God to exist in eternity without a creation. Maybe that involves a relative timelessness. What is certain is that God has made a temporal creation and is able to act temporally in it. God is not timeless because he experiences a succession of events and faces a partially unsettled future.[103]

With God, I suppose, the past would be perfectly preserved in his memory, all the realities of the present would be known to him, as would all the possibilities of the future, including events which he has promised to bring about. It would be hard to take God's actions in time seriously if God were timeless, just as it would be hard to imagine God entering into personal relationships if he were unable to change. I suggest God knows the passage of time as a dimension of his own endless existence. Even before there was a world, God would have had the experience of temporality in the missions of the Son and Spirit that echo the eternal processions in the divine being. I sense a correspondence between the sending of Son and Spirit by the Father and the perichoretic relations of trinitarian life. God's time cannot be precisely like our time, if only because God pre-exists the world when our kind of time did not yet exist. But God, being a personal agent, cannot be timeless either. Though the passage of time in the divine life must be different from what we know, there were always the inner dynamics of the everlasting Trinity. God is above time in the sense that he is above our finite experience and measurement but not beyond sequence itself. There was a before and after for God when he created the world and there always will be the sequences of the trinitarian communion.[104]

8. Omniscience

Everyone agrees that God is omniscient and knows everything that any being could know. He knows everything that has existed, everything

---

[103] Cf. Barth, *Church Dogmatics* II/1, 617, 619.
[104] Swinburne, *Coherence*, 217–29; *Providence*, 253.

that now exists, and everything that could exist in future. He know these things vividly and not in a remote way. He also knows what he will do. Thus, God can respond in creative ways to everything that happens in the world. But no being, not even God, can know in advance precisely what free agents will do, even though he may predict it with great accuracy. My assumption is, and the Bible seems to share it, that exhaustive foreknowledge would not be possible in a world with real freedom. Luther agrees from the opposite direction: what God foreknows must necessarily happen; otherwise God could be mistaken. God's not knowing aspects of the future does not reflect on God's knowing ability because that is not dependent on a complete and perfect knowledge of the future. It is simply the nature of the creation project that its future is not altogether settled and, therefore, not altogether knowable.[105]

God, in order to be omniscient, need not know the future in complete detail. Were he to know it, we would have to suppose that it is already determined that human freedom is illusory. Our decisions would then settle nothing because there is nothing left to settle. We would have no 'say' in the way things turn out. Such omniscience would threaten our, and God's, functioning as persons. God's omniscience is not like a huge encyclopedia with the totality of facts – past, present and future – in it. That would cancel aspects of the future, which are in some way contingent on our decisions. If history is real, the future must be open in ways that only creaturely decisions can close. The idea that God knows every detail of the future is not taught in Scripture and is philosophically questionable. Of course, God has the power to deal with every circumstance that arises but he cannot have, and does not need, total knowledge in advance of every detail. God is a highly resourceful and capable person. Not everything, including his actions, has been determined since before creation. God is the living God who deals with situations that confront him, responding accordingly. The reason the Bible often says that God 'changes his mind' is because he is working with finite agents, so that when one course of action proves futile he tries another. How boring it would be for God to have to reign over a creation project, each molecule of which has its predestined place! There would be nothing for God to do.[106]

---

[105] It was the editors who entitled my essay, 'God Limits his Knowledge' in Basinger and Basinger (eds.), *Predestination and Free Will*, ch. 4. I do not in fact think that God limits his knowledge – having present knowledge means he knows all that can be known. So, Fackre, *Christian Story*, 256–8.
[106] Cf. R.C. Sproul, *Not a Chance: The Myth of Modern Science and Cosmology.*

How could a temporal flow be timelessly known or postulated ahead of time if freedom is involved? In fact, God as temporal knows the world successively and does not know future acts, which are freely chosen in a libertarian sense. The absence of such knowledge does not negate God's omniscience because he still knows every possible choice and every possible consequence of it. The open view of God holds that he knows all that can be known of past, present, what is possible in the future and what he plans to do. But the future is open to what God and humankind will yet freely decide to do. This seems to be the biblical picture – the future is partly settled and partly unsettled.[107]

The idea of exhaustive divine omniscience has, nevertheless, been a persistent belief from early times and few theologians have considered the possibility that God might have created a universe, the future of which could not be totally foreknown. I presume the reason for this assumption lies in the instinct to preserve the divine control of everything and to rule out risk as a possibility. It is time to reconsider the alternative, which is very attractive. Imagine the delight of genuine interactions and loving relationships, and the elements of novelty and surprise that a world with an open future would offer God! Why not think of God as cognitively dependent on the world and his knowledge changing as history changes? True, there would be a degree of uncertainty as God faces a partly unsettled future because genuinely free decisions cannot be entirely predicted prior to being taken, but what a beautiful context. Instead of a future that is totally fixed and foreknown, there is one that stretches before us. It is a future that is full of opportunity and promise as we go forward with God.[108]

God knows all there is to be known and the fact that some things cannot be known does not diminish the perfection of his knowledge. God knows the past, which is unalterable, the entire present, which is accessible, and a great deal about the future, so far as it can be foreseen, because he knows the constitutions, tendencies and powers of each person and has a full knowledge of his own purposes and how he plans

---

[107] So Fretheim, *Suffering of God*, ch. 4; Boyd, *God of the Possible*, ch. 3; and Swinburne, *Coherence*, ch. 10.

[108] It is a hopeful sign that Tiessen, a Calvinist, has brought middle knowledge into play in his model because it conveys the impression of divine responsiveness to what is going on in the world, *Providence and Prayer,* part 2. Unfortunately, to me it is only an impression because God's decree is logically prior to any real dynamism and does not really take account of what creatures do. This differs from the usual Arminian appeal to middle knowledge which is compatible with the open view of God.

to carry them out.[109] History is not yet completely settled but is still being actualized. It has not been videotaped in advance. The possibilities have not yet all become actualities. God is still deciding exactly what he will do in matters of detail, but not overall. Recall the dialogue between God and Abraham over the fate of Sodom, which had not yet been decided (Gen. 18); or the conversation between God and Moses over what to do with Israel now that she had become so resistant to grace (Exod. 34); listen to God asking himself what he is going to do next in Hosea 6:4. All this makes much sense in our own experience of having to decide what the future will be by means of our choices, we sense that everything has not been decided and not everything foreknown.[110]

Black theologian Major Jones grasps this truth out of reflection on his people's oppression:

> We believe human actions to be truly free, such that whereas God's knowledge of the past is total and absolute, God's knowledge of future events is not yet complete, particularly so far as acts of human freedom are concerned. The perfection of divine omniscience then must be construed to be God's always perfectly increasing knowledge, taking in, with the passage of time, all knowable reality as it expands. Not to know as real and sure what is, as yet, neither sure nor real is not imperfection; to know the unreal and the unsure as uncertain and still forming is to know perfectly whatever is to be known.[111]

9. Wisdom and resourcefulness

God is a wise and resourceful person. Had God ordained everything before creation, he would not really have to be wise because there would be nothing that required wisdom. Wisdom is only required if God is governing a world with free creatures in it who have to be responded to moment by moment as time goes by.[112] But God is and has to be resourceful, because the world is an open project. God has to be resourceful, competent and innovative to carry it out. It takes wisdom to

---

[109] Sanders, *God Who Risks*, 194–206.

[110] This view of how God relates to the future is also vehemently opposed. B.A. Ware writes: 'For the sake of fidelity to Scripture, for the sake of the strength and well-being of the church, and for the sake of the undiminished glory of God, Sander's presentism must not be accepted within evangelicalism.' See his review of Sanders' *God Who Risks*, in *Journal of the Evangelical Theological Society* 43 (2000), 342.

[111] M. Jones, *The Color of God: The Concept of God in Afro-American Thought*, 95.

[112] Ware seems to miss this point when he claims that it is the open view that conducts an assault on God's wisdom; see *God's Lesser Glory*, 154–9.

do that if things do not go well. God has to think about how to bring his purposes to completion. I see this in Romans 9–11 where God wants to have mercy upon Jew and Gentile alike, but faces the problem of Israel's unbelief. Paul explains how God is working on it.[113]

Conventional theism likes the scenario of a problem-free world where everything is planned and settled from the beginning. Deity might as well go into retirement because there is nothing left to do. By contrast, in the open view, God is involved in history, in give-and-take relationships, and always has a lot to deal with. Fortunately God is supremely wise, knowing all things, knowing what can be done, and knowing the best way to do it. God's purposes can be thwarted because he gave freedom to the creature, but he has the requisite patience and skill to deal with anything and everything at any time.

I suppose that the main reason people hold so tightly, maybe desperately, to meticulous sovereignty and exhaustive foreknowledge is the anxiety that, without them, God could not be sure, and we could not be sure, that his plans will come to fruition. We wonder how, unless with iron fist and crystal ball, he can succeed in the work of redemption. We worry that God, unless he controls everything, cannot achieve anything. The open view trusts God to accomplish what he said he would accomplish and does not let fears take over. We take God at his word. This is far from a diminished concept of God. Rather, it is an exalted view according to which God is resourceful and wise enough to handle any and all challenges that arise from his having created a significant universe. God knows all the possibilities and is, therefore, never caught offguard. God also knows what he is planning to do and the necessary consequences that will flow from present and past. There is a degree of uncertainty about the future but God understands the range of possibilities contained in it.

Some find exhaustive foreknowledge comforting, but I find it frightening because it tells us that 'whatever will be will be' and that there is nothing we can do about it. It is more scriptural and practical to take the path of trusting God. He is the one who walks with us through the dark valley and can deliver us from evil because nothing is inevitable. Trusting God to make a difference in the future only makes sense if the future is partly open. As Boyd puts it: 'Only if God is the God of what *might be* and not only the God of what *will be* can we trust him to steer us away from what should *not be* and in the direction of what *should be*.'[114]

---

[113] Sanders, *God Who Risks*, 181–4.
[114] Boyd, *God of the Possible*, 153.

Clark H. Pinnock

Conventional thinking has been led astray in the direction of certain ideals of divine perfection and has developed tendencies, though there are variations of emphasis, that alienate it from the biblical witness and from Christian experience. It is time to be more straightforward in facing up to the problem of the pagan legacy and make the necessary modifications. Let's be done with half measures and try to make sense of the biblical picture in a coherent way. The dynamic biblical portrait requires theologians to rethink aspects of the divine perfections and stop allowing the influence of philosophical assumptions to blur them. It is a tragedy of Christian theology that, having begun with a revelation of the living God, our thinking should have turned away to notions of God that are alien to the original message. It is ironical that, having challenged metaphysical inertness and sheer power so effectively in the New Testament itself, theology should have so soon returned to these very errors.

Scripture, Tradition, Culture

The editorial in the 7 February 2000 edition of *Christianity Today* exhorted us not to attempt to read Scripture outside the context of tradition. It said that the Holy Spirit has not been inactive since inspiring the New Testament and we should read Scripture with the help of those who have gone before. (This is a good idea in my opinion too, as long as it does not rule out fresh insight altogether.) So what gives offense in the open view apparently is not its biblical basis, which is strong, but its novelty. Critics say it is not traditional enough; it is after all so very different from the Augustinian tradition. One wonders though how traditional is 'traditional enough' given how Zwingli, for example, tossed out the whole sacramental system of thinking which regarded baptism and the Lord's Supper as means of grace. Charles Hodge boasted that nothing new was ever taught at the Princeton Seminary of his day, but he was much too modest because Warfield's response to evolution and the overall endorsement of Scottish common sense realism at Princeton were certainly modern ideas. But then what is wrong with fresh insight into God's inexhaustible word?[115]

---

[115] The point about being traditional was re-iterated by R.J. Neuhaus, *First Things* (April 2000), 93. Neuhaus is a Roman Catholic priest but one wonders how much tradition our evangelical critics plan to accept. Is N.T. Wright not within his rights to challenge even so cherished an idea as Luther's justification by faith in Paul's writings? Isn't it a good thing to be more biblical even at the

It is better to think of the open view of God as we think of its alternatives (say, Thomism or Calvinism) as a sincere response to the witness of Scripture and open to discussion. All of us worship one God: personal, self-existent, creator, separate from but active in the world, perfectly good, all-powerful, all knowing, and eternal. Anathemas are not called for. Our mutual faith in Jesus Christ is prior to and more fundamental than a detail in a theological model. We are saved by the grace of God in Jesus Christ, not by opinions about divine eternity or foreknowledge.[116]

Historically, the early church's first theological move concerning the matters under discussion was to go with a free will theistic model out of which various Arminianisms came, of which the open view of God is a recent variant. The fathers before Augustine believed that human beings possessed libertarian freedom and that God does not act irresistibly on the unwilling. One might even call this model 'classical', given its great antiquity and current popularity! In any case, the term 'classical theism' is of recent coinage and by no means the property of any one group.[117]

Soon afterwards came Augustine's model of God that would issue in, *inter alia*, Thomism and Calvinism. Though called classical by some conservatives today, it is not a normative model. It is simply a legitimate, neo-Platonic, pattern of interpretation, deserving of the discussion it is being given. But let us remember that Augustine was in many ways the innovator here, while the open view connects with more ancient traditions.[118] The open view is also a 'traditional' view and it belongs to a family of theologies that witness to the dynamic nature of God. Though free will theism is now being criticized for being novel, it should be remembered that in this, as in other matters, it and Augustinianism have co-existed for most of the history of the church. Why can they not continue to co-exist?[119] Besides,

---

Footnote 115 (*continued*) expense of tradition? Of course he had better have a strong argument but what if he does? See N.T. Wright, *The Climax of the Covenant: Christ and the Law in Pauline Theology.*

[116] One may speak of a basic theism held by us all as John Sanders does in an unpublished paper delivered to the Northeastern Regional meeting of the Evangelical Theological Society (March, 2000).

[117] See Geisler, *Chosen But Free*, 145–54, taken from Forster and Marston, *God's Strategy*, 243–88.

[118] H. Küng, *Christianity: Essence, History, and Future*, 288–308. The deeper he got into the controversy with the Pelagians, the more his position on many issues hardened.

[119] Process theists join fundamentalists in labeling Augustinianism 'classical' for their own reasons. They want to set process theism over against everything else and squeeze free will theism out of the picture. Both groups have something to

discussions are taking place among our critics about many of these very same issues, e.g. immutability (Ware), eternity (Nash), impassibility (Tiessen) and sovereignty (all the Arminians). Why draw the line at foreknowledge? Why not discuss the whole package of attributes? Maybe it is not the open view that has gone 'too far'. Maybe conventional theism has not yet gone 'far enough'. It is the neo-Platonism, not the Christian faith, which has to go. I just wish our critics would stop equating these two things.[120]

The open view of God grows out of the ideological, if not the ecclesiastical, soil of Wesleyan-Arminianism. It belongs to traditions that affirm human freedom and deny total divine control. At the same time, the open view differs from them in its understanding of certain of the divine attributes. Wesley and Arminius, for example, held to traditional definitions of categories like unchangeability, eternity, and omniscience, which openness theists believe jeopardize the reality of the divine/human relationship. The open view calls for more extensive modifications of tradition than Arminianism normally does. But traditions change and develop whether they are Wesleyan, Calvinist, Catholic or any other. The open view is not unusual in this regard. The question is whether making the Arminian model more coherent is a reasonable thing to attempt or beyond the boundaries?[121]

A specific point which many have found controversial in the open view of God is its understanding of divine omniscience. In adopting present knowledge as our view, we have placed ourselves beyond what

---

Footnote 119 (*continued*) gain from distorting the situation. Conservative critics want to place openness theists in the process camp, thus proving the rule that my enemy's enemy is my friend.

[120] If my critics were Thomists, they would hang tough on immutability and impassibility and reject any whiff of determinism but, as it is, they tend to be Calvinists so they focus on sovereignty and omniscience while being more liberal in their views of immutability and impassibility. For me, the package of conventional attributes is tightly bound, which means everything has to be on the table to be discussed.

[121] Given the way in which the open view differs from classical Arminianism, I might have entitled my essay, 'From Augustine to Arminius and Beyond' in Pinnock (ed.), *Grace of God*, ch. 1; see also R.A. Muller, 'Grace, Election, and Contingent Choice: Arminius' Gambit and the Reformed Response' in ibid., ch. 11; R.L. Maddox, 'Seeking a Response-able God: The Wesleyan Tradition and Process Theology' (typescript, 2000); and D.A. Tiessen, *The Openness Model of God: An Examination of its Current and Early Expression in Light of Hartshorne's Process Theism.*

the Arminians have said because we think that exhaustive foreknowledge is not a scriptural concept, is detrimental to relational theism and indeed the life of faith. If we are God's covenant partners, it is important that the future is not completely settled, because that would mean there is no room for us to participate in shaping the future as disciples in the service of God. An open future means that things can turn out differently on account of our participation in them. It was not, I think, wise for Arminius to put such emphasis on exhaustive divine foreknowledge, because it gives the impression that history is already decided and not something that we are involved in shaping.

Some even say it is heretical to hold to present knowledge since who, apart from Socinians and process theists, has ever embraced this notion?[122] The hope is to dispose of openness theology by tying it to some known heresy. One begins by identifying a version of traditional theism, for example Thomism or paleo-Calvinism, as orthodox and then associating the open view with some dubious school of thought like Socinianism. The fact is, there is no single version of classical theism whose terms are undisputed and there is no reason to declare the open view of God out of bounds. In the case of divine knowledge, one need not go back to Socinus when there is a more natural root in evangelicalism itself. Methodists like Lorenzo McCabe and Adam Clarke, who were orthodox Christians and also lived prior to the rise of process theology, held to divine present knowledge.[123] The fact is, open theists are trinitarian believers, which means the Socinian charge is wide of the mark.

But why has the open view of divine omniscience been rare? Gregory Boyd writes

This is because almost from the start the church's theology was significantly influenced by Plato's notion that God's perfection must mean that he is in every respect unchanging – including in his knowledge and experience. This

---

[122] R. Strimple notes that the open view of God differs in this respect from classic Arminianism and labels it Socinian. To be fair, he should have noted that openness theists are unlike the Socinians trinitarian and orthodox in their Christology. A theory of omniscience has not been the test of orthodoxy hitherto. The tactic is to position free will theists with known heretics if at all possible; see J.H. Armstrong (ed.), *Coming Evangelical Crisis*, 139–153.

[123] L.D. McCabe, *The Foreknowledge of God* (1887) and *Divine Nescience of Future Contingencies* (1862). The origin of an idea can be important and she who constructs the best typology may win the debate. Ware explores possible origins of openness in a fairer way in connection with Basinger's book *Case for Free Will Theism* in *Journal of the Evangelical Theological Society* 43 (2000), 165–68.

108 *Clark H. Pinnock*

philosophical assumption has been losing its grip on Western minds over the last hundred years, which is, in part, why an increasing number of Christians are coming to see the significance of the biblical motif of divine openness.[124]

If divine passibility is a point of vulnerability for conventional theism, because it pulls the thread that unravels the garment, denying exhaustive omniscience is a point of vulnerability for the open view. Not because it is unscriptural (it enjoys a good deal of testimony) and not because it is not meaningful (it is extremely meaningful), but because of a lack of faith. Our critics cannot bring themselves to trust in a God who would create a world with an open future. They cannot believe in a God who would make himself that vulnerable. If this is true, as it appears to be, we are dealing with a spiritual pathology, not theology. Ask yourself this question: could the Creator, if he so chose, create a world the future of which would be partly settled and knowable, and partly unsettled and unknowable? If he could do so, does not this world have the appearance of being such a place? If you think he cannot, then who has diminished divine sovereignty?

Should it be troublesome that Arminians and other free will theists hold to exhaustive foreknowledge and we break with it? I do not think so. The view has scriptural support and, in any case, is not an article of faith.[125] There have always been vigorous debates about the various attributes of God. Why not just continue to discuss them and resist the temptation to label one another heretics? Being traditional is not everything either. Tradition is not infallible: Luther questioned it. (You can hear Luther's colleagues in the monastery advising him to accept tradition and stop insisting on his own private interpretations!) How amusing to have Baptists and other assorted Protestants telling us to heed tradition when reading the Bible, as if they themselves always do so! What are we to think of Michael Horton advising people, when they read the Bible, to bring the confessions with them? (On the other hand, I think he is right – how else are they to find deterministic ideas if they don't?)[126]

---

[124] Boyd, *God of the Possible*, 115.
[125] Even as I wrote these lines the Southern Baptist Convention changed its faith statement in June 2000 to include belief in exhaustive divine foreknowledge, as did the Baptist General Conference a week later. In reporting it, the editors of *Christianity Today* expressed doubt that it was a wise move to cut off discussion in this way (7 August 2000), 36.
[126] See Michael Horton in J.H. Armstrong (ed.), *Coming Evangelical Crisis*, 262.

Who among us Protestants believes everything in tradition anyway? For example, do we want to defend infant baptism, infused grace through the Eucharist, the celibacy of the priesthood, the *theotokos*, the images, and a state church that can call councils just because they are in the tradition? We all, at certain points, place our interpretations above those of tradition. One cannot, at the same time, use the Bible against Catholics and then use tradition to overturn fresh openness exegesis.

Are we not aware (for example) that Zwingli overturned a virtual consensus in tradition with regard to baptism as a means of grace in his own views about it? He turned a sacrament into a mere ordinance and major novelty.[127]

Concepts like timelessness and impassibility are not written in stone. They are opinions of the past that are important to discuss, but they are not dogmas of the church. Tradition is precious but not infallible or monolithic. It plays a role in our thinking but cannot rule out fresh thought. All of us sift through tradition to some degree. Granted, there are basic traditions we would not, and do not, revise – Trinity, incarnation, atonement and resurrection – but definitions of immutability and power do not stand among them. We insist on our liberty to wonder about these matters. Tradition deserves respect but we are not slaves to it. One can be cautious about new interpretations and ask for strong evidence on behalf of any novelty but not rule out fresh insight. Ask yourself which Protestant belief was not labeled heretical when it was first proposed? The duration of a belief does not by itself prove it; we must go to the word and the testimony. Sometimes 'new' beliefs can be found in Scripture which were there all the time and which the Spirit is giving us to help meet the needs of our time.

Conventional theism is traditional in a way, but has to explain its indebtedness to classical culture. It needs to deal with the legacy of pagan influence that is present in it. We must not pass off as orthodoxy truth mixed with alien notions. The very people who usually repudiate syncretism are in this case defending bad syncretism. The real issue, of course, is inerrancy of the assumptions being used to interpret the Bible and not the inerrancy of Scripture itself. Included are assumptions that dictate that God cannot take risks, even if he chooses too; that God cannot create a world, the future of which he does not totally foreknow; and that God cannot be emotionally affected by what happens in the world, even though he plainly is.

---

[127] See Jack Cottrell, 'Baptism in the Reformed Tradition' in David W. Fletcher, (ed.), *Baptism and the Remission of Sins*, ch. 4.

These habits are so engrained in the thinking of conventional theists that they are unaware of them. Yet they stand in the way of God's people knowing God truly.[128] It is right to be cautious about new interpretations but we must not be apoplectic about them. The church needs fresh insight to help in her thinking and acting as she enters the new millennium. We should be welcoming new ideas not shunning them. Do Protestants now want to put aside the ongoing reform of the church?

In raising the issue of the divine foreknowledge, we have not transgressed some rule of theological discourse and placed ourselves outside the pale of orthodoxy. Why can an evangelical not propose a different view of this matter? What church council has declared it to be impossible? Since when has this become the criterion of being orthodox or unorthodox, evangelical or not evangelical? We tolerate all kinds of differences of opinion about important matters. Many want to re-open the ancient discussions concerning God's timelessness and impassibility. Surely we do not want to shut such discussions down and question each other's faith. Why do I get the feeling that some critics are trying to marginalize us so that evangelicals won't have to discuss certain issues?

An irony of evangelicalism is that, while it contains disparate traditions, it doesn't like to admit its own theological pluralism. The impulse is to assume that only one tradition is valid and true, while fellowshipping with several in the evangelical big tent. The fact is, evangelicalism is large enough to permit several paradigms to interact peacefully. We have grown up enough to discuss them without rancor. I would hope that a number of systematic statements of Christian truth will be forthcoming, each with a distinctive direction, and that we would grow as hearers of God's word. The providence of God and the movement of history will sort out the valid from the invalid and the significant from the insignificant. We don't need to be so anxious about that.

Evangelicalism is a vital movement with great promise for the renewal of the church, but intellectually it is prone to biblicism, rationalism and determinism. Evangelicalism, however, also has a pietistic root that deviates from these characteristics. Luther and Calvin have had a turn and now the call for reform is coming from Arminians, Wesleyans, and Pentecostals. They are asking us to forsake our mental idols and

---

[128] P.R. House sees the conventional model as virtually divinely revealed in 'Evangelical Christianity must re-assert its inerrantly-revealed biblical definition of God', *Southern Baptist Journal of Theology* 1 (1997), 5. Surely our models are not inerrantly revealed but human constructions.

worship the Lord God revealed in Jesus Christ. They are saying: 'There is room for fresh insight – more light can still break forth from God's holy Word.'[129]

Up to this point I have devoted much of the space to answering criticisms from the right that the open view of God is not biblical or traditional enough. Now I have to face a very different criticism from the left that it is too biblical and traditional. More liberally minded theologians will by now be feeling that sticking as closely to the Bible and tradition as the open view does will disappoint readers who want a more modern and intelligible model. They want help with commending belief in God in the present context and may be feeling that I am not sufficiently conscious of the need to address changes in human understanding, scientific and philosophical, which have taken place since biblical times. But, whereas some might stick to the biblical and traditional issues that in the evangelical context would be safer, I see the importance of entering into philosophical and existential issues. The question is, can I sustain the biblical root while exploring intellectual issues independent of the text?

---

[129] H.H. Knight III, *A Future for Truth: Evangelical Theology in a Postmodern World*, 33–5.

Chapter Three

The Metaphysics of Love

Having considered the biblical witness to the openness of God and how we might bring it to a more appropriate theological expression, the next task is philosophical in nature. Besides establishing faithfulness to the word of God, we must also strive for a timely presentation for the sake of a more effective contemporary witness. Having explored the truth of the message, we need now also to interpret this truth for the present generation, so that on the basis of revelation we can also commend the timeliness of God's word. Theology ought to seek to be biblical and traditional. It must also be intelligible and coherent because we want to be understood by people in the present day. Those who would communicate must communicate coherently or they will not be understood and they will not, therefore, be in a position to critique anyone else.

There may be truth to be found from entering into dialogue with modern thought. Did not the Israelites leaving Egypt take the jewels of Egyptian culture and reshape them into furniture for the sanctuary? Have not all the great theologians made use of philosophical reflection to give force to their own convictions?[1] It is not a bad thing to be philosophically engaged. Surely a failure to grapple with intellectual issues is a weakness from a theological standpoint. Pope John Paul II sees faith and reason as the two wings on which the human spirit can soar in contemplation of the truth. His encyclical *Fides et Ratio* (1998) is a summons to the pursuit of wisdom in which theology and philosophy are harmoniously integrated to the advantage of both and the detriment of neither.[2] What Augustine did in his day, we have to do in ours. A synthesis does not have to be a bad thing so long as it does not hinder the proclamation of the gospel.

---

[1] Lovelace, *Dynamics*, 172–84; G.R. McDermott, *Can Evangelicals Learn From World Religions?*.

[2] Cf. A. Dulles' criticism of D.G. Bloesch in E.M. Colyer (ed.), *Evangelical Theology in Transition*, 73; Dulles, *Craft*.

Having a vision of reality helps one navigate the world because it offers categories to help formulate doctrine and holds a promise of apologetic gain. Theology never operates without some regard for philosophy and is philosophically influenced to some degree. The question is not so much whether but how it is influenced, not whether but how philosophy plays a role. Naturally, there has to be discernment as to which philosophical resources serve the proclamation and which hinder it, but philosophy may have something to offer. There is even the possibility that, if philosophy played a role in getting theology off track, philosophy may help to restore things. The fact is that many today get more help from Christian philosophers than from theologians because the former are less cautious and more willing to test hypotheses. It just might turn out that there may be useful insights, Pascal notwithstanding, in philosophy for theology to use in interaction with modern thought.[3]

It was, therefore, proper (let me say this candidly) for early theologians to engage Hellenistic thought, even though they sometimes did so naively. Similarly, it is proper for us to engage modern ideas, even though we too run the risk of making mistakes. We have no choice. We have to consider both the role which ancient philosophy played in shaping conventional theism and how far modern philosophy might be influencing the open view. How will it look in fifteen hundred years in relation to modern thought? I still look for philosophical resources to help us express our distinctive vision of God. In particular, we need a philosophy which values change and can imagine God, not as distant from the world and immobile, but as intimately involved with the world and dynamic. At the same time, we do not want the open view to be negatively impacted by modern philosophy in the way that conventional theism was negatively impacted by ancient philosophy. We seek an apologetic breakthrough but not at the price of unwise accommodations. In this matter of alleging accommodation though, let him who is without sin cast the first stone.[4]

---

[3] W. Hasker in Pinnock, et al., *Openness*, 126. On the general issues, see Dulles, *Craft*, ch. 8. In reading this the reader may feel a real shift in the book from the emphasis up to now.

[4] Roger Olson's early review of *Openness of God* in *Christianity Today* was entitled, 'Has God been held Hostage by Philosophy?' (9 January 1995), 30. I understand the title, but for open theists it has always been a question of biblical and not philosophical theology. Nevertheless, paradoxically, we are interested in philosophy too and Erickson even detects the influence of our philosophical assumptions, see *Evangelical Left*, 107; *Father Almighty*, 27. Wright remarks harshly, 'The entire structure of free will theism is based on reconstructing evangelical theology

We are all influenced by historical settings that enhance or detract from our interpretations of Scripture. It is truly said that no one comes 'from nowhere' but that everyone comes 'from somewhere.' Critics have charged that alien philosophical assumptions distort our perception of what the Bible says about the openness of God. A specific charge states that, in accepting libertarian freedom, we have allowed an alien assumption to distort our exegesis. Holding freedom in such a strong sense, it is said, causes us to deny divine determination and exhaustive omniscience.[5] Now I agree that libertarian freedom does rule out all-controlling sovereignty and exhaustive omniscience, but not that this view of freedom is an alien import into exegesis. The Bible itself assumes libertarian freedom when it posits personal give-and-take relationships and when it holds people responsible for their actions. Compatibilist or determinist freedom cannot easily account for such things. On this matter I am moved by the Bible itself, even though I also do believe that libertarian freedom is a hard-core common sense notion in human life which is characterized by the strong sense that our actions are, at least in part, self-determining.[6]

It is not the open view of God that is philosophy-driven so much as conventional theism itself. Anselm and Aquinas both derived important aspects of their theism from reason and not from Scripture. Having provided a logical proof for God's existence, they both went on, without much appeal to Scripture, to state the attributes a perfect being must have. For example, he must be impassible because if he had passions it would mean that he could be affected by creatures and somewhat be dependent on them, which, they supposed, would be

---

Footnote 3 (*continued*) to conform to the presupposition of the autonomy of the human consciousness', *No Place for Sovereignty*, 227. The early church wrestled with similar issues – how to come to terms with the philosophies of its day. Olson, *Story*, 54, 84, 103.

[5] Piper accuses me of being philosophically seduced in this way; see *Pleasures*, 70–4.

[6] Piper's own view of freedom, so-called compatibilist freedom (named thus because of its 'compatibility' with determinism and therefore more appropriately labeled deterministic freedom) was itself imported into theology by theological determinists like him who wanted some sort of 'freedom' in sync with determinism. It seems to me that they prefer it because of public relations and the need to support conventional theism, not because the Bible suggests it. What if they just came out and said that they were determinists and didn't believe in freedom at all, like Luther once said? They would come under ridicule. Helm, however, calls it 'deterministic' freedom, which is exactly what it is; see *Providence*, 66–8.

improper for a being greater than which cannot be conceived.[7] A tragedy of theology has been that, owing to philosophies which privilege changelessness, it has been difficult to express the central Christian truth claim that the Word was made flesh. Theology needs philosophy that can handle themes like perfection-in-change, incarnation and pathos. It needs philosophical thinking which has room for a God who can be affected and not unaffected by relations to the world.[8]

The Two Horizons

The early theologians of the church articulated the Christian faith in the language of their day and sought to give an intellectually responsible account of it. They brought the biblical witness into relation with ancient philosophy and, inevitably, its ideas of divine perfection. In this way, it gained admission intellectually into the Hellenistic world. Despite what I have said against what happened, I think it was a responsible decision. We all do metaphysics – the challenge is whether the metaphysics we do is of the right kind and there are always gains and losses. On the one hand, the Greek influence helped theology mature and develop a worldview; on the other hand, certain influences from that quarter on the doctrine of God have been harmful. Discernment is crucial, some things we can embrace but other things we must eschew.[9]

One way to picture the difference between the ancient and the modern horizon in philosophy is to say that the ancients preferred permanence to change, while moderns opt for change over permanence. What characterized the ideal of perfection on the ancient horizon was changeless Being. The influence of ancient philosophy on the formation of Christian theology is often illustrated by the early interpretation given to Exodus 3:14, where God says 'I am who I am.' Instead of taking this to mean that God is the living and faithful God who keeps covenant and never forsakes his people, it was taken to mean that God is Being itself as the Septuagint had already rendered it. So what was originally a historical promise became a metaphysical definition in the abstract of God's essence. It introduced into Christian thinking the concept of God as an infinite, unbounded

---

[7] Olson, *Story*, 322.
[8] Hallman, *Descent of God*, ch. 6.
[9] I like the discernment I see in C. Stead, *Philosophy in Christian Antiquity* and in W. Pannenberg, *Basic Questions* II, ch. 5.

ocean of being and as a subsistent Being in which all beings share, one who is infinitely and qualitatively different than the world.[10] Having made this move, philosophy goes to work. As Being itself, God is an absolutely perfect and pure actuality and is not subject to any deficiency. This entails God's immutability and simplicity and means that, in relation to time, God is timeless and does not realize his essence in successive moments. God's eternity means simultaneity not everlastingness. It means that God is always in full possession of the perfection of his being. God does not owe his being to any other; he exists by himself as completely unconditioned. Pure actuality means there is no becoming in God. God cannot change because change would presuppose a transition from potency to act and require change either for the better or the worse. This affects God's relationship with the world. God cannot have real relationships with a changeable world because that would involve give and take. God can impact us, but we cannot impact him in any mutual way otherwise he would change. But God never changes and cannot change in relation to the world – only the world can change in relation to God. There cannot be reciprocity of relations between God and the world because then the world would be able to affect God. God must also be apathetic, unaffected by our joys or sorrows. We are in the presence of an immobility package of attributes shaped by philosophy not Scripture, i.e. immutability requires timelessness requires impassibility requires omniscience.

This has left us with a double problem. First, as I have been saying, this is not biblical thinking. The difference between the biblical portrait and this philosophical definition is obvious. The Bible uses personal not absolutist language. It talks of God's being-here and his being-with and for us. The Greek definition is incapable of rendering the living God and his intensely personal nature. It makes God an abstraction without personality and cannot do justice to the witness of Scripture. One cannot pray or relate to such a God. Theology has relied too heavily on Greek thinking and must open itself to better resources. The dialogue with philosophy has to be broadened. Not every philosophical resource is equally valid for theology. In the end, divine self-revelation has to control what philosophy we use.

Second, it is not intelligible and this leads to a crisis of faith. If God undergoes no change, can have no real relations and is unaffected by the world, the world is hardly relevant to God and it makes little difference

---

[10] Kasper, *God of Jesus Christ*, 147–57. Geisler tries to rebut the point about Exodus 3:14 in *Creating God* 75–80, even though he does not have the commentaries on his side.

whether we love him or not, or even exist. No wonder people are abandoning 'God', if they think that is who God is. Can anyone blame them? How can one love a remote God, indifferent to what happens, and unable to suffer or respond? A good deal of atheism is a child of traditional theism that cuts God off from human life and undercuts the very meaning and value of life.[11]

Theological integrity and the credibility of the concept of God in our time are both at stake. It is difficult to believe the conventional model of God because of its intellectual contradictions and lack of existential appeal. It says, for example, that God is timeless yet acts in time; that God's knowledge is exhaustive yet freedom is real; that God's power is all-controlling yet things happen contrary to his will; that God is unchangeable and yet knows and relates to a changing world. It makes God seem like a metaphysical iceberg and a solitary Being suffering from his own completeness, and then tries to deny it. This model is hard to connect with the categories of Scripture and also hard to present with conviction to people today.

Theologically, the God of Abraham, Isaac and Jacob is distinct from the God of the Hellenistic philosophers. The Greek idea was that because God transcends history so completely he is not changed by anything or ever placed in a position of being conditioned or affected by anything. The Bible, on the other hand, associates God with events and affirms God becoming flesh in Jesus Christ and suffering for us. Theology must summon up the courage to take these things seriously and stop sweeping them under the rug. Apologetically, the open view of God embraces a modern understanding of reality as dynamic not static. It invites us to see reality and God's experience of it as open not closed. This affinity with modern thought, however, is based in the Bible and is not an accommodation to philosophy. Ironically, it is our critics who are overly indebted to (ancient) philosophy, which prevents them being biblical or relevant. The real issue is not the inerrancy of the Bible but the inerrancy of the assumptions that are being used to interpret it.

Theology has labored under a heavy burden. The philosophy available to the early church was rather unsuitable for rendering the Christian idea of God. Theology has needed new points of departure, new thinking which could better express the personal reality of the God of the Bible in philosophical ways. In its own way, the Greek vision was a powerful one and it continues to challenge us today. But what are

---

[11] O'Donnell suggests this in *Mystery*, ch. 1. Along the same lines, A. Kenny also doubts the coherence of the classical model of God in *The God of the Philosophers*.

needed now are philosophical resources that can handle deeply revelation-based ideas like incarnation, suffering, relationality and perfection
in change.

The ideal of perfection under the modern horizon, however, is associated with ideas like personhood, freedom and dynamism (on both the
existential and physical levels). Ancient metaphysics started with Being
and moved to freedom, viewing God's freedom as the highest form of
being, namely, a Being that exists in itself and for itself. The modern
way, in contrast, starts with the subject and freedom, not abstract being,
and proceeds to think about being along these lines. Freedom is what
sheds light on the nature of the world, and happily it is easier to
commend faith in God in relation to this philosophical horizon. Modern
thinking, in some ways, makes it easier to commend the portrait of
a personal, loving God. One is not stuck with the requirement to think
of God as fully actual, unchangeable, timeless, immobile and all-
controlling.[12]

This does not mean that we should posit an internal relation between
the gospel and modern thinking, as if modern thought were a miracu-
lously secularized version of biblical thought. This would ignore the
dangers present in modernity – the danger, for example, that God would
be reduced to a function of human freedom and not be the transcendent
creator. Nevertheless, the category of person is positive and helpful. The
gospel says that the human person finds fulfillment in relation to the
divine, understood as person not as substance. God is seen as alive and
abstractness is avoided. The category spells relationality since persons
exist in relation to other persons. It also spells love: God is love; the
meaning of being is love. The category of person holds to the truth that
God is not an object or a thing that can be pinned down. He is a subject
who exists, speaks, and acts in freedom. The category of person holds
fast to the truth that God is Lord of the world and not a function of it. It
asserts the existence of God as a unique subject from whom, through
whom, and to whom are all things. It conceives of the most ultimate
reality not so much as substance existing by itself, but as self-communicating love.

The openness model places us in a happy position relative to the
modern context because it enjoys biblical support and helps us establish

---

[12] Kasper discusses the definition of God's essence on the horizon of traditional
western metaphysics and then on the horizon of the modern philosophy of
freedom in *God of Jesus Christ*, 147–57. We may need 'a theistic metaphysics of
freedom' to help us imagine God as both the ground of being and as personal
(tripersonal) being; see P. Clayton, *The Problem of God in Modern Thought*,
495–505.

a positive relationship with aspects of modern experience. Although critics try to convert the asset into a liability, by charging that we obtained the model from modernity, the fact is that the open view helps us speak convincingly to contemporary hearers. Its concept of God lacks the disadvantage of feeling like a relic of ancient philosophy and can present itself as a challenging, contemporary option. People do not want and do not need a God distant from the world and untouched by its suffering. But they do need a God who enters into history, becomes incarnate, dies on a cross and rises again. They do need a God who, though he transcends the world, identifies himself with temporality and even with death, and whose truest being lies in his coming and becoming. God's being is not static and without movement. It is an eternal becoming in the liveliness of God's triune being and in his reaching out to creatures. God does not leave himself behind when he comes to us. He is most fully God in his coming. God's becoming is the highest point of his self-revelation, in sharp contrast to the ancient ideal.[13]

The way we think about the world will shape the way we think about the creator. In early theology, the world was pictured as a hierarchy with all creatures occupying a rung on the ladder of reality. God was being in contrast to becoming; he dwelled in the ultimate ivory tower.[14] But the picture that we work with today is very different. With the rise of the biological sciences, we now think of the world as a living organism and a community of relationships in process of development. The designer of a machine stands back from their work, but the designer of a community works inside the project and even experiences its growing pains. Influence and persuasion become important factors. Thinking of the world as an organism encourages us to think of God in an openness fashion, as an interactive and suffering God. God's closeness to the world and his involvement in it are celebrated. This celebration is rooted in God's freedom as the creator to bestow freedom on others and not in necessity. For some time we have needed a different philosophical point of departure in order to express what the gospel has had to say.[15]

There has been a shift from substantialist to relational categories in modern times. We now understand the world as an interrelated process. Conventional theism relates poorly to this kind of world but trinitarian thinking relates well. Nowadays dynamic relational categories are more fundamental than substantialist categories, and the open view is in a better position to communicate because its worldview is more dynamic.

---

[13] Jüngel, *Trinity.*
[14] Norris, *God and World.*
[15] Fiddes, *Creative Suffering* 37–45.

Conventional theism tends to be unbiblical and unintelligible, whereas the open view is both scriptural and timely. We are witnessing the demise of the traditional understanding of reality based on Greek philosophy and Enlightenment rationalism. The emergence of a more dynamic view of reality allows people to read the Bible better and even do philosophy in new ways. In theology, the metaphysics of substance no longer rule. Likewise, in philosophy a mechanistic view no longer holds sway. A modern framework has developed which offers fresh prospects for specifying dimensions of the relationship between God and the world that are both conceptually adequate and fit the biblical data.[16]

Nature is seen as a dynamic process and not an essentially static structure of immutable forms. It is characterized by development and change and there is spontaneity and novelty as well as openness to God's action. The patterns of life in the world have been re-interpreted and transformed from a fixed hierarchical order into a dynamic process, a complex of interacting forces in organic interdependence. God can be seen as sovereign, the one who is above all and who transforms creatures.[17] Boyd writes

> Throughout this century, and especially in the last several decades, we have been stepping out of the Newtonian worldview into a worldview which is thoroughly dynamic, relativistic, and relational. Such classical concepts as substance, absolute time and space, and thing in itself, are losing their viability among modern people. Such concepts as process, force, energy, and relationally defined essence, are gradually taking their place.[18]

The essence of a thing now depends on its relationship with other things. Everything is related to everything else. The network of relationships is more basic than substantial individuals. An open view of God fits better into this new climate. It suggests a more appropriate ontology and cosmology. We have shifted from static to a thoroughly dynamic understanding of the world where change, and not timeless stability, is a familiar idea. The world is composed of dynamic microscopic events, not solid little atoms. The more we move in this direction, the more out of sync conventional theism will be and the more relevant the open view of God will become. God's dynamic creation is the place for the flourishing of creatures. Whereas formerly we fought for the truly interactive relationship between God and the creature in the matter of salvation,

---

[16] Boyd, *Trinity and Process*, 1–11.
[17] I.G. Barbour, *Issues in Science and Religion*, 86–7, 439–52.
[18] Boyd, *Trinity and Process*, 3.

now we can see it also in the workings of the universe itself and God's relations with it.[19]

Conventional theism was shaped in an intellectual climate that favored being over becoming and stability over change. Accepting these assumptions bestowed on it temporary intellectual power but it also distorted Christian theism. The climate has now shifted and new possibilities now exist for theology. The opportunity exists for a fresh intellectual relevance of the doctrine of God. The open view holds promise for apologetics and philosophy of religion. Of course, at the same time, there is always the risk of a new enculturation but that is a risk we always have to take. It would be worse if we just stayed put, defended the pagan heritage, and lost intellectual traction and appeal. Much as I want to defend the open view on scriptural lines, I also want to take intellectual issues as seriously as the early theologians did.[20]

Biblical Philosophy

Theology can join with and even stimulate philosophy because it is truth-seeking and addresses ultimate issues. The Bible has truth to offer when it speaks about the nature of God and the world, about human nature and ethical values, about human significance and the undecided future. It is a joy to be a philosopher but how much more to be a philosopher with life changing convictions about God, incarnation and resurrection to inform our thought. Theologians do not embrace a ready-made schema of philosophy, but they do seek to put into expression the vision of reality implied in revelation. Though I approve of natural theology, I also find it productive to tease out philosophical aspects of the biblical witness itself (Christian natural theology) and plan to explore the contribution of openness theism, which views God as a personal agent related to and involved in the world, to the Christian worldview. Biblical theology can have philosophical relevance.[21]

---

[19] Boyd, *God of the Possible*, 107–11.

[20] A fly in the ointment for some evangelicals might be that the modern outlook welcomes a theistic evolutionary outlook which may stick in their throat if they are creationists; see C.H. Pinnock, 'Climbing out of a Swamp: The Evangelical Struggle to Understand Creation Texts', *Interpretation* 43 (1989), 143–55.

[21] As a natural theologian, I most admire Richard Swinburne and as a truth-seeking revelation-based theologian, I most esteem Wolfhart Pannenberg; the latter's concern comes out clearly in *An Introduction to Systematic Theology*, ch. 1. Pannenberg also acknowledges, however, 'the inconceivable majesty which transcends all our concepts', *Systematic Theology* I, 337.

Seeking a 'biblical philosophy' casts light upon open view thinking. It seeks for truth about reality in the biblical metaphors rather than in currently available philosophical propositions and hopes to realize intelligibility in this way. It also cares about coherence and cruciality. A process theist, on the other hand, places priority on identifying a contemporary conceptuality but also gives thought to biblical teaching. Thus, both positions see value in what the other is trying to do but would feel that their own approach and priority is the wiser of the two.[22] I see the open view of God contributing to philosophical insight in the following ten areas.

1. Being and knowing

What is first in the order of being may not be first in the order of knowing. Theologians must be sensitive to those who do not assume that there is a God, even though the sense of divinity seems to be intuitive for most people.[23] Beyond that, the only real 'proof' of God would be the elaboration of a theory that is fully descriptive of the world, within which God holds an essential place and which explains the other elements. We cannot achieve that and the best we can come up with is something with explanatory power greater than comparable schemes. There may be no single knockdown proof of God, but there may be a soft-rational, cumulative case for God that is feasible and gives intellectual support to the intuition of deity. Why is there something rather than nothing? Why is this something intelligible? Whence the design distributed so generously in the dynamic structures of the world? Whence the system of laws and conditions by which life and personality were brought forth? Whence the interconnectedness, coordination, and harmonization of the different levels of existence? Why is there consciousness? Why is there moral obligation? Why is there a universal religious quest? Although such reasoning cannot offer irrefutable proof, it can make theism plausible. The existence of God certainly explains why the world is such an amazing place.[24]

A strong appeal for ordinary people as regards belief in the existence of God arises from existential considerations. It lies in the fact that God, if there is a God, could, assuming the necessary attributes, supply the basis in reality itself for the ineradicable confidence humans seem to

---

[22] See J.B. Cobb and C.H. Pinnock (eds.), *Searching for an Adequate God: A Dialogue Between Process and Free Will Theists*, xiii– xiv.

[23] So, Calvin, *Institutes* I, chs. 3–5; Pannenberg, *Systematic Theology* I, 116–8.

[24] M. Peterson, et al., *Reason and Religious Belief*, 87–8; and B. Hebblethwaite, *The Ocean of Truth: A Defense of Objective Theism*, ch. 6.

have in the final worth of their existence. I refer to that confidence
without which one could scarcely go on living. Without a sense of
worthwhileness grounded in reality, it is difficult to be committed to
anything or undertake any significant task. If, on the other hand, there
were a God who loves us freely, an objective deity who really exists, then
there would be a ground in reality itself for confidence in the final worth
of our existence. Everyone has the sense that life is meaningful and not
absurd, and theists know this is because underneath there are everlasting
arms. This witness does not testify to just any God, to a deity aloof and
indifferent, in short, to a conventional God. Rather, it witnesses to a
divine reality that is genuinely related to life in the world and to which
we and our actions make a real difference, i.e. it testifies to God as
understood in the open view of God.[25]

2. The importance of revelation

Natural theology can take us part of the way but revelation has a much
fuller picture to offer as to the nature of ultimate reality. Christians celebrate a relational trinitarian God of unfathomable love, incarnate in
Jesus Christ and experienced by the catholic community.[26] This is based
on historical reality, not on speculative philosophy, and is confirmed by
the resurrection of Jesus. It yields a relational ontology and metaphysic
of love, and identifies a God who is antecedently actual and self-sufficient, yet self-giving. It also witnesses to a God who does not need an
external world to experience love because he experiences goodness and
love within himself apart from it, but who, at the same time, is open to
the world and experiences the goodness of the created order.[27]

The deepest and most ultimate reality, according to the gospel, is personal and relational rather than mere substance. The absolute God is
supremely beautiful and benevolent, loving and lovable. God is a
dynamic event of communion and communication, sometimes envisaged by the church fathers as a 'dance' of trinitarian life; he is not a fea-
tureless, isolated and motionless monad. Loving mutuality and
relationships belong to God's essence rather than static substance or
overwhelming power, categories which make it so hard to express the
self-revelation of God and grasp how God relates to a changing world.
Ours is an internally and externally relational God, a God who enlarges

---

[25] S.M. Ogden says that it points to the God of process theism in *The Reality of
God and Other Essays*, ch. 1. In fact the argument is shared between us – we
both find it compelling but employ it in slightly different ways.
[26] So O'Donnell, *Mystery*, ch. 2.
[27] Boyd, *Trinity and Process*, 374–92.

himself as he grows into more and more relationships with an increasing number of souls.[28] This may be the beauty of the Lord that the psalmist longed to behold (Ps. 27:4). Think of it, the ground in reality itself for the final worth of our existence is the God of incarnation and resurrection who pitches his tent among us and is the very epitome of perfection-in-change. This is a God who is not alienating of humanity, who does not exist at human expense and who is not a superpower threatening to crush us.

3. The world exists by grace
The self-sufficiency of the triune God underlines the fact that the world exists by grace, not by necessity. A creation exists because God freely decided to make it. It gives pleasure to God, even though he does not strictly need it. It is a product of God's overflowing love and echoes in its own creaturely way some of the dynamism of the triune God. God does not choose to be alone. He wills the creature to co-exist with him and to stand alongside him as the beloved covenant partner. This is our core identity – to be loved by God. This is our daily discipline – to claim our belovedness.[29]

The foundation of the significance of our creaturely existence is the fact that God delights in us and wants a relationship with us. In freedom, God created and then chose to interact in the temporal processes of the world, while being, at the same time, eternally and self-sufficiently actual. God enjoys the goodness of the world and, by grace, creates (unnecessarily) in order to share his own bliss with others. Creation is a more than necessary fact and God is no greater for having done it. God is unsurpassable, whether or not there is a world. But God is also delighted with it, as an artist who loves to express creativity. Creation gives God an occasion, as it were, to express his unsurpassability. God is able, by creating the world, to actualize his own potential: not the potential to be God, but the potential to be the creator of a non-divine world and the potential to appreciate it. The world thus becomes part of God's experience and in this way is deeply meaningful to him. He values it even though, as I said, it doesn't make God more God than before. Creation satisfies God's eternal disposition to love and to communicate. It reflects an abundant source of self-creativity and an intensity of love and delight.

---

[28] S. Lee, *The Philosophical Theology of Jonanthan Edwards*, chs. 7–8. Edwards illustrates the possibility that an orthodox Calvinst could appropriate process type thinking without being a panentheist.
[29] Morris, *Idea*, ch. 8.

4. Love

God created the world out of love and with the goal of acquiring a people who would, like a bride, freely participate in his love (Rev. 19:7). He could have pre-programmed creatures to love him, but instead created them with the liberty to choose to love him freely. Love was the goal and freedom the means to the goal. Humankind had to be granted real freedom, i.e. a capacity to respond, if we were to be able voluntarily to enter loving personal relations with God. He values freedom, not so much as an end in itself, but as an instrument to make possible what he really longs for, love. God gives us real freedom because of his desire for loving relationships. God is inviting us to join in his own ongoing trinitarian communion and conversation. He wants us to join in and share the intimacy of his own divine life. God is committed to lead us to glory, even if it proves costly to himself. It is a mark of the divine wholeness. The more 'whole' God is, the more perfectly God can suffer with and for others. God's weakness demonstrates how strong he is. God is Lord precisely in becoming a servant. His love is more than necessary. The Trinity expresses itself by creating new partners for the dance. God is emphatically interested in how we respond to his overtures.

Freedom was one of the noblest of all the characteristics with which God endowed us. A whole world of noble goals is made possible thereby. C.S. Lewis writes

> Why did God give them free will? Because free will, though it makes evil possible, is also the only thing that makes possible any love or goodness or joy worth having. A world of automata – of creatures that worked like machines – would hardly be worth creating. The happiness which God designs for his higher creatures is the happiness of being freely, voluntarily united to him and to each other in an ecstasy of love and delight compared with which the most rapturous love between a man and a woman on earth is mere milk and water. And for that they must be free.[30]

God made creatures capable of doing much good, and much bad. He made them able to make moral choices, not predetermined by prior causes. It is the glory of humanity that we act freely and not out of necessity. God sovereignly created responsible free beings and wants them to be creative in their own way.[31] Here is a point of appeal of open theism. It is positive about human significance. Persons make real contributions

---

[30] C.S. Lewis, *Mere Christianity*, 49.
[31] Swinburne, *Providence*, 105–7; Geisler, *Chosen but Free*, 19–37, 175–80, 221–5.

to history. It does not endorse autonomy, but it does support significant human agency.

This is not to deny the partial truth of predestination. There is a destiny that is given to us from the past with which we work in the present, as we bend and reshape it to our own particular ends. Destiny only becomes fate when its weight overcomes freedom. We all actualize our own being in the present out of a destiny that comes to us from the past, combined with the possibilities that confront us from the future, as God challenges us to go forward. Belief in real freedom is something like belief in God, it is difficult but possible to deny. This is because we intuitively accept freedom. Ask yourself how many people in real life doubt that they, or their associates, are responsible beings. How many believe that that their choices are nothing more than the products of previous states of mind? They know that they shape the influences they have received in significant ways and that they cannot excuse themselves when they do wrong. Certainly there are inputs into human behavior from nature and the environment, but as persons we also partly transcend these forces. Human nature essentially emerges and is not predetermined.

What I call 'real freedom' is also called libertarian or contra-causal freedom. It views a free action as one in which a person is free to perform an action or refrain from performing it and is not completely determined in the matter by prior forces – nature, nurture or even God.[32] Libertarian freedom recognizes the power of contrary choice. One acts freely in a situation if, and only if, one could have done otherwise. Free choices are choices that are not causally determined by conditions preceding them. It is the freedom of self-determination, in which the various motives and influences informing the choice are not the sufficient cause of the choice itself. The person makes the choice in a self-determined way. A person has options and there are different factors influencing us in deciding among them but the decision one takes involves making one of the reasons one's own, which is anything but random.

Assuming libertarian freedom does not betray an unwarranted indebtedness to modern ideas, since the Bible itself implies it in many ways when, for example, it portrays God as seeking freely chosen and reciprocal relationships with us; it portrays grace as something one can receive or decline; it sets before us moral choices; it implies that God declares himself outraged by human sin; and when God grieves over what we freely decide to do. These are not conditioned responses to prior influences. Belief in freedom is not so much a modern belief as it is a perennial commonsense

---

[32] Swinburne, *Providence*, 33–5; K.J. Clark, *Return to Reason*, 69–70.

notion that is very difficult to deny in practice. It is a form of the experience of voluntary action in which we sense that real alternatives lie before us. It is an intuition that is also an important clue to the nature of the world. What Scripture implies is also what makes most sense.[33]

The alternative view of freedom, called compatiblist or determinist freedom, judges an act to be free when there is an absence of external constraint. Actions flow necessarily from what the person wants to do. They are based on what they have inherited and are not the product of external coercion. God or destiny could be in complete control and freedom would still exist under this arrangement. Thus it appeals to theological, and other, determinists. This view is not without merit. Things like our culture, upbringing and biology affect our choices. We do act on the basis of our desires and out of who we are. Those who know us well can predict lots of our actions. God knows us better than anyone so he will have a much clearer idea of what we are likely to do. When God revealed to Paul that 'all Israel will be saved,' I suppose he knew that, not because he possessed a crystal ball, but because he knows what will bring his people around (Rom. 11:26). But recognizing these factors does not require one to rule out the possibility of novelty and the reality of self-determination. How else can there be loving relationships? How else can there be moral responsibility? How else could sin have come into the world? How else can we explain why agents are held responsible for their choices?[34]

A defense of real freedom starts from the human experience of deliberation, decision, and action. Human creativity is as unpredictable in principle as it is in practice and freedom is the act of the whole person. Think of it in relation to the present conversation. Are we not trying to influence each other to accept one model of God or another? Do we not think of ourselves as existing in an open situation in which one can move one way or another intellectually? Surely the reader and I are more interested in the evidence and truth than each other's pre-existing states of mind. I hope nobody holds that that we are pre-determined to believe what we now do believe. I hope someone might be persuaded to change his or her mind. I think that I might be. It is apparent to me that God does not force himself upon us but delights in the chorus of voices as we seek

---

[33] W.S. Anglin argues that if people do not have libertarian freedom: (1) they lack true rationality, (2) they lack genuine artistic creativity, (3) they lack significant moral responsibility, (4) they cannot choose values, (5) they cannot cooperate with others, (6) they lack the power to love, and (7) they cannot make promises in a meaningful way; see *Free Will and the Christian Faith*, ch. 1. See also Hasker, *Metaphysics*, 47–9.

[34] Cf. P. Helm, *The Grace of God, The Bondage of the Will*, ch. 21.

to understand, even in this very discussion. God's mustard seed is hardly visible yet it grows and prospers.[35]

Stephen Wellum expresses the fear that a weak view of sovereignty might lessen our ability to think of the Bible as entirely the word of God because, if freedom is libertarian, God cannot control every aspect of the inspired text.[36] True enough, but do we want to affirm what amounts to a dictation of the text? It seems that when we read Scripture we have an interplay of divine initiative and human activity. God is overseeing the process but human authors are also active. God is always present, not always in the mode of control, but often in the manner of stimulation and invitation. God works alongside human beings in order to achieve by wisdom and patience the goal of a Bible that expresses his will for our salvation.[37]

5. A preconditioned and dynamic creation

In order to supply freedom for the sake of love, God made the world a subtle and supple place. He made a natural order incredibly fruitful and serendipitously creative as a womb and then a home for us. God equipped it with a whole set of preconditions that would make life possible and make room for freedom in the context of the world's own natural becoming. He made an environment where not everything would be predictable and where novelties can happen. He made a world with an open future as a proper setting for life and the development of freedom. It is no wonder that God declared it 'good, very good' (Gen. 1:31). At a certain point in time, according to his own sovereignty and not by timeless necessity, God created the world. It was the gift of a creative being who chose to actualize forms of value that would not otherwise exist. He made creation with purpose and an open future, and a world genuinely contingent, full of creatures capable of free action.[38]

---

[35] I.G. Barbour, *Issues in Science and Religion*, 305–13. A point of tension in Francis Schaeffer's apologetic was his attempt to hold to both all-controlling sovereignty and libertarian freedom; see S.R. Burson and J.L. Walls, *C.S. Lewis and Francis Schaeffer*, 92–8. J.I. Packer gives the same impression but one suspects that he, like Carson and unlike Schaeffer, holds to compatibilist freedom, which unties the Gordian knot. A puzzle remains as to why Packer thinks there is an antinomy if freedom is compatibilist.

[36] S.J. Wellum, 'The importance of the nature of divine sovereignty for our view of Scripture', *Southern Baptist Journal of Theology* 4 (Summer 2000), 76–90.

[37] Pinnock, *Scripture Principle*, 100–5.

[38] J. Polkinghorne offers a scientifically based cosmology to fill in the picture; see *Serious Talk: Science and Religion in Dialogue*. J. Moltmann speaks of the

There has been a change in thinking about the world, from static to a dynamic understanding, which assists us theologically. What is most real for us today is not timeless stability but dynamic changefulness. We now think that the universe is composed of dynamic events more than solid things. There has been a shift in thinking from mechanistic and deterministic terms to non-deterministic and quantum terms. We have moved from the assumption that science could theoretically predict everything to the view that a measure of unpredictability is intrinsic to these complex systems. The beauty is that, given the open view of God, there is no need to deny this shift and every reason to affirm it. Seeing the future as partly open and partly settled fits hand in glove with what we are discovering about dynamic systems in science today. God, through his word, injects information into the system, while he by his Spirit indwells the process.[39]

God created a world governed by laws of physical and moral order. He also created intelligent, libertarianly free, and morally responsible creatures, and sustains them in existence. His summons to them is that they act wisely in accordance with God's created order. It is not God's normal policy to protect creatures from the consequences of their actions or from the actions of others. In a sense, the history of the universe, as it unfolds, is an enormous act of God's, within which we live out our lives. At the same time, God is not far away and uninvolved but willingly subject to influences outside of himself to which he responds. Ours is a dynamic worldly order in which God influences the world, ordinarily through persuasion, and in love seeks to move us in the direction of greatest good, in spite of possible resistance to his influence.

God has established a flow of creativity in which there are systems so exquisitely sensitive to circumstances that the smallest disturbance produces large and ever-growing changes in the world. The natural world now seems to be more complex and open than we have assumed and the network of causal connections less restricted than we had imagined. We see a world where a wider causality is available for the service of love. It is a context in which God would seem to have more ready access into history.[40] We used to think of human beings enjoying freedom but nature being the realm of strict causation. But now it seems that the path to human freedom lies in nature itself, where God works with and

Footnote 38 (*continued*) 'play' of God's Sabbath in *God In Creation: A New Theology of Creation and the Spirit of God*, 276, 296. See also J.-J. Suurmond, *Word and Spirit at Play: Toward a Charismatic Theology*.
[39] Barbour's recent book is replete with suggestions how a dynamic God might relate creatively with a dynamic universe; see *When Science Meets Religion*.
[40] M.A. Corey, *God the the New Cosmology: The Anthropic Design Argument*.

within the indeterminacy of the world. This does not mean the world is out of control. Though there is uncertainty at the sub-atomic level, the processes yield patterns and regularities in the aggregate. Indeed, randomness itself is the precondition of order, as God works with and through the uncertainty of nature. Nature supplies an environment for the emergence of intelligent life, capable of loving God freely. Indeterminacy is a fundamental ingredient of the world and creates the possibility for the flourishing of creatures. People sometimes talk as if it would be easy for God to create free beings. Think again. The age of the universe suggests that it is not easy. It suggests that this work of divine artistry takes a lot of time and care.[41]

Usually we affirm freedom in the human realm but not in nature itself. It now seems that God has built the possibility of freedom deeper down than we have assumed. We now recognize factors in nature that make human freedom possible – it is factors like indeterminacy, randomness and uncertainty that create the possibility of flourishing. This is a very special world, finely tuned for life. It is a world which God allowed to make itself to a large degree – a self-making which takes place in a setting of finely tuned potentiality. Creation in all its particulars is an intricate process that involves God interacting with sensitivity, patience and love; not something that came ready-made from God's hand.[42] It has become easier to understand divine action in and with the world, thanks to contemporary science. There are new places of openness for God to move about in and previously unheard ways of understanding how God influences the world, e.g. quantum mechanics, chaos theory, dynamic systems and top-down causation in nature.[43]

6. The problem of evil
The open view of God helps with the problem of evil. It yields 'a logic of love' theodicy that can be sketched along these lines:

(a) God created for the sake of loving relationships.
(b) This required giving real freedom to the creature that it not be a robot.

[41] See D.J. Bartholemew, *God of Chance*; P.R. Meadows, 'Providence, Chance, and the Problem of Suffering', *Wesleyan Theological Journal* 34 (1999), 52–77.
[42] J. Polkinghorne, *Quarks, Chaos, and Christianity*, chs. 2–3
[43] P. Clayton, *God and Contemporary Science*, ch. 7; H. Gruning, *How in the World Does God Act?* It might be easier to understand God's actions if God were thought in some way to be embodied. Cf. Jantzen, *God's World,* 85–93.

(c) Freedom, however, entails risk in the event that love is not reciprocated.
(d) Herein lies the possibility of moral and certain natural evils – those which appear irredeemably malicious and demonic.
(e) God does not abandon the world but pledges a victory over the powers of darkness. In such a theodicy, God does not will evil but wills love and, therefore, freedom that opens the door to things going right or wrong.
(f) Though God does not protect us from ourselves, God is there redeeming every situation, though exactly how, we may not yet always know.[44]

If love requires freedom and if freedom entails risk, God could not create such a world and be absolutely certain what the creatures would do with it. God took a risk when he made this kind of a world since freedom entails the possibility, if not the necessity, of genuine evil because love can be refused. Risk was involved in creating this kind of non-divine order because rebellion and defection are possibilities. Evil was not what God willed, though he did make it possible by giving freedom for the sake of love.[45] Theists in the past have tried to exclude the category of risk in God's experience but risk is integral to loving relationships. By trying to exclude it, they have had to put responsibility for evil at God's feet. The open view of God, on the other hand, freely accepts the obvious – things do not always go the way God wants them to. For the sake of love, God created a world that would require tremendous resourcefulness on God's part and radical trust on ours.[46]

Evil has been difficult for conventional theism because of its reluctance to see divine power as something which is shared with creatures. As long as God has a monopoly on power, any response to evil becomes extremely difficult. If God had such a monopoly, one would have to deny the existence of genuine evil because evil is something God wanted to happen. Conventional theism, with its obsession for control, makes God the author of evil and condemns itself to defending something untenable. We have to face the fact that, if nothing happens outside the

---

[44] We await G. Boyd's *Satan and the Problem of Evil*. B. Ware contends that the open view of God does not help us as much with suffering as it may seem in 'Despair amidst suffering and pain: A practical outworking of open theism's diminished view of God', *Southern Baptist Journal of Theology* 4 (Summer 2000), 56–75.
[45] Basinger, *Free Will Theism*, ch. 4.
[46] Helm (*Providence*) and Tiessen (*Prayer and Providence*) exclude risk, while Sanders (*God Who Risks*) and Boyd (*God of the Possible*) embrace it.

will of God, there is no genuine evil. If he is in control in a monopolistic sense, everything that happens has to have a reason. Even the Holocaust has to have a reason and has to contribute in some way to the greater good, if only we could see it from God's point of view. In this way evil is taken up into God and a dark shadow is cast over God's goodness. Augustine was on the right track early in his career when he proposed a free will defense to deal with the problem of evil. Unfortunately, it came to naught when his thinking moved toward a doctrine of all-controlling sovereignty in later years. Surely there is no way that sinners can be held responsible for evil if God secretly controls them.[47] Indeed, the strongest, and perhaps only, argument for atheism is the existence of evil, which, if God secretly planned it and had a reason for it, makes belief in God impossible. The blueprint model of divine providence, in which each evil serves a higher purpose and every gruesome detail contributes to the beauty of God's work, makes the problem of evil insoluble. No wonder the discussion of theodicy shows so few signs of progress. Belief in a God who ordains and/or allows every evil to exist (including the burning of children) cannot be sustained.[48]

The open view of God lets one affirm the reality of genuine evil because it does not see God as the only source of power and does not have to figure out why, in God's mysterious providence, horrors come upon us. The openness model accepts that certain evils ought not to be. God is not in control of the powers of evil at this time in history, so they do not always play into the hands of God. There is not always a reason for every occurrence of evil. God, though he established the structures of the world, does not always get what he wants in every situation. Much of the difficulty in theodicy arises from attributing all-controlling power to God. Things look quite differently when you realize that God does not always get his way and is not responsible for everything that happens. Why do we forget that there is a war on between God and the powers of darkness? Angels and humans, being in possession of real freedom, have rebelled and are able to create havoc at the present time.

Logic of love theodicy even helps us cope with natural evils that originate independently of human action. It can rationalize certain evils that seem to lack a moral agent and whose cause seems to lies somehow in the natural order. Why does the non-teleological lie alongside the teleological? Some natural evils are an inherent part of the natural order and are

---

[47] Despite J.S. Feinberg, 'God, Freedom, and Evil in Calvinist Thinking' in T.R. Schreiner and B.A. Ware (eds.), *Grace of God, The Bondage of the Will*, ch. 20. J. Hick, *Evil and the God of Love*, chs. 3–4.

[48] Boyd presses the issue in *God at War*.

needed for life. Some of them may arise from the randomness that underlies creativity and be the byproduct of the orderly natural process that sustains life. Thanks to medicine and engineering we learn to cope and deal with threats and serious challenges to life that we face. Other natural evils, however, and this is often overlooked, may be due to the free will of spiritual beings who, unlike ourselves, also possess a degree of control over nature. After all, Scripture speaks of the demonic and spiritual warfare. Are there not times when one detects a diabolical dimension to natural evil? We see nature red in tooth and claw – tornados, typhoid and plagues that savagely kill the innocent – and conclude that this did not come from the hand of God. We say with Jesus, 'An enemy has done this!' and refuse to blame God for it (Mt. 13:28). It is not only biblical but also experiential to contend that some evils originate in the kingdom of Satan, and the reason that the world looks at times like a war zone is that it is a war zone. Jesus did not attribute things like deformity, blindness, leprosy and fever to the providence of God. He viewed them as evidence of the reign of darkness, which he was engaged in defeating. Nature, as it now is, does not unambiguously reflect the will of God. There is good evidence for the existence of the demonic, not only in Scripture, but also in practically all the cultures of the world.

7. The Holy Spirit

An asset of the open view of God in relation to the problem of evil is the confidence we have as Spirit-filled believers in the power of God to deliver from evil here and now.[49] The signs and wonders that accompanied the gospel in the first instance and in the flow of charismata that flooded the earliest Christian communities impress us. Healing the sick, casting out demons and works of power signaled the inauguration of the kingdom of God in Jesus' ministry; they portrayed the end of Satan's reign and the coming transformation of the world. The powers of death were put on notice by the gracious working of God and by a release of divine life. Signs accompanied those who believed God's own testimony to the truth of the gospel (Mk. 16:17; Heb. 2:3–4). The proclamation was in word and by a demonstration of the Spirit and power (1 Cor. 2:5). The healing of the sick, a prominent feature of Jesus' ministry, represented, in Cullmann's words, 'a proleptic deliverance of the body.' Jesus' resurrection has consequences for our bodies, although their transformation will not occur until the dawn of new creation.[50] Similarly, exorcisms also signal the coming of the

---

[49] Pinnock, *Flame*, 129–41.
[50] O. Cullmann, *The Early Church*, 165–73.

kingdom and the overcoming of the powers of evil. Signs and wonders signal a new phase of history, which will culminate in the new creation. The outpouring of the Spirit and his gifts on the church is characteristic of the age of the messiah and his reign in the kingdom of God.[51]

We all know, however, that the level of the manifest presence of God can vary and we may wonder where God is when we really need him. If God can involve himself in the world in natural, and unusual ways, how can we explain God's non-involvement? If God can do miracles on occasion, why does he not do more of them? If God can alter states of affairs, why does he not alter them more consistently? Why does God tolerate the ongoing activities of evil agents so liberally? In the Bible itself, in traditions of lament, believers voice this very concern (Ps. 10:1).

Part of the answer, according to the open view, is a lack of faith on the human side. Mark tells us that Jesus could do no mighty works in Nazareth because of unbelief (Mk. 6:5). Limited expectations on our part diminish God's freedom to act. Often there is a worldview impediment. We may shrink from believing in God's promises and close ourselves off from the full range of God's gifts because of the effect on us of western materialism.[52] The fact is, God may want to move but may be prevented because, though he has the power, he wants to work hand-in-hand with the covenant partners with whom he shares dominion over the world. Without openness to God there is no power. God likes to act when we ask him to and, in effect, limits his power to do mighty works. God makes himself dependent on the prayers of his people. Putting it positively, God loves to move in response to our prayers. Our failure to pray impacts the world negatively.[53]

Furthermore, owing to the situation of spiritual warfare, God's power to act can also be obstructed in ways that we do not readily understand. On one famous occasion Daniel's prayer was heard, but the answer delayed because, it is stated, of the opposition of the angel of Persia (Dan. 10). The anecdote suggests that God cannot just do anything he wants, when he wants to. It suggests that his power can, at least temporarily, be blocked and his will not be done in the short term. The early Christians were aware of this dimension and, therefore, did not ask

---

[51] J. Ruthven has written a fine book defending the ongoing charismatic dimension of Christianity; see *On the Cessation of the Charismata: The Protestant Polemic on Postbiblical Miracles*.

[52] C.H. Kraft, *Christianity With Power: Worldview and Your Experience of the Supernatural*.

[53] The open view shares this insight with the school that Tiessen calls the church dominion model: *Providence and Prayer*, ch. 6.

why they continued to suffer. They knew a spiritual war was going on. Instead, they asked how long it would be until the final victory of God and had to trust the commander in chief.[54]

There are other factors too, for example the relative irrevocability of freedom and the stable natural order God has set in motion. Having created free agents, God cannot simply terminate them and their evil deeds. God has committed himself to working with finite powers. To prevent his creatures working evil would be to act against the liberty God gave them and removing that freedom would show that God was not serious in giving it in the first place. He made a kind of covenant of non-coercion with creatures, which involved the necessity of his enduring their decisions as free agents for a time. Thus, he also accepted the need to work around their evil influences. There are certain metaphysical constraints that even God cannot avoid, though he made them. God is not free to just 'delimit' himself at any time.[55]

God's decision to make this kind of world constrains his freedom to act. God's self-limitation began with that decision and is not a moment-by-moment affair. Creation placed limits on God's freedom to act subsequently. As creator, God cannot and will not scrap the conditions, including the stable natural environment required to sustain life, which underlie the project,. Heat and cold are good things but not in excess. Learning to cope with dangers is positive but can lead to accidents. Some evils are the unavoidable by-products of an orderly natural process which is life giving and at the same time gives opportunity for noble responses. I do not think when we pray that we want God to forsake the basic design that the universe has.

Process theology has a stronger version of this principle. It locates freedom inherently in the world, which it says God did not create 'out of nothing'. It posits limitations on God's power that are inherent in the structure of the world. These constraints on God's power, including freedom, are never retractable. The open view of God, on the other hand, does not construe God's relationship with the world as necessary and handles the issue with the idea of a binding covenant. Though God does struggle with powers of evil, the powers are not metaphysically ultimate; they are created and finite.

In this way the open view can make sense of the fact that the biblical witnesses lament God's inaction in respect of evil. In lamenting, they express the thought that God could be doing more than he is now doing

[54] See W. Wink, *Engaging the Powers*, 308–17; Boyd, *God at War*, 9–22.
[55] MacGregor, *He Who Lets Us Be*. This has been a concern of Inbody, *Transforming God*, chs. 7–8.

and wonder why he isn't doing it. They do not recognize inherent limitations in God but (with Woody Allen) wonder why God is such an underachiever. They ask God, in effect, 'Do you know what you are doing?' Why can't you do more? In the open view, it is possible to question God's wisdom and the ways in which he is employing his power. It accepts how complicated the world is and how many variables there are to deal with in it and does not deny God's lordship over the world.[56]

8. The future

Philosophically speaking, it makes sense to think about the future as partly settled and partly unsettled, otherwise it would be the realm of settled actualities and not open possibilities, which would undercut meaningful human life. In *A Christmas Carol*, Ebenezer Scrooge, in reference to the tombstone which he saw in the vision, asks: 'Are these the shadows of the things that will be, or are they the shadows of the things that may be, only?' He adds: 'Men's course will foreshadow certain ends to which, if persevered in, they must lead, but if the courses be departed from, the ends will change.' Thus he pleads, 'Assure me that *I may yet change* these shadows you have shown me, by an altered life. Oh, tell me that I may sponge away the writing on this stone.' Scrooge wanted to know if the future was still being shaped and, if so, whether his actions could affect it.

If the future is not open, then neither God nor humanity can contribute anything to it. If it is open, however, our decisions are possibilities until we actualize them. Therefore, we are motivated to make the best choices and not fall back into resignation. Knowing that what will transpire in the future is still being decided inclines us to assume responsibility for the future. Why pour out your life if, 'whatever will be will be?' Why pray, if prayer changes nothing? Why exercise the authority the Lord has given? Boyd comments

> Knowing that what transpires in the future is not a foregone conclusion but is significantly up to us to decide, we will be more inclined to assume responsibility for the future. We will be more inclined to pursue what could be rather than resign ourselves to what will be. Life is life indeed when there are possibilities not just certainties.[57]

---

[56] J.D. Levenson makes this point in the preface to the 1994 edition of *Creation and the Persistence of Evil: The Jewish Drama of Divine Omnipotence*, xv. He rejects the process position and defends the open view of God on this point.
[57] Boyd, *God of the Possible*, 94.

God knows everything that any being can know. He knows everything that has ever existed, everything that now actually exists, everything that could possibly exist in future, and everything that he has decided to do. The details of his knowledge change as creatures act in new and free ways. This is not a limitation on God as knower; it has to do with the nature of the future as partly settled and partly unsettled. God knows everything that can be known and that is perfection enough.[58]

If love requires freedom and freedom entails risk, risk too suggests a certain kind of knowledge on God's part. One cannot be said to be taking a risk when engaging in activities the outcome of which is, and always has been, completely certain. Risk implies that an outcome could go one way or the other. You do not take a 'risk' when investing in a stock if you have insider information about the stock you are investing in. If God had exhaustive foreknowledge, there would be no risks. God who risks does not have insider information on everything that is going to transpire. God did not know all along what Hitler, or Adam, would do with his freedom. If he did, it would imply that he thought that Hitler's evils could serve a purpose and that it was better that, on balance, they happen rather than they not happen. Surely not! God gave Hitler freedom but it was not settled ahead of time how he would use it. It was always a possibility rather than a certainty what he would do. The future is partially open and partially closed.

9. God's faithfulness
Rebellion notwithstanding, God remains faithful to the creation project and has committed himself to redeem it. Having judged the world in the flood, God vowed not to do it again. Having scattered the nations at Babel, God raised up Abram to put into effect his desire to save them. God shows us where he stands in his willingness to suffer for us. God assumed our nature, bore our pain and created a new humanity in Christ by the Spirit. Through self-sacrifice, the intensity of God's love is expressed and provides for the reconciliation of the world. God does not relish suffering but he does enjoy the restored relationships made possible by it. As a fellowship of loving persons, God is willing to be involved in the world, even at cost to himself. He is willing to be vulnerable. God

---

[58] See 100, n.105, ch. 2. I do not believe that God limits his knowledge. Rather God created a world the future of which is partly unsettled and he knows it truly. God knows everything that can be known. I was surprised to hear Swinburne say, 'To maintain his freedom, God limits knowledge of his own future choices.' See, *Coherence*, 178. See also, Boyd, *God of the Possible*, 15–7.

does not stand aloof from human suffering. At Auschwitz, someone asked, 'Where is God?' The answer came, 'God is there on the gallows', meaning God is at work transforming the situation from within.[59]

God is committed to putting things right and has promised to redeem what was lost. The problem of evil can be debated intellectually but cannot be solved by argument. God himself can only resolve it in the ordinary persuasive ways we are familiar with and by a revelation of his glory. God will overcome wickedness through his wisdom, power and resourcefulness. He allows the creature to wreak havoc on the world for a time but not forever. The gift of freedom was not unlimited in scope or duration and therefore the power to do evil is finite.[60]

God can keep his promise even though creatures contribute to history and can resist his will. He can still reinstate his sovereignty over the universe, even though the future is open and even though he respects human freedom. God's own resourcefulness, wisdom, and patience can guarantee the end of history. Granted, it would be easier if he always carried a big stick, but doing so would not lead to the outcomes he seeks. We trust that the One who promised to make all things new knows how to do it and how to accomplish it. Nothing arises which God does not anticipate and handle; he has lots of options at his disposal. God is a flexible and effective worker. One sees in the Bible how God moves along one line and switches over to another. One sees it in the surprising ways he fulfils his promises in the New Testament. God knows how to play the game. He is the master chess player. He knows the extent of the risk he is taking. He is the consummate guide to lead us through the wilderness to the Promised Land.

The universe expresses the purposes of God. The act of creation asserts that the world's source and ground are in God. The doctrine of providence maintains that every phase of history is under God's guidance. Hope lies in the goal of the project being achieved. Creation and history are steps toward the realization of God's purposes. Eschatology, far from being a frivolous topic, is fundamental and deals with the goal of the entire process. We have already seen in Jesus Christ what the character of ultimate reality is like and now by faith we declare that, despite the obstacles, the purposes of the God and Father of Jesus will prevail. Despite the fact that aspects of the future are unsettled, we have confidence in the victory of God, because of his resourcefulness, and because

---

[59] Inbody, *Transforming God*, ch. 8.
[60] Pannenberg, *Systematic Theology* III, 632–46. In contrast to process theism, in which God is restricted to using persuasive power only, Pannenberg defends a larger sense of God's power.

of the resurrection of Jesus and the gift of the Spirit. Concerning the end of history, 'God has given us assurance by raising him from the dead' (Acts 17:31). Concerning our participation in God's glory, God has placed the Spirit in our hearts 'as a first installment' (2 Cor. 1:22). Confidence in the victory of God rests upon redemptive facts that have already occurred. History is indeed heading toward the goal of becoming the kingdom of God. We have glimpsed its beginnings and we await its full realization.

10. Was creation worth it?

One might ask if God was wise in creating humanity with all the trouble that has happened and still happens. Was it worth it? Why didn't God content himself with apes and porpoises? Why not be content with deterministically 'free' human beings? They could be delightful creatures and would not cause half the bother. I think it is because God is a serious lover who wants these relationships of love most deeply. It is a desire in God we humans can easily identify with because we know how precious they are. By creating such a world, high-level values became possible. In spite of evils, how many would conclude that creation was not worth it? What a spectacle the world is! It is an emergent, evolving system, which moves from elementary particles to complex personal life. How can one not be impressed by what appears to be the self-expression of divine purpose, limited as it is by certain metaphysical constraints yet moving toward something marvelous – a community of persons living in a freely chosen relationship with God![61] How many would advocate that, in order to avoid Hitler and Stalin, God should have precluded Moses, Plato, Aquinas, Leonardo, Beethoven, Picasso, Mother Theresa and more?[62] In addition, the gospel assures us that it has been and will be worth it all. 'The sufferings of this present time are not worthy to be compared with the glory which will be revealed in us' (Rom. 8:18).

The Relation to Process Philosophy

Critics may counter with the charge that the open view of God appeals to modern people because it is a modern outlook. It has a pagan heritage of its own, reflecting as it does certain modern values! It is anthropocentric and not centered on God. But is this so? All we have done is to lift up the scriptural principle of relationships of love with freedom, which

---

[61] Ward, *Holding Fast to God*, ch. 9.
[62] D.R. Griffin, *God, Power, and Evil: A Process Theodicy*, 309.

upholds human dignity and significance. Too often tradition has estimated the value of humanity at near zero. A biblically grounded humanism is on the mark.

A specific charge often laid is that the open view is a thinly disguised version of process theology. How is the open view of God related to process theism?[63] This is a fair and strategic question because there are some similarities. Conventional theists often characterize the open view as a form of process thought that, in an evangelical context, is tantamount to proving it heretical without any further ado. If openness theology could be shown to be a version of process theology, guilt by association would be established, which would be very handy for the severest critics. But the question is valid – if Augustine picked a pagan inheritance, anyone can, including me. Maybe modern influences, which create a distorting tilt in the direction of divine immanence, are present in my work. Many critics of openness thought think so mainly because it feels like a modern accommodation to them. But is it necessarily so? Maybe a dialogue is possible.[64]

Some give process thought a very wide berth so as not to face this possibility. But I, deploring as I do the politics of establishing guilt by association, believe it is good to dialogue, even if there is the risk of being misunderstood. Process thought is an impressive modern conceptuality with a lot to offer and I for one do not allow fear to dictate with whom I will consult. At the same time, any fair judge would have to conclude that the charge that the open view is a process view is very wide of the mark. One cannot equate them. D.A. Carson, a critic of the open view, comments, 'In fairness to Pinnock, he sharply distinguishes himself from process theologians by insisting that God created the universe and could, but chooses not to, constrain his creatures.'[65] The falsity of the charge is highlighted by process theologians themselves who do not think that open theism is a form of process thought.[66]

---

[63] A topic for another day would be how the open view relates to traditions of finite theism like those of E.S.Brightman, J.S.Mill and even Mormon theology. Cf. Beckwith and Parrish, *Mormon Concept of God*, 29, 127.

[64] If lines can be traced between Jonathan Edwards and Alfred N. Whitehead, why not take up the challenge? See J.B. Cobb, *A Christian Natural Theology*, 224; and S.H. Lee, *The Philosophical Theology of Jonathan Edwards*, 5.

[65] Carson, *Gagging of God*, 225. D.F. Wells, on the other hand, speaks of 'the process theology being advocated by Clark Pinnock, John Sanders and Gregory Boyd.' See, *Modern Reformation* July (2000), 10.

[66] D.R. Griffin critiques free will theism vigorously in *Evil Revisited: Responses and Reconsiderations*, 14–22, before giving an account of process theism, 22–40. More recently, he subjects it to another strong critique to which free will

Open theists are evangelicals who look to Scripture, not to White-head. We object to the way process theology imposes a philosophical worldview – a kind of totalizing meta narrative – on the Bible.[67] Theologically, we are orthodox Christians who hold to the Trinity, the ontological otherness of God and divine activity in history, including miracles. We do not think that God is tied to creation necessarily or that God is limited to exercising only persuasive power.

As an open theist, I am interested in authors such as Hegel, Pierre Teilhard de Chardin and Whitehead because they make room in their thinking for ideas like change, incarnation and divine suffering, ideas which are central to the gospel but awkward for conventional theology influenced by ancient metaphysics. While they may not suit our pur-poses ideally – I do not want to be their disciple – at least they point in the direction of a more helpful orientation in which God's becoming human is celebrated and not seen as a problem. At least they encourage theolo-gians to take their own themes seriously without being embarrassed. It is refreshing to find philosophers who entertain ideas like pathos without feeling that perfection is compromised. The open view shares something with process thought: what we want to overcome is the tilt towards a metaphysic of being and attain a metaphysic of becoming.[68]

Besides, there are things about process theism that I find attractive and convictions that we hold in common.[69] We:

- make the love of God a priority;
- hold to libertarian human freedom;
- are both critical of conventional theism;
- seek a more dynamic model of God;
- contend that God has real, and not merely rational, relationships with the world;
- believe that God is affected by what happens in the world;

Footnote 66 (*continued*) theist W. Hasker replies in 'Process Theology and the Christian Good News: A Response to Classical Free Will Theism' in Cobb and Pinnock (eds.), *Searching for an Adequate God*, ch. 1.

[67] So D. Hurtubise, 'Difficult Connections: Philosophical Process Theology and Christian Faith'; and W. Pannenberg, *Metaphysics and the Idea of God*, ch. 6.

[68] See H. Küng, *The Incarnation of God: An Introduction to Hegel's Theologi-cal Thought As Prolegomena To A Future Christology*, 530; and *Does God Exist?*, section B. Also, Macquarrie, *In Search of Deity*, part two.

[69] Erickson lists seven positive features in process thought and eight points of difference in *Father Almighty*, 60–6. Also R. Basinger, 'Evangelicals and Process Theism: Seeking a Middle Ground', *Christian Scholars Review* 15 (1986), 157–67.

- say that God knows what can be known, which does not amount to exhaustive foreknowledge;
- appreciate the value of philosophy in helping to shape theological convictions;
- connect positively to Wesleyan/Arminian traditions.[70]

As for Whitehead himself, how could anyone not regard him as an illustrious thinker? H.P. Owen writes, 'Next to F.H. Bradley, he is beyond doubt the greatest metaphysician who has written in the English language in this century.'[71] The possibility that Whitehead might help us in the area of natural theology, and maybe even in theology, cannot be ruled out. Here is a theology that tries to work with modern science and has a dynamic metaphysic that doesn't equate God with everything superior and the world with everything inferior. I find the dialectic in its doctrine of God helpful, for example the idea that God is necessary and contingent, eternal and temporal, infinite and finite. I think it is right about God affecting everything and being affected by everything. I agree with it that God is temporally everlasting rather than timelessly eternal. I agree that God is passible not impassible and omniscient in the sense of exhaustively knowing all that can be known – that does not include knowledge of future free contingents. In fact, I appreciate Whitehead and Hartshorne much the way that conventional theists appreciate Plato and Aristotle. We are both indebted to philosophers, in their case ancient and in my case modern, but one must still measure the extent of indebtedness and the propriety of what is being borrowed. Candidly, I believe that conventional theists are more influenced by Plato, who was a pagan, than I am by Whitehead, who was a Christian.

Concerning resemblance on the doctrine of God, Rice writes

> The openness concept of God shares the process view that God's relation to the temporal world consists in a succession of concrete experiences, rather than a single timeless perception. It too conceives God's experience of the world as ongoing, rather than a once-for-all affair. It also shares with

---

[70] Things may not be what they seem, however. By God's love I mean the favour of a God who is ontologically other, while a process theist is thinking chiefly of a sympathetic response. A modest dialogue has begun; see Cobb and Pinnock (eds.), *Searching for an Adequate God*. Earlier I approached the subject in 'Between Classical and Process Theism' in R.H. Nash (ed.), *Process Theology*, 313–27; and in 'Neo-Classical Theism,' in Kantzer and Gundry (eds.), *Perspectives*, 37–42. See also B. Stone and T.J. Oord (eds.), *Nature and Thy Name is Love: Process and Wesleyan Theologies in Dialogue*.
[71] Owen, *Concepts*, 76.

process theism the twofold analysis of God or dipolar theism. It conceives God as both absolute and relative, eternal and temporal, changeless and changing. It assigns one element in each pair to the appropriate aspect of God's being – the essential divine character or the concrete divine experience.[72]

Less positively, there is a methodological difference. Process theology is a natural theology based on the metaphysics of Whitehead, whereas openness is a biblical theology not obliged to a developed philosophical schema. Process theology is a philosophical theology that explicitly draws its way of speaking about God from Whitehead and Hartshorne (cf. core doctrines such as naturalistic theism, the idea of spontaneity rooted deep down in the universe and a non-sensationist doctrine of perception). The openness model, on the other hand, is more revelation-based and less dependent on philosophy. The fact that process theology is a natural theology, while openness is a biblical theology, also reflects in part their ecclesial locations – process in the mainline liberal churches and openness in post-fundamentalist evangelical circles. Ironically, there is a closer resemblance between conventional and process theists methodologically than between openness and process theists in that conventional theism agrees with process thought that the nature of God can be known by natural reason and often treats Scripture as a second source!

There are also significant conceptual differences between openness and process theism. They are seen in the fact that process theology teaches that God's love is metaphysically necessary, does not affirm the doctrine of creation out of nothing, and does not hold the biblical hope in a definitive victory over evil at the end. In contrast, openness theist David Basinger writes, 'God not only created this world *ex nihilo* but can, and at times does, intervene unilaterally in earthly affairs.'[73] Like process, we want to preserve the transcendence of God while denying the separation of God and the world but unlike process we want to conceive the relationship as a voluntary, not a necessary, one.[74]

Most important is the issue of the transcendence of God, the ontological difference between God and the world. The open view holds that creation is an act of sovereign freedom, not merely the imposing of order

---

[72] R. Rice, *God's Foreknowledge and Man's Free Will*, 33. He has given a fuller account of the similarities and differences in 'Process Theism and the Open View of God: The Crucial Difference' in Cobb and Pinnock(eds.), *Searching for an Adequate God*, ch. 4.

[73] D. Basinger in Pinnock, et al., *Openness*, 156.

[74] In contrast to Clayton, *Problem of God*.

on pre-existing matter. God is the mysterious other on whom everything that exists totally depends. Creation is an act of free grace and generosity, the work of a God whose disposition is to be generous and who is disposed to create and welcome the creature into union with himself. The openness view asserts that God sovereignly created the world out of nothing and does not exist in a kind of dualistic relationship with everlasting and primordial matter. It denies the process conviction that God is ontologically dependent on the world and that God always has and must have a world to experience. He does not need a world in order to be God. True, God essentially loves and the world (any world) is the object of his loving, but creation remains a gift not a necessity. Imagine a happily married couple, already fulfilled in their love for one another, having a baby. Having a baby is something they could freely choose to do and they would certainly love it. But one must say that, while their love for the child expresses their love for one another, they are not required to have a child in order to love. God's love for the world expresses his loving essence too, but it is not a necessary expression of his essence. Whether to create a given world or not is a free choice. This is what makes it gracious. Putting it bluntly, God's nature would be complete and his love fulfilled even without a world to love.

The open view holds to an asymmetrical view of the relationship of God and the world, i.e. that God is ontologically independent of the world, whereas the world is ontologically dependent on God. In process thinking, there always is a world with which God is necessarily related, making God and the world interdependent. The world is not as radically dependent on God as it is in the openness model and in conventional theism. From the process point of view, openness is a form of classical theism. (This is amusing given the way conventional theists consider us to be a version of process theism!) For Whitehead, God is not really the creator but one who provides the existing flux with possibilities. Thus, we are only partly indebted to God for our existence: that part which God is able to lure or persuade into being.

The open view sees God as a self-sufficient, ontologically other trinitarian being who voluntarily created the world out of nothing and graciously relates to it in self-limiting ways out of respect for the freedom that he bestowed on the creatures he made. We hold that God is ontologically other than the world and, in a certain sense, 'requires' no world. God does not have to relate to some other reality because he is internally social, loving and self-sufficient. Nevertheless, God wills a dynamic world and relates to it in appropriate loving ways. According to openness, the world is contingent because God created it freely and, therefore, the existence of the world is not necessary. Contrast this with the process view, which suggests that there was always a world; God did not create the world, it just exists. There is a second everlasting something and thus a kind of dualism. On the issue of creation out of nothing, I believe that God originates all that exists and is the source of all that is. I believe that God is ontologically independent of the world and that creatures are dependent on God but real and good. I believe that the world depends on God and not God on the world – the relation is asymmetrical.[75]

At the same time, I agree with process theology exegetically that Genesis 1 does not itself teach *ex nihilo* creation but presents God as imposing order on chaos – for *ex nihilo*, I look to Hebrews 11:3 and Romans 4:17. The Genesis text describes a power of chaos present at God's forming of the world (Gen. 1:2). What this signifies is not made clear. It might indicate a metaphysical dualism and thus an inherent limitation on God's power, but I link it to the major biblical theme of spiritual warfare and believe the chaotic situation to be due to rebellious angels 'who did not keep their position but left their proper dwelling' (Jude 6; 2 Pet. 2:4). This rebellion could explain resistance to God's will prior to the (re-)creation described in Genesis 1. The chapter describes a shaping of creation, not a *creatio ex nihilo*. Thus, at the time of (re-)creation God is facing opposition that could explain particularly vicious, noxious and horrible forms of natural evil as having been introduced into the world by rebellious spirits. In that case, certain ugly features of the world may reflect the ugliness of a battlefield.[76]

Another significant conceptual difference has to do with divine activity. Open theists believe that God acts upon the world as well as within it such that he sustains the world and acts in history. We find the process God too passive to do justice to the biblical testimony. The Bible does not limit God to influencing the world by persuasion only. He not only remembers and experiences but also makes moves in the history of salvation. We are not 'naturalistic' theists like process theists, who consider that God's power is always and only persuasive and never coercive or unilateral. In process thought God can only try to persuade creatures to follow his way and little else. If God influences everything but controls nothing, little room is left for miracles and final victory. Open theists, on the other hand, believe that God is not bound to persuasion alone, but

---

[75] P. Copan, 'Is Creatio ex nihilo a Post-Biblical Invention? An Examination of Gerhard May's Proposal', *Trinity Journal* 17 (1996), 77–93.

[76] So B.K. Waltke, *Creation and Chaos*; Levenson, *Creation and the Persistence of Evil*; Boyd, *God at War*, 283–7; and Boyd, *Satan and the Problem of Evil*. Griffin has added belief in the demonic to his own system and thereby strengthened it: *Evil Revisited*, 31–4.

attribute more power to God. We believe that God can decide that certain things will happen in the future because he plans to do them. Thus the future is settled to whatever extent the Lord decides to settle it. God can predetermine, and foreknow, whatever he wants to about the future. This does not change the fact that he also leaves much of it open and allows other issues to be resolved by the decisions of free agents. God could have created a universe in which he would determine everything but has chosen not to do so. Instead, God elected to create a world reflective of his own spontaneously free and triune self. God made the decision to limit the exercise of coercive power out of respect for creaturely freedom, which, in turn, placed (voluntary) constraints on God's acting.

Over and above God's providential guiding of history, the open view holds that there have been and can be specific revelations of the purposes and power of God at particular points in history. Certain events in world history can be the special effects of divine activity. Though all reality witnesses to God the creator and ruler, God also manifests himself in special ways. Though he sustains all of history, he also acts at times as an agent in history, for example when he was uniquely active in that strand of history that culminated in the life, death, and resurrection of Jesus. In Jesus, God allowed a unique discernment of God's purposes by raising things beyond their natural powers. That God might interfere with nature is intelligible – it need not mean a violation of nature or be a sign of failure. It may simply indicate God's decision to utilize the causal order for his ongoing purposes, as we use it ourselves for our own freedom. God can make a difference, just as we can make a difference in the natural order by what we do. The causal structures of the world are not impediments to the accomplishments of God's purposes. The more we learn about the amazing complexity of sub-atomic reality, the easier it is to imagine it.[77]

The people of Israel, for example, depended on miracles for their survival. The idea of holy war in pre-monarchical times meant casting themselves, weak as they were, upon God to deliver them from their enemies. Because they could trust in God as their king, they did not need to rely on the crutches of worldly might. They depended on God for their survival.[78] In Jesus' resurrection something unexpected happened which still evokes astonishment. It represented not only a vindication of Jesus' claim but laid a foundation of human hope. His resurrection was an

---

[77] Barbour, *When Science Meets Religion*, ch. 6.
[78] J.H. Yoder, *The Original Revolution*, ch. 4. Holy war is a very difficult concept and Yoder's explanation is one of the best.

unexpected providence in unusual circumstances. Here the natural was taken beyond its normal powers for a higher purpose. What happened to Jesus was a sign of what will happen to us all beyond history. His resurrection was the historical anticipation of the destiny of humanity and the seed from which the new creation will grow. Such an event goes beyond persuasion. God brought it into effect unilaterally without consultation. There are not many incidents like this – God usually prefers ordinary and everyday activity – but they can happen when in the wisdom of God they need to happen. Coercive power is available to God, even if he uses it sparingly. In the early days of the universe, it probably was the rule but now the preferred *modus operandi* leans toward persuasion.[79]

At the same time, we should not exaggerate how easy it is for God to intervene. There are constraints upon God's acting, as I have suggested, such that he cannot just do anything, anytime, anywhere as is so often supposed. God interacts with the givens of the situation. For example, there is:

(a) The variable of irrevocable freedom whereby God cannot just terminate the existence of created agents, having made them and committed himself to them. God's is not play-acting.[80]

(b) The complexity of the cosmos, unthinkably vast and tightly woven, with the element of spontaneity on every level, is also a factor. Rabbi Kushner interprets God's answer to Job in this way: 'If you think it's so easy to run the world, *you* try it.' Where is our admiration for the works of God?[81]

(c) Then there is the factor illustrated in Daniel 10:12–14 where the answer to Daniel's prayer was delayed by the activity of an evil power. A prayer to God was blocked.[82]

(d) Similarly, in the New Testament we read that Jesus could do no mighty works because of unbelief (Mk. 6:5–6). God may well be doing all that he can do in every situation given the variables.[83]

Process philosophy can be helpful but must be refashioned and cannot be adopted wholesale. Philosophy has its limits. It is not located at the end of history and cannot by itself clarify the structure of the world

---

[79] Kirkpatrick, *Together Bound*, ch. 6; Polkinghorne *Serious Talk*, ch. 6. For a kenotic theology of voluntary divine restraint, Murphy and Ellis, *Moral Nature*.

[80] Boyd, *Satan and the Problem of Evil*, ch. 8.

[81] H.S. Kushner, *When Bad Things Happen to Good People*, 43.

[82] Boyd, *God At War*, 9–11, 136–42; Wink, *Engaging the Powers*, 308–13.

[83] Tupper, *Scandalous Providence*, 323–35.

completely. We also need theological symbols to do the work. Randy Maddox comments

> While the longstanding Wesleyan commitment to God's response-ability resonates strongly with the process emphasis on God's temporal, creative, and persuasive nature, it should be no surprise that this same commitment renders many Wesleyans less happy with the apparent restriction of God's role in the ongoing process of the whole of reality to only that of 'lure.' Is such a God still truly response-able? Where is the basis for eschatological hope within this restriction? Is there not a place for God to engage us more actively than this, without resorting to coercion?[84]

Process thinkers find difficulties with the open view of God too. They argue that a God who is ontologically independent of the world would possess coercive power to do anything he wanted at any time. Even if he voluntarily limited it, the monopoly on power would still be in effect. And if it is, they ask, why doesn't God stop evildoers from performing atrocities and nature from wreaking havoc? If God can act, why doesn't he act unilaterally more often? Process theism avoids this problem by limiting God to persuasive power only. Surely, they reason, God would stop genuine evils if he could. They make a good and, to me, painful point.[85] As an open theist, I cannot accept that God is metaphysically limited, and try to emphasize his commitment to a free world. I am forced to say that God has made a commitment to the creation project that constrains his actions. The positive side of it for me is that I line up with Israel's counter-testimony, which bombards God with questions – How long, God, will you hide your face? Why do you stand far off? Where are you when we need you?[86]

Has process theism influenced the open view? Perhaps indirectly it has because both are part of the Arminian tradition and a larger cultural

---

[84] R.L. Maddox, 'Seeking a Response-able God: The Wesleyan Tradition and Process Theology' (typescript, 2000), 31. See also M.L. Petersen, 'Orthodox Christianty, Wesleyanism, and Process Theology', *Wesleyan Theological Journal* 15 (1980), 45–58.

[85] W. Hasker continues the dialogue which surfaced in *Searching for an Adequate God* in 'The Problem of Evil in Process Theism and Classical Free Will Theism' (forthcoming in *Process Studies*).

[86] The decision of the open view to adhere closely to the biblical text creates problems for intelligibility that can be avoided by the more liberal approach of process theology which feels free to engage in more radical reconceptualisations. But it may feel to readers that the open view has the merit of maintaning a biblical tension and not eliminating it. So Brueggemann, *Theology*, 400–3.

context. There are common themes – the emphasis on human freedom, the interrelatedness of reality and understanding God in terms of love – and there may even be direct influences. I have read process theology and appreciate some of the things I find there. It is helpful to dialogue with it because it helps me see some issues more clearly. I appreciate it as modern, dynamic metaphysic but reject important aspects of it as foreign to the gospel. Thus, I prefer the open view of God both to the immobility of conventional theism and to the flux of the process view. Openness theism involves a synthesis that does not burden theology with pagan elements.

Theology, Philosophy, Apologetics

Let me be candid, we are all influenced by philosophy. We are all helped by the careful thinking that good philosophers do when they sort out puzzles and conundrums. Open theists should, however, be careful not to be overly dependent on process philosophy. Likewise, conventional theists should be candid about their dependence on the great Hellenes. Given the emphasis we both place on the Bible, we should be scrupulous with respect to extra-biblical influences. It surprises me that some critics are so loyal to what they take to be normative tradition and are blind to the influences of pagan thought on their doctrine of God.

Theology has labored under a heavy burden. The available philosophical resources for the early church were not altogether suitable for rendering Christian ideas. Theology has needed new points of departure and fresh thinking that could better express the personal reality of God. In its own way, the Greek vision was a powerful one and one which continues to challenge us today, but we do need resources that are able to more naturally handle revelation based ideas like incarnation, relationality, suffering and perfection in change.

We can be grateful for the shift from substantialist to relational categories in modern thinking. The emergence of a more dynamic view of reality allows us to read the Bible with greater profit in some areas and an opportunity exists for showing the fresh intellectual relevance of Christian doctrine. A framework which offers fresh prospects for discussing the relationship between God and the world that is both biblically sound and conceptually adequate has developed in modern times. With the world now being understood more as an interrelated process, dynamic trinitarian thinking assumes ever greater plausibility.

No amount of proof can make belief in God's existence plausible, if God is understood to be a static substance and/or an alienating being. If, on the other hand, God is understood more biblically and, to moderns, more intelligibly as a power that is internally related to the world and the ground of our own worth as persons, Christian theism can be become intellectually compelling again.

Chapter Four

The Existential Fit

A.W. Tozer wrote, 'A right conception of God is basic, not only to systematic theology, but to practical living as well.'[1] In this chapter, we explore practical implications of the open view of God. Ideally, mind and heart ought to be in agreement and theology ought not only to make intellectual sense, but have transforming effects on the lives of believers. What difference does the open view make? How does this understanding of God help make sense of life? All too often theology has become abstracted from life and is not the practical wisdom that helps disciples live out their faith.[2]

Paul's challenge to the Galatians (3:4) is apropos, 'Did all that you experienced mean nothing at all? Surely it meant something!' We need a view of God which has practical reason and pure reason on its side to give it existential backing. Ideas have consequences and beliefs affect behavior. It is important, therefore, that doctrines are credible in practical terms as well as biblically and rationally sound. They ought to have the ring of truth and make a difference to life. They ought to be relevant to real life situations, motivate us and affect how we live. The open view, like any model, needs to ring true in the light of experience and be adequate to the demands of life.[3]

---

[1] A.W. Tozer, *The Knowledge of the Holy*, 6. M. Horton views this with suspicion and detects a liberal move in any desire to relate theology and practice; see 'Is the New News Good News? Shifting Views Concerning God in our Day', *Modern Reformation* 8 (1999), 11–2.

[2] I credit interest in the open view of God in large part to the urgent practical issues it addresses. For example: Why pray? Is everything settled? Can we make a difference? Is there a plan B? Is God relational? Is God open to us? Does God risk? We are meant to live out doctrines. If God is relational, image bearers are meant to live relationally. If God is love, we must become lovers ourselves. See R.P. Stevens, *The Other Six Days: Vocation, Work and Ministry in Biblical Perspective* (USA edition; UK, *The Abolition of the Laity: Vocation, Work and Ministry in Biblical Perspective*), part 1.

[3] Immanuel Kant spoke of 'practical reason,' the kind of reason which detects truths of living, truths that we know on the basis of experience. Human

Though not impossible, it is difficult to believe in a God, the understanding of whom is existentially repugnant. If God is apathetic to the world, why should we be committed? But, if God is solicitous of us, what a motivation! Thomas Merton wrote, 'If we believe God is a stern, cold lawgiver who has no real interest in us, who is merely a ruler, lord, a judge and not a father, we will have great difficulty living the Christian life.'[4] How can one relate to a God who is far away and who cannot, or will not, respond? The open view of God possesses strong practical appeal and close existential fit, because it upholds human significance and motivates human action. It sees human beings as God's covenant partners and co-laborers. In speaking of partnerships, it highlights interactive personal relationships (dialogical, reciprocal and mutual), and in speaking of co-laboring it insists that people's lives make a difference as to how history works out. Thus, openness supplies tremendous motivation for living and a positive mental attitude. One of the strengths of the open view is that people see the way it makes sense of their lives and are drawn to it. It is hard to refute on the existential level.[5]

Putting it the other way around, it is difficult to live on any other basis. The open view describes our experience so admirably, whether or not we consent to it intellectually, that it commends itself on that basis. In practice, believers relate to God as a person and face an open future, which is what the open view posits. Life has the character you would expect it to have if the openness model were true. Thus it illuminates the living of life and commends itself on that basis. One is almost forced to live as if it were true, even if one thinks it is not. If our lives make no impact on God and if what you decide makes no difference to the blueprint of history, why go on? A conventional theist can, of course, persevere because the gospel requires it but they cannot give an account of why they do so. They have to live as if their view of God were different than it is, i.e. they live as if it were, in fact, the open view. Openness theists, on the other hand, are able to live life on the basis of the model. According to openness thinking, God has real relationships with humans and lets them share in shaping the open future, which is what practical reason requires we posit. Experience and the open view

---

Footnote 3 (*continued*) freedom is an example of this – one encounters its truth in the experience of living as moral persons. One may deny it intellectually but not practically.

[4] T. Merton, *Life and Holiness*, 31. On practical implications, see Basinger in Pinnock, et al., *Openness*, ch. 5; Erickson, *Father Almighty*, ch. 13; Geisler, *Creating God*, ch. 7; and Boettner, *Predestination*, ch. 27.

[5] Ware devotes part three of *God's Lesser Glory* to a discussion of the difference the open view of God would make in daily life, specifically in relation to prayer, guidance, and suffering.

both assume that history is the sphere of real divine relationships with creatures. They both say that we are not players on a stage, mouthing a script and repeating the lines we were directed to say. We are, instead, real participants. Thus the open view promotes action not resignation. We face possibilities, not just foregone conclusions; there are things to be settled.[6]

Conventional theism in its various forms undermines this in one way or another. It suffers from the condition of existential self-contradiction. One may think that everything is settled but not act like it, because that would lead to paralysis; most people will pray anyway, as if it were not. Why get up in the morning, if you think everything about the day is already decided? Believing that would rob you of every purposeful impulse; why move a finger? You cannot even fight evil without fighting God. Though it is safe to live on the basis of openness thinking, it is not safe to live on the basis of conventional thinking. It may be exhilarating to discuss it intellectually, but you cannot take it seriously practically because it can destroy your sense of personal responsibility. It can make prayer meaningless and evangelism unnecessary and undermine one's will to live and act.[7]

As If Not

The open view of God enjoys an 'as if' asset. That is, it is safe to live as if the model were true. Conventional theism, on the other hand, has an 'as if not' problem. It has a streak of existential irrationality running through it. Suppose that God has ordained everything you will ever do and it is all completely certain. You would be wise to live as if this were not true from a practical standpoint, otherwise you could have a crisis of motivation. Prayer would be undermined because it cannot change anything. People could not be held responsible for what they do. God would have to be considered the author of evil. You may believe the doctrine but it is certainly better to live as if it were not true.[8]

---

[6] In *A Christmas Carol* Scrooge asked, in reference to the tombstone: 'Are these the shadows of things that will be or are they the shadows of things that may be, only?' He wanted to know if the future was still being shaped and, if so, whether his actions could affect it. He saw the need for an open view of God.

[7] Geisler sees the bad practical effects of 'extreme Calvinism' but not the bad effects of his own views; see *Chosen But Free*, 131–8; and *Creating*, ch. 7.

[8] Boettner is burdened by many practical difficulties. He knows that it sounds fatalistic; that it is inconsistent with free agency and moral responsibility; that it makes God the author of sin; that it discourages motives to exertion; that it represents God as a respecter of persons and unjustly partial; that it is unfavorable

Suppose, in particular, that God decided from eternity to save a certain number of people unconditionally and will not fail to do so whatever they do or do not do. It would be better to live as if this were not true, not only because it would make God a respecter of persons, deliberately giving to one the mercy he withholds from another, but because it subverts any motive for seeking God since the outcomes are settled, and undermines any mission to preach the gospel to every creature. If one must believe in such a doctrine, it would be advisable not to give it much thought for practical purposes. It would be better to operate on the basis of God's love for all humanity as constant and sincere, which, thankfully, most conventional theists do.

Suppose that God, as Thomas Aquinas taught, is unchangeable as a stone pillar and cannot entertain real relationships in his essential nature. Suppose that in God there are no real relations to creatures – that they may move in relation to God but God cannot move in relation to them. Since the Christian life is at the heart a personal relationship with God, it would be best to live as if this view of immutability were not the case, as I am sure Aquinas himself must have done in his life.

Suppose that God were timeless and experienced events in the world simultaneously, as most conventional theists think. Would God know what time it is now and would God be able to pursue purposes within history? And, what could it possibly mean to say that God knows Julius Caesar and Winston Churchill as living at the same time? How does God plan, think, remember and respond? What sort of a person would a timeless person be? Clearly it would be better, whatever our concept of this, to live as if God were everlasting and not timeless.

Suppose that God were impassible and could not be affected by what transpires in the world, as conventional theism has always said. Does this mean that God is not wounded by injustices, as Calvin said, and cannot feel our pain, as Anselm said? Is it true then that God does not grieve when we grieve and that God surveys with uninterrupted bliss what transpires in this vale of tears? This is existentially intolerable. Clearly, whatever your doctrine, it would be better to live as if impassibility were not true. Only a suffering God can help.

Suppose that God knows the future exhaustively and that things that will happen in the future are already as settled as things that have

---

Footnote 8 (*continued*) to morality; that it precludes a sincere presentation of the gospel to the non-elect; that it contradicts universalistic Scripture passages. These are, he says, 'objections commonly urged against the reformed doctrine of predestination.' See Boettner, *Predestination*, chs. 15–22.

already happened. This would mean that nothing that God might decide to do and nothing that we might decide to do could change the fact that everything is now known and decided. Surely it would be wise to ignore that belief and act as if it were not true. Practically speaking, it is wiser to think of the future as a realm of possibilities not actualities because if what will happen in detail is not a foregone conclusion, we will be more likely to take responsibility for the future and not be resigned ourselves. Whatever your doctrine, it is surely better to live as if God did not know the future exhaustively.

Conventional theists pay the open view of God a compliment when they live their lives on the basis of something like the open view rather than their own. Ordinary Christians untutored in theology are drawn to it because it commends the view of God that they have picked up through a simple reading of the text and makes such good sense of what they experience.[9]

Let us now consider some of the practical aspects of the open view.[10]

1. Lives that matter

What makes the open view of God convincing on the practical level is the way it views God as a reality genuinely related to our lives and to whom our lives make a difference. Such a God is not an alienating being or at all existentially repugnant. Quite the contrary, God is the basis in reality for the significance of our lives and gives them a firm foundation. The open view commends God even to those who do not yet acknowledge God. It provides the reason why our lives and our actions have significance. Our lives matter to and impact God because he is a reality genuinely related to life in the world and to whom our actions and ourselves make a difference. God is a necessary being, relative to nothing as to its existence, and a solid foundation to the meaningfulness of our lives. He is also supremely relative, entering into real relations with us

---

[9] The downside of this appeal of the open view to ordinary believers is its possible naiveté: theologians should not read the Bible as naively as lay people do. This is true – we ought not always be literalistic – but there is a sense of the faithful here to be heeded.

[10] Being a philosopher, Geisler's ideas of the practical are not issues of day-to-day living but issues of epistemology. For example, he says that if God does not have exhaustive foreknowledge there could not be predictive prophecy or biblical inerrancy. His idea of a practical issue is tied to having rational certainty. Even so, the point is weak – since prophecy does not require exhaustive foreknowledge and the question of inerrancy does not come up. Geisler, *Creating God*, ch. 7.

and affected by what we do. God, as the open view understands God, is a tremendous existential asset.[11]

It is more difficult for traditional theism to make practical sense because our lives lack that kind of significance, since God is not supremely relative. If God cannot have real relations with us (Thomism), or if he is the solo performer who cannot make room for significant human agents (Calvinism), or if he is pure actuality, impassive, and timeless, or if the entire future is settled already, the basis of the significance of our lives is undercut. If we make no real difference to God, we might as well not be. I am sure that most Christians believe that their lives make a difference to God. The nice thing about the open view of God is that it gives this understanding a theological rationale that it usually has not had before.

2. The friendship of the Lord

In terms of the life of faith, the open view sees God as capable of genuine personal relationships. It allows us to think of our relationship with God as a transforming friendship in which we interrelate. The psalmist says, 'The friendship of the LORD is for those who fear him, and he makes his covenant known to them' (Ps. 25:14). Abraham and Moses were called God's friends (Exod. 33:11; Is. 41:8). Jesus called his disciples friends, not servants (Jn. 15:15). Such relationships of love cannot be forced, on the one hand, and involve give and take, on the other: God created us as persons for love and fellowship. He gave us freedom to be his covenant partners and has granted us a special role in the creation project. God made us able to encounter him and respond to his word. All this would be undermined if God had no real relationships with creatures that were nominal and external, and not real.

Whether we love God or not, whether we cooperate with God or not, are genuinely free decisions. God cannot push a button and make a human person love him. If he could, the person would not be truly the beloved; they would only be an appliance whose behavior only resembles that of a lover. Love does not exist where lovers are compelled to love. God could have wired us to behave in love-like ways but did not do so because he wants the real thing. Whatever precisely the situation in heaven will be as to our loving or not loving, it is the case that in this world we have the possibility of oving or not loving.

In his later years, Henri Nouwen saw the relationship in the work of certain high wire trapeze artists. One day, as he was sitting with the leader of the troupe, he heard him say:

---

[11] Ogden, *Reality of God*, 37.

As a flyer I must have complete trust in my catcher. The public might think that I am the great star of the trapeze but the real star is Joe, my catcher. He has to be there for me with split-second precision and grab me out of the air as I come to him in the long jump.

Nouwen asked how it worked.

'The secret,' Rodleigh said, 'is that the flyer does nothing and the catcher does everything. When I fly to Joe, I have simply to stretch out my arms and hands and wait for him to catch me and pull me safely over the apron behind the catch bar. The worst thing the flyer can do is to try to catch the catcher. I am not supposed to catch Joe. It's Joe's task to catch me. If I grabbed Joe's wrists, I might break them; or he might break mine; and that would be the end for both of us. A flyer must fly, and a catcher must catch, and the flyer must trust, with outstretched arms, that his catcher will be there for him.'[12]

The open view of God is alive to the delicacy and sensitivity of God's interactions. Ever responsive to our needs, God possesses the subtle awareness of every nuance of changing situations. God can be compared to the male dancer who assists the ballerina as she gracefully leaps into the air and lands with everything in perfect balance. God can be seen as the responsive partner who practices a delicate art, leaping at the right moment, steadying at others, and keeping perfect balance with the living reality to which he is responding. Gordon Kaufman writes: 'God's perfect responsiveness is the quality which enables him to deal with every new happening in the created order with freshness and creativity, bending it toward his ultimate objectives without violating its own integrity.'[13] Such sensitivity is possible because of God's perfect knowledge of us. He always understands what is needed for us to become the persons he intends us to be. He also has an empathy that perceives and feels from within the situation of the other. In this way, there is always a rightness and appropriateness in his dealings with us.

As creator and redeemer, God loves to interact. Like any good parent, God wants us to feel his presence, tell him things, and ask for things. God in turn wants to tell us things (revelation) and cooperate with us in doing things (mission). He wants us to ask for things for ourselves and for others, things that he will bring about only if we ask him, since, in that way, the good that he gives will be the better for our involvement in it. The open view of God makes good sense of the relationship we have with God.[14]

---

[12] J. Beumer, *Henri Nouwen: A Restless Seeking for God*, 68.
[13] Kaufman, *Systematic Theology*, 239.
[14] Swinburne, *Providence,* 111–5. Tiessen places this idea under his 'church dominion model' in *Providence and Prayer*, ch. 6.

3. Freedom

The open view of God also has appeal because it resonates with and affirms the human intuition that there is freedom. This is important because freedom is part of the God-human relationship, which is personal and mutual, not manipulative or causal. God could have arranged things differently; there are many kinds of conceivable relationships. God might have made a creature that he would completely control – that is in the realm of possibility. But it seems that God wanted a creature with whom to interact freely in love a creature, therefore, with a measure of self-determination. Imagine, Hasker asked me in a personal correspondence, if you were faced with the decision before the birth of a child whether you would like a child which would obey you automatically without any awareness that it lacked real freedom or a normal (sic) child which has a will of its own and may resist what you may want. Is there really much doubt what most people would choose?

In the movie *The Truman Show*, the hero, Truman Burbank, lives in a controlled environment, unbeknownst to him. His world is actually a movie set where everything is staged. In order to keep Truman on the island, the director has his father (an actor) drown to instill in Truman a fear of water so that he will 'freely' choose to remain and not want to leave. Day after day the controllers plug in the conditions that ensure that Truman will do what they have planned and it works very well, apart from a few glitches, until Truman begins to be suspicious. A pretty female actress tries to warn him and his 'dad' breaks onto the set and tries to alert him. Truman gradually begins to notice signs of manipulation and wants to escape. He sees the attempts to control him in sinister terms, even though the master controller, Christoff, claims to have his best interests in mind. Truman begins to feel like a puppet and a prisoner in his world. He makes the decision that it would be better to live in the real world (off the set), with its dangers, than in this controlled environment. Something inside makes him long to be a free man among free people, risks and all. He does not want to be a safe puppet. When he makes the break to freedom, the TV audience cheers because they too sense that manipulation is wrong. They scream, 'Go for it, Truman!' The movie portrays the fact that people rebel against living in a controlled situation. Religiously they are drawn to a God who is sovereign over his sovereignty and does not manipulate us, even for our own good, because he seeks relationships of reciprocal love.

There is an intuition in us that is difficult to shake. I refer to the deep sense that human behavior is not entirely shaped by causal factors but is partially self-determining. It is an intuition that people hold in practice even when they deny it intellectually. For example, we hold others responsible for their actions, whether praiseworthy or blameworthy; we do not believe God is the only significant agent; we do not consider the fact that a person holds a different viewpoint than ours as something they were predestined to do; and we exhort one another because we assume that people can change their ways. Freedom is, in Griffin's words, 'a hard-core common sense notion,' a notion presupposed in practice, even when denied verbally. Life itself requires us to posit it and we all live *as if* it were true. God has given us the experience of voluntary action in which alternative possibilities present themselves and we hold to it, unless some clever person talks us out of it.[15]

Composing a symphony, for example, is more than a complex outworking of one's total background situation. In creating a work of art, one brings forth something that is not just implicit in the past. The circumstances of the artist will influence it but not supply the vision of what becomes the work of art. Or, when I make a promise, I do not say 'provided it is not determined that I do otherwise.' I promise to do something whatever happens. In giving a promise I intend to transcend any and all causalities and do what I said I would do. In moral matters, if a person is held responsible for an action, it cannot be that the decision was the outworking only of the past state of the universe. It cannot be that God or nature arranged it that this decision was inevitably reached. In moral matters, it makes sense to say I am sorry, I should not have done that. It makes sense to say how well you did and you deserve a lot of credit for that. The fact is, we believe our actions make a difference and that we are blameworthy or praiseworthy. This is a common sense belief that keeps us going and prevents us falling into resignation and despair. It informs us that we are not part of a deterministic system. We could be mistaken about it but why would anyone suppose that? Whatever we think intellectually, it will be more natural to live as if we were free. A psychologist may even believe that we act out of nature/nurture and that our decisions are wholly predictable. But they know that it is important that we do not believe it, because if we internalize it progress and healing will stop. We will not take responsibility for the future. Even if we think God ordains everything, it would be wise not to live on the basis of this belief. It would be better to act as if it mattered what we decide.

Freedom is finite, however. What I am as a human being is largely due to factors over which I have no control. But, at the same time, such factors do not determine everything about me. There is also the possibility that I may change and grow beyond my present circumstances. I can

---

[15] Griffin, *Evil Revisited*, 3.

affect the lives of others for good or ill and they can affect mine. I can contribute to shaping the future. Therefore God takes human beings seriously. He values the potentials and regrets the failures. He does not prevent us choosing not to love him, though it saddens his heart, because the love he seeks must be freely chosen.

Believers are commended for their faith because of freedom (Heb. 11:2, 6, 39). They would not be commended if it were inevitable. Similarly, sinners are condemned for not exercising faith. How can that be, if this too is inevitable? God wants all of his children to come home but they have to choose to come home. We have to choose God if we want to be with God. Humans are not robots who have no choice. God loves us and wants to be loved in return. Love cannot be forced; it must be freely given. Hell is an important indication of how seriously God takes human decision-making. It is the bitter fruit of saying 'no' to God. We have the freedom to refuse his love, even at the risk of destroying ourselves. It is our choice, not God's choice. Freedom is even the reason for hell because one may accept God's proposal or reject it.[16]

Conventional theism of the determinist type tries to sustain human significance but can't really do so if what we do is determined by pre-existing factors. If what we decide has already been predetermined, the significance of who we are is greatly diminished. It makes us like characters in a novel, determined by the author; then, we are not persons in real life. If God controls all things, how can our actions have real meaning?[17] John Frame says that the unity of the church requires the efforts of human beings. He notes that we are commanded to keep the unity of the Spirit in the bond of peace and summoned to avoid attitudes detrimental to unity. God's sovereignty, he claims, does not entail passivity. It encourages human efforts and does not undermine them. But it seems to imply it if God's pre-ordination is as all-inclusive as Frame holds.[18]

Conventional theism struggles with fatalism. Fatalism and predestination are not the same thing – one is impersonal, the other is personal – but they imply much the same thing for practical purposes, i.e. the certainty of all future events. For example, if I am to die today, I will die; if not, I will continue to live. Nothing I do can change anything at all. All incentives are removed. I can only pretend to be making a difference.

---

[16] H. Nouwen, *Bread for the Journey*; P. Kreeft and R.K. Tacelli, *Handbook of Christian Apologetics*, 297–8.

[17] It is not easy to make determinism practical; see J. Bridges, 'Does Divine Sovereignty Make a Difference in Everyday Life?' in T.R. Schreiner, and B.A. Ware (eds.), *Grace of God*, ch. 8.

[18] J. Frame, *Evangelical Reunion: Denominations and the Body of Christ*, 29.

Divine control rules out free agency and any responsibility. How can a person be a free and responsible agent if their actions have been foreordained from eternity? They are only nominally free. Genuine agency contemplates the future as open, not settled. There's room to make a difference by what we do now.[19]

4. Persuasive love

The open view of God has practical appeal also because of its notion of relationships being freely chosen and genuinely personal. It presents a non-coercive model of salvation, holding that God relates to us as I-thou not as I-it and that human persons can say 'yes' or 'no' to him. Although God has taken the initiative in loving us first and has said 'yes' to us in Jesus Christ, he wants to hear our 'yes' in return (1 Jn. 4:19; 2 Cor. 1:19). God wants us freely to accept his invitation. Screwtape, explaining why the enemy, God, does not employ irresistible power in salvation, remarks: 'Merely to over-ride a human will (as his felt presence in any but the faintest and most mitigated degree would certainly do) would be for him useless. He cannot ravish – he can only woo.'[20] A man may woo a woman but he cannot make her love him. God's longing for us is, therefore, accompanied by restraint and longsuffering. He has made himself vulnerable in relation to us. God puts the question and does everything possible to win our consent but, as Lucas says, 'the final decision, the final right of refusal, he has vested in us, and we, not God, are answerable for the answer we return.'[21]

God's grace is a persuasive not a coercive power. God does not force people to love him, as if that were possible, but pursues personal relations. In the gospels we read of lepers and blind people who were incapable of healing themselves and were challenged to respond to the grace of God. When grace presented itself to them in the person of Jesus, they had to decide whether or not to ask for help. Jesus healed them if and when, and only if and when they called upon him. Salvation depended on a response of faith in Jesus. Could they do anything to help themselves? In one sense no, but in another sense yes, because they could call upon the Lord![22]

God is the Savior and takes the initiative but does not give the response to his own offer. If God did that, and if salvation were not in

---

[19] Tiessen, *Providence and Prayer*, ch. 12. Cf. Helm, *Providence*, 141, 218, 229.
[20] C.S. Lewis, *Screwtape Letters*, 128.
[21] J.R. Lucas, *Freedom and Grace*, 15
[22] R. Latourelle, *The Miracles of Jesus and the Theology of Miracles*, 258.

any way conditioned on human response, why would God not save everybody in this way? The truth is that, although humankind can do no good apart from grace, grace is given to all and calls for a response. As persons, we cooperate with the grace of God because it is part of our very being. Scripture upholds the primacy of grace and the inability of human nature to do good, but it also teaches that it is the responsibility of the person to respond to God's gift.[23]

In Charles Dickens' *A Christmas Carol*, Scrooge addresses Marley's ghost, 'You are fettered. Tell me why.' The ghost replies: 'I wear the chain I forged in life. I made it link by link and yard by yard. I girded it on of my own free will and of my own free will I wore it.' Concerning Scrooge, he says, 'Would you know the weight of the strong coil you bear yourself? It was full as heavy and as long as this seven Christmas Eves ago. And you have labored on it since. It is a ponderous chain.' He goes on to say, 'I am here tonight to warn you, that you have yet a chance and hope of escaping my fate'. That is the human situation; it expresses both the tragedy and the hope.

God's love for us is prior to our love for God. John writes, 'We love God because God first loved us' (1 Jn. 4:19). God's love for us motivates us to love him in return but the offer has to be accepted for the relationship to happen. Grace motivates the sinner to come home; it does not compel. The prodigal had to decide to re-enter the relationship with his father. He did so when 'he came to himself' (Lk. 15:17). God takes the initiative and offers us a relationship, but we have to choose to enter it. God reveals his love for us in Christ and inspires us by the Spirit to respond. God enables us to make the choice, but he empowers by motivating inspiration and not through irresistible force.[24]

Salvation does not arise out of sinful human nature. It is God who saves us; we do not save ourselves. The grace of God at work in us is always preparing us to receive more grace. There is a role for human participation in salvation but it is grounded in God's gracious empowering, not in our inherent abilities. Our cooperation is possible because of God's empowering Spirit working within us.[25] God elects a people in Christ – we do not elect ourselves – and wants all people to belong to it. Individuals receive their own election by becoming part of the elect body. We find our own identity as God's chosen by participation and

---

[23] This lies at the heart of Wesley's theology. It is an important way in which he took the Reformation further. See J.B. Cobb, *Grace and Responsibility: A Wesleyan Theology for Today*, 35–41.
[24] V. Brummer, *Speaking of a Personal God*, 86–9.
[25] R.L. Maddox, *Responsible Grace*, 83–92.

incorporation in the body of Christ. William Klein writes, 'Election is not God's choice of a restricted number of individuals who he wills to save but is a description of the corporate body which, in Christ, he is saving.'[26] The election of individuals is not irresistible. God longs for creatures to elect God in return and not isolate themselves from him by resisting the election that has been given to us all in Jesus Christ.[27] God wills our salvation conditionally; it is by grace through faith. God wants but does not compel our response.[28]

The determinist model is causal rather than personal on the matter of salvation. God is free to say 'yes' or 'no' to us but we are not free to say 'yes' or 'no' to him. God causes our responses to him, even the positive ones.[29] Paul Helm writes, 'Our plight is such that only a God who can effectively bring about his redemptive aims, a God who works all things after the counsel of his own will – that is, the God of Scripture – can help us.'[30] The causal model focuses on humanity's damaged condition rather than on the broken relationship. The idea is that the sinful nature has to be destroyed by a unilateral action of irresistible grace. The sinner is not able to respond until God compels them. The relationship is a manipulative one and basically impersonal. Any 'love' is a product of compulsion.[31] But relationships do not occur under such circumstances. Rather than thinking of God as creating a new state in us, we should think of God as motivating us to make a choice. Sinners remain persons even in sin and God addresses them as such. God wants to heal relationships that cannot be restored unless and until we respond. God has already reached out to us in Christ and invited us to respond, but he does not compel faith. He wants a personal relationship and therefore enables, and does not compel, us. Grace is not irresistible because it is personal. As the author to the Hebrews says, 'the good news came to us

---

[26] W.W. Klein, *The New Chosen People: A Corporate View of Election*, 266. See also R. Shank, *Elect in the Son: A Study of the Doctrine of Election*.
[27] Barth, *Church Dogmatics* II/2, 67–8, 178, 449.
[28] Most Christians have been synergists, believing that divine agency and human agencies cooperate in some way in salvation and in history. See Olson, *Story*, 256, 271, 276, 280, 469–71; H.J. McSorley, *Luther: Right or Wrong? An Ecumenical-Theological Study of Luther's Major Work, The Bondage of the Will*; and Geisler, *Chosen But Free*, 87–98, 145–54, 181–91, 232–4.
[29] Boettner, *Reformed*, ch. 13; Sproul, *Chosen by God*; Sanders, *God Who Risks*, 237–51.
[30] P. Helm, 'Openness theology and God: Project for the Future', *Modern Reformation* 6 (Nov/Dec, 1999), 50.
[31] V.Brummer, *The Model of Love: A Study in Philosophical Theology*, 156–63.

just as to them; but the message they heard did not benefit them, because it did not meet with faith in those who listened' (Heb. 4:2). The fact that we have to respond to God does not make salvation a matter of works though. There is a difference between earning grace and receiving it. Accepting a gift is not a meritorious act (Rom. 4:16). Accepting a gift is not work. The response makes for a personal relationship.[32]

Are sinners able to respond to God's motivating inspiration? They cannot attain salvation but, yes, they can receive the gift of salvation. They are, after all, persons not corpses. Thus the Bible is replete with invitations and exhortations. God repeatedly invites sinners to respond, implying the capacity to do so. All are invited to the wedding feast (Mt. 22:9). God rewards those who seek him (Heb. 11:6). 'God's kingdom is like a merchant in search of fine pearls' (Mt. 13:45). 'Repent and believe the good news' (Mk. 1:15). 'Ask and you will receive' (Mt. 7:7). 'Come, everyone who thirsts' (Is. 55:1). I suppose that the divine inspiration is fruitful in us because of an ember still glowing in us.[33] God helps people by grace to respond but grace is not irresistible. Jesus cries out in Matthew 23:37, 'Jerusalem, Jerusalem, the city that kills the prophets and stones those who are sent to it! How often have I desired to gather your children together as a hen gathers her brood under her wings, and you were not willing!' Stephen cried out in a similar vein, 'You stiff-necked people, uncircumcised in heart and ears, you are forever opposing the Holy Spirit, just as your ancestors used to do' (Acts 7:51). When people reject God he feels it keenly because he wanted them to repent but they were not willing. Our very desire to respond to God reflects the grace of God at work in us, but its effectiveness depends on our cooperating with it. God does not save us without our participation.

If the Bible viewed salvation in causal terms it would be difficult to explain why God would not save everyone that way. More glory would surely accrue to God if he did. In that case, it must be that he does not want to be so generous and prefers to be a respecter of persons. He must be refusing to make grace available to those equally in need of it, which would deny God's omnibenevolence and loving nature. One would have to say that God may choose to love but not that God is love. He could just as well hate as love and would be justified too because what glorifies God in this system is the freedom to love or not to love 'sovereignly'. Critics sometimes talk of heresy in relation to the open view, but is it not

---

[32] I.H. Marshall, *Kept*, 194–5, 204; Boyd, *God of the Possible*, 137–44.
[33] V. Brummer, *Speaking of a Personal God*, 83–9; H.R. Boer, *An Ember Still Glowing: Humankind in the Image of God*, ch. 5; Geisler, *Chosen But Free*, 56–66.

heresy to teach that God does not essentially love? Does it not deny that 'God is light and in him is no darkness at all?' (1 Jn. 1:5). In the open view God essentially loves; creatures can rely on him loving them because he is love. Calvinism can offer no such assurance.[34]

Barth comments in the preface to *Church Dogmatics* II/2, 'I would have preferred to follow Calvin's doctrine of predestination much more closely, instead of departing from it so radically, but I could not and cannot do so. As I let the Bible itself speak to me on these matters, as I meditated on what I seemed to hear, I was driven irresistibly to reconstruction.'[35] With this Barth makes reference to his belief in a Christ-centered and humanity-inclusive concept of election. (He would not, I should add, have approved of taking his revision of Calvin in a synergistic direction.[36]) The fact is, however, that synergism not monergism has been the majority Christian view. It does not glorify humanity unduly but keeps the relationship personal.[37]

5. Sanctification

The open view also makes sense of the experience of sanctification, since growth in grace illustrates the personal character of salvation. Again, God gives us everything we need for life and godliness but it is up to us to make use of the provisions (2 Pet. 1:3–4). God wants us to pursue holiness but his will for us can be frustrated by our unwillingness to cooperate. Holiness cannot be attained without the Spirit but the Spirit cannot sanctify us without cooperation. The open view makes sense of the call to holiness as something that does not happen automatically but as something we have to attend to. The Christian life is from beginning to end a work of grace and progress comes through a diligent exercise of the means of grace. God's will can be resisted and God's Spirit grieved by believers who ignore God's plans for them. God wants us to aspire to be better Christians but whether we will do so or not is uncertain.

According to theological determinism, however, whatever state you are in now is the will of God since God's will covers everything that happens, including states of mind and heart. If one does not desire to grow in holiness, this lack of desire is God's will too. If God wants someone to desire holiness he will make them want it. According to compatibility freedom, we are not responsible for our desires but only

---

[34] Ibid., 49, 85–7, 235–42.
[35] Barth, *Church Dogmatics* II/2, x.
[36] Tiessen demonstrates how Calvinistic Barth remains, despite this comment, when it comes to the sovereignty of God; see *Providence and Prayer*, ch. 10.
[37] Olson, *Story*, 535–6, 595, 612.

for our actions. We, therefore, cannot be blamed for not wanting a higher level of holiness. One's condition of wanting or not wanting it is part of what God has planned. If my desire is at a low level, it must be God's will that it is. One reason why Wesley opposed predestination so vigorously was that he thought it would undercut commitment to holiness. His instincts were correct. It surely does.[38]

I have put emphasis in this book on God wanting relationships of love but that is not all he wants. God wants to dwell in the midst of a holy people. God wants relationships that are holy and fruitful. It could be that I have portrayed the relationship in too familiar a way, as if there was no thunder at Sinai and no awful judgments, as if God were not a consuming fire. Make no mistake, God has high expectations for relationships. Like marriage, to which they are compared, they require wholehearted commitment on both sides. In this life God expects our wholehearted love of him and our neighbor. He requires clean hands and a pure heart, and he expects us to pursue these holy ends.

6. The call to discipleship

The open view also makes good sense of the call to discipleship that requires strong motives for exertion and action on our part. It implies that God is not the sole actor and that human beings exercise power and 'say so.' According to a parable, the master gave his servants different amounts of capital and told them to invest it. He was serious about this and held them responsible. In the same way, God expects us to put our God-given resources to work in order to gain a return. We will be held responsible for the kind of investments we make (Mt. 25:14–30). Discipleship implies a genuine partnership.

We are God's covenant partners. God depends on us. He calls us to take responsibility and exercise dominion over creation. He calls us to obey the commandments and sends us forth in mission. He expects us to exercise social responsibility. His will gets done on earth through human action in the power of the Spirit. God is looking for people to join him in the battle and rise up against the powers. We are called to reclaim aspects of the creation that the enemy has seized. Thus Jesus urges us to hear the word, use our talents, exercise our faith, seize the opportunity and be ready for the kingdom. He calls us to active radical faith and holy boldness. The fact that God is depending on us is tremendously motivating.

---

[38] Sanders, *God Who Risks*, 240, 249; Maddox, *Responsible Grace*, 57.

God expects us to take responsibility for the future. He wants us to reflect upon and choose among the possibilities. He expects us to be passionately alive; not waiting for the future to happen to us, but intent on creating it with God's help. Ebenezer Scrooge asked the third ghost of Christmas: 'Are these the shadows of the things that will be or are they the shadows of things that may be only?' He is really asking whether the future is fixed or whether he can change it. He wants to know if everything has been decided or whether his decisions can shape it. At stake is our basic life orientation. Are we resigned fatalistically in the face of everything having been settled or are we committed to tearing down strongholds and extending God's kingdom reach?

The fact is that our input makes a difference to God and to historical outcomes. God takes co-workers seriously. We are God's hands and feet; whether God's will gets done on earth depends in part upon us. How will the poor be helped if we do not help them? How will the nations be evangelized if we do not tell them? We bear responsibility for much of what has gone wrong in the world and we can be the part of the solution. Creaturely decisions, as well as divine decisions, affect the course of history. Obedience is important to the realization of God's purposes. We can be responsible for something happening or not happening. Our action or inaction can influence another person's relationship with God. There is a degree of human responsibility in the open view of God not found in the conventional models.

We must take responsibility for things. We are responsible for addressing evils in the world that are not the will of God. The decisions are ours to take or not to take. God has planned that good works be done and it is up to us to do them (Eph. 2:10). We bear primary responsibility for what is or is not done. This is true in the realm of evangelism. Do people hear the gospel or not? It has been decided by God that they should hear and it is up to us whether they do. William Carey was told by the hyper-Calvinists that God, if he wanted to reach the heathen, could do it without Carey's help. As Calvinists, they spoke the truth. But Carey knew, instinctively, that he could make a difference if he went to India. He knew that the future could be different if he went. So he put aside his own Calvinism and acted like an open theist would, as Calvinists usually do when it comes to practical matters. Their theology fosters indolence but, fortunately, they ignore it in practical matters.[39]

---

[39] See W. Travis, 'William Carey: The Modern Missions Movement and the Sovereignty of God' in T.R. Schreiner and B.A. Ware (eds.), *Grace of God*, ch. 14; Piper, *Pleasures of God*, 58–60.

7. Perseverance

The relationship continues to be personal to the end. The reception of God's word must be followed by faithful retention. This is implied by frequent calls in Scripture to abide in Christ and persevere. Paul says that we will be presented holy to God 'provided that you continue securely established and steadfast in the faith, without shifting from the hope promised by the gospel' (Col. 1:23). Security is linked to our faith-union with Christ. The relationship must be maintained and not be forsaken. We are kept by the power of God, through faith (1 Pet. 1:5). The continuation of salvation depends, in part, on the human partner because the relationship is personal and reciprocal. One perseveres by persevering, through the power of God. As in the parable of the sower, some respond but later turn back (Lk. 8:9–15). The book of Hebrews is replete with warnings not to fall away from the living God (e.g. Heb. 3:12; 6:4–6). There is no good reason to take them as merely hypothetical. Believers are secure under the condition that they continue in faith, which is a process not completed until the end of the journey. One may fail to persevere until the end and not receive what was promised. Our hope is in the grace that will be brought to us at the revelation of Jesus Christ (1 Pet. 1:13). The process has a beginning, a middle and an end. It is not over until it is over.[40]

I cannot pretend that the open view of God is very appealing at this point. It may make sense of the biblical exhortations and it may follow from a personal model of salvation but it does not appeal to our self-interest. From a biblical and theological point of view, eternal security is the first petal of Calvinism's TULIP that should fall; from the point of view of self-interest it is surely the last. Cheap grace has appeal. There is in the flesh a desire for security apart from reciprocity born of a lack of trust in God. On the other hand, our experiences of the struggles of the life of faith mesh with the open view of perseverance. It is not the experience of a done deal. We who have the Spirit groan inwardly as we wait for the redemption of God (Rom. 8:23).[41]

At the same time, character becomes more predictable over time: the longer we persist on a chosen path, the more that path becomes part of who we are. Hence, generally speaking, the range of viable options diminishes over time. As I grow older, my relationship with the Lord deepens and is strengthened. It may even be that in heaven there will be

---

[40] R. Shank, *Life in the Son: A Study of the Doctrine of Perseverance*. Having plucked the Calvinist TULIP of four of its petals, Geisler leaves one, perseverance, hanging in *Chosen But Free*, 98–100, 117–30.

[41] Sanders, *God Who Risks*, 249–51.

no possibility of falling away. The element of risk may belong to the time of our earthly probation and our ability to choose may diminish; as choices become habits, habits become character, and character becomes our very being. In a sense, we are becoming our choices. We are moving from possibility to actuality, one way or the other. Some are becoming fixed in ungodliness, while others are becoming steadfast in goodness. Our experience of self-determination may be temporary. It may exist to determine what we will be, whether we will participate in the everlasting love of God or eternally repudiate it. Each person is now fixing their heart, either toward or away from God's kingdom, but the possibility of going one way or the other may not last forever.

For some, it is inconceivable that a believer might fail to be saved in the end. How could God's purpose for a person be thwarted in this way? They reason that if the Spirit awakened them to faith, why would they be allowed to perish? The answer is that God respects his covenant partners and does not override their freedom. Believers can be confident about persevering – perseverance in being faithful to the divine Lover who upholds us by his unwavering faithfulness[42] – but must not ignore obstacles to their persevering. Apostasy is not a hypothetical danger: the risk is a real one, even though God does not want it and works against it. Our desire for security can be a carnal thing, the wanting of an ironclad guarantee apart from the proper source of security, Jesus Christ.

8. Prayer

The open view of God meshes well with the activity of prayer, particularly of petitionery prayer that is such a good indicator of the interactive nature of our relationship with God. We stand, like those adoring early Christian figures depicted in the catacombs, upright with heads raised and eyes open, with arms stretched out and hands open in an attitude of expectation and readiness. Even the posture is different. We stand erect and do not just prostrate ourselves or bow with eyes closed and hands folded as if to make ourselves as small as possible and powerless.

In prayer the practicality of the open view of God shines. In prayer God treats us as subjects not objects and real dialogue takes place. God could act alone in ruling the world but wants to work in consultation. It is not his way unilaterally to decide everything. He treats us as partners

---

[42] Marshall, *Kept*, 191–212; Shank, *Life in the Son*. From the Calvinistic standpoint it is not very different. How does it help to know that God will save all the elect when one cannot know whether one belongs to that company. It is always possible that God is encouraging us to think we belong in order to magnify his name by damming us.

in a two-way conversation and wants our input – our gratitude, our con-
currence, our questioning, even our protests and our petitions. He
enlists our input because he wants it, not because he needs it. He treats us
as responsible agents with whom he has a dynamic relationship. Prayer
validates the open view of God because it is so revealing of the interactive relationship. God does not stand at a distance but gets involved,
becomes conditioned, responds, relents, intervenes and acts in time.
Prayer changes things because God allows it to influence him so that
prayer becomes an effective contributor to the flow of events. As Samuel
puts it, 'Far be it from me that I should sin against the Lord by ceasing to
pray for you' (1 Sam. 12:23).[43]

   People pray passionately when they see purpose in it, when they think
prayer can make a difference and that God may act because of it. There
would not be much urgency in our praying if we thought that God's
decrees could not be changed and/or that the future is entirely settled.
Then we would pray more out of obedience than hope. Why pray if
nothing depends on our praying or not praying? But if God's plans can
change and the future be altered, prayer makes good sense. Then we may
hope that God will respond and act because we asked him. In prayer
God makes himself dependent on us, in a certain sense, and allows
himself to be affected by our praying. What happens on earth affects
what happens in heaven. As Jesus said, 'Whatever you bind on earth will
be bound in heaven and whatever you loose on earth will be loosed in
heaven' (Mt. 18:18). As James puts it, 'You have not because you ask
not' (Jas. 4:2). Certain things happen because we ask for them, things
that might not otherwise have happened. Clearly God wants to act in
answer to prayer, not apart from it. Jesus gave the example of a widow
who pestered a judge until he heard her and praised the faith of a centu-
rion who believed that Jesus could heal even at a distance. Obviously
God is looking for serious faith that he might respond to it. Jesus says,
'Ask and you will receive' (Mt. 7:7). It appears that God's actions can be
conditioned by our praying and that our not praying may thwart God's
will.[44]

   Scripture is full of examples. God told Abraham that he was about to
judge Sodom and Abraham debated with him about it (Gen. 18). Evidently the decision was not set in stone but was refined through

---

[43] V. Brummer, *What Are We Doing When We Pray?*; Berkhof, *Christian Faith*,
490–7. In this whole area, see Tiessen, *Providence and Prayer*. Ware acknowledges the appeal of the open view of God at this point and sees that the conventional model is vulnerable in *God's Lesser Glory*, 164.
[44] See Basinger on petitionery prayer in Pinnock, et al., *Openness*, 156–62;
Sanders, *God Who Risks*, 268–74.

dialogue. God told Moses that he was going to destroy Israel but Moses countered with reasons why he should not do so (Ex. 32). In that case, God listened to Moses and relented and did not follow through on his plan. Manasseh ignored God and was taken by the Assyrians.

> While Manasseh was in distress, he entreated the favor of the Lord his God and humbled himself greatly before the God of his ancestors. He prayed to him and God received his entreaty, heard his plea, and restored him again to Jerusalem and to his kingdom. Then Manasseh knew that the Lord indeed was God. (2 Chr. 33:12–13)

In the book of Revelation God responds when intercessors pray. It is almost as if their prayers create opportunities for God to work. Prayer expands God's effective presence in the world.[45] Our prayers make a difference because of the personal relationship that God has entered into, in which he lets himself be dependent on us to some extent. He weaves our prayers into his planning. God takes us seriously because we are his partners, and lets our prayers change history. This makes us collaborators with God in the writing of the story of redemption. God likes to do things in partnership. He is preparing us ready to reign with him. We may miss a blessing because we fail to ask for it.[46]

Richard J. Foster writes

> In our efforts to pray, it is easy to be defeated right at the outset because we have been taught that everything in the universe is already set and things cannot be changed. And, if things cannot be changed, why pray? We may gloomily feel this way but the Bible does not teach that. The Bible prayers prayed as if their prayers could and would make an objective difference. The apostle Paul announces that we are 'co-labourers with God'; that is, that we are working with God to determine the outcome of events (1 Cor. 3:9). It is Stoicism that demands a closed universe not the Bible. Many people who emphasise acquiescence and resignation to the way things are as 'the will of God' are closer to Epictetus than to Christ. Moses prayed boldly because he believed that his prayers could change things, even God's mind. In fact, the Bible stresses so forcefully the openness of our universe that, in an anthropomorphism hard for modern ears, it speaks of God changing his mind in accord with his unchanging love (Exod. 32:14; Jon. 3:10). This comes as a genuine liberation to many of us, but it also sets a tremendous responsibility before us. We are working with God to determine the future! Certain things

---

[45] Wink, *Engaging the Powers*, ch. 16. He speaks of history belonging to the intercessors.

[46] Brother Andrew, *And God Changed His Mind*, 13, 15, 77. See Tiessen, *Providence and Prayer*, ch. 6.

will happen in history, if we pray rightly. We are to change the world by prayer. What more motivation do we need to learn this loftiest human exercise?[47]

Dallas Willard writes

> God's response to our prayers is not a charade. He does not pretend he is answering our prayers when he is only doing what he was going to do anyway. Our requests really do make a difference in what God does or does not do. The idea that everything would happen exactly as it does regardless of whether we pray or not is a specter that haunts the minds of many who sincerely profess belief in God. It makes prayer psychologically impossible, replacing it with dead ritual at best. And (of course) God would not respond to this. You wouldn't either.[48]

Prayer makes sense in the context of personal relationships and the open view of God. It is less meaningful for conventional theists, because either God cannot respond to the creature (Thomism) or prayer cannot change what has already been decided (Calvinism). This forces us to pray out of obedience because God asks us to pray but robs us of the sense that prayer plays a role in determining what will happen. It cannot change the predestined blueprint in which the prayers themselves are foreordained. If God should decide to help Mary on a certain day, God may ordain that I pray for it. But, in that case, my prayer is a predestined means to a predestined end, and, if I didn't pray, God would have ordained that too making the exercise of prayer a charade. God has to pretend to be answering prayer when he is only doing what he was going to do anyway. Such prayer does not bespeak personal relationships, not when prayer is effective only as a carrying out of what God predetermined.[49]

At the same time, we do not want to go to extremes. We are not suggesting that God needs our counsel and has no ideas of his own to implement, only that God values relationships and wants to take our prayers into

---

[47] R.J. Foster, *Celebration of Discipline*, 35. In a letter, Richard wrote, 'I want to thank you and the others for this excellent resource (*The Openness of God*) that challenges our thinking and encourages us in a world view which makes sense of many things, for example, prayer.'

[48] Willard, *Divine Conspiracy*, 244.

[49] Observe the Calvinists' struggle with this: Erickson, *Father Almighty*, 283–286; C.S. Storms, 'Prayer and Evangelism under God's Sovereignty' in T.R. Schreiner and B.A. Ware (eds.), *Grace of God*, ch. 9; and J.I. Packer, *Evangelism*, ch. 1. See also Grudem, *Systematic Theology: An Introduction to Biblical Doctrine*, ch. 18; and P. Helm, *Providence*, ch. 6.

account. We are not under the illusion either that we can get what we want if only we pray hard enough. No, God has other resources than just us and we have to accept the will of the Lord when it becomes plain to us.

9. Guidance

The open view of God also meshes with the experience of guidance. If in prayer we share our thoughts with God, in guidance God shares his thoughts with us. God said, concerning Abraham, 'Abraham is my friend – shall I not tell him what I am going to do?' The apostle speaks of Christians being led by the Spirit of God (Rom. 8:14). This is the way it is with friends. God has goals for our lives but they have open routes. Even if we fail in some way, God continues to work for our good. His ways with us are marked by flexibility and we need not trouble ourselves with the thought that there is a detailed plan and we missed it (as if we could miss it if it was foreordained). Guidance is not found by our prying into the classified divine blueprint – such does not exist. Guidance is an ongoing and dynamic process in which God is with us every step of the way and leads us into an open future of promise.[50]

David Basinger writes

> Since we do not believe that God has exhaustive knowledge of the future, it makes no sense for us to think in terms of some perfect, preordained plan for our lives and, hence, to worry about whether we are still within it. Accordingly, we need never feel – no matter what has happened in the past – that we must now settle for second best.[51]

God may have a specific piece of guidance about what we should do in a given situation. Mostly though, he wants us to be a certain kind of person who loves and obeys him. God wants us to go through life together with him, making responsible decisions as we go. There is no crystal ball; as we live our lives, we decide what the future will be in dialogue with him. We seek God's wisdom in actual situations, not hidden secrets about tomorrow.[52]

God does not have a definite event in mind for every future circumstance and does not have the future entirely planned. There is no

---

[50] Basinger in Pinnock, et al., *Openness*, 162–8; and Sanders, *God Who Risks*, 275–8. See Ware's critique in *God's Lesser Glory*, 177–89.

[51] Basinger in Pinnock, et al., *Openness*, 164.

[52] G. Friesen agrees that we should seek wisdom not secrets but still harbors a belief in a blueprint inaccessible to us which he wisely counsels us to ignore for practical purposes; see *Decision Making and the Will of God: A Biblical Alternative to the Traditional View*.

document with detailed information on it about such things as whom you will marry, when you will die, etc. That would lead to a fatalistic attitude, which does not please God. Even if there were a detailed plan, we do not have access to it so, in effect, we have to live as if it did not exist. Since we do not know what God has ordained, we face the future as if it were open. One could affirm the blueprint intellectually but would have to ignore it practically.[53] Guidance does not consist in asking God to check the future and give us the secrets. It is about facing the future together with God. It is about going together through life and deciding with him what its course shall be. Whatever its actual course in detail, the goal is the same – God will have us conformed in the image of Christ. That can happen whether one is a preacher or an undertaker. It can also fail to happen if we do not want it to happen.

One could object to this picture and say that a God who does not control everything and does not even know the future exhaustively cannot be much of a guide. But then again if God is in total control one doesn't need to trust and doesn't need a guide. Whatever will be will be! It is because there is risk, there are things to be settled, and a war to be won, that we keep close to our Lord and trust him to find the way through. Even our critics have to do so; there's no other way to live practically speaking.

10. The problem of evil

The open view of God also helps us deal with the problem of evil. Unlike conventional theism with its much stronger doctrine of divine control, we can say that God does not want horrors like the Holocaust to happen. They are genuine tragedies that God did not will and which are not part of some greater good. He did not ordain them and, in fact, weeps over them. We too are entitled to be outraged by them. Practically speaking it means that one can fight evil without fighting God.[54] Though God can bring good out of evil, it does not make evil itself good and does not even ensure that God will succeed in every case to bring good out of it. Greater goods do not arise out of every occurrence of evil. In reference to evil, God is not the author of it but is a very present help in time of trouble. Though not the cause of our suffering, God is always alongside, helping us through it.

Conventional theism tends to make God the author of evil because evil arises in a world controlled directly or indirectly by him. Whatever

---

[53] Helm, *Providence*, ch. 5.
[54] Recall *The Plague* by Albert Camus where the doctor asked the priest if he could fight the plague without fighting God. The open view says, yes, of course we can! God takes no pleasure in it. It is not mysteriously his will for humanity.

happens is thought to be God's will so it is difficult to see there can be genuine evil. Evil turns out to be in every case something good in disguise. Evil things happen because they fit somehow into his plan, which makes it hard to hate evil without hating God. Why, God may be teaching us a lesson or something. When you get mugged, you should thank God for it! How can there be genuine evils if God wills everything? There must be a reason for what happens in every case. Every evil must contribute to a greater good. As Joni Eareckson says, in effect: I broke my back because God wanted it. The open view would rather say, God wept when she was hurt but has brought good out of it, thanks in large part to Joni herself.[55]

If God's sovereignty extended to all things it would extend to evil too and even sin. Despite efforts to blame creaturely agents for their part in it (e.g. God hires A to kill B and doesn't do the deed himself), God's power is so decisive that it is difficult to think of God as good. It casts a shadow over God's character. It makes God inscrutable because he simply does what he pleases and we have to submit.[56] In fact, God does not control the world completely. God works alongside and even against creaturely agents who have a degree of influence. There is no all-determinative power that steers everything. We are caught up in real warfare and should not be surprised by evil. Evil was not a problem in the New Testament; it was an enemy that they expected to overcome by the power of God. They did not try to explain evil based on the false problematic of exhaustive sovereignty, they set about defeating it. They did not wonder why Jesus got murdered, they knew why: the powers of darkness conspired against him. What they wondered about was how God was moving redemption forward through it. What caused lament for them was the delay, 'O Lord, how long?' (Rev. 6:11).

Theology and Experience

Besides being biblical and coherent, the open view of God is also adequate for the demands of life and relevant to concrete situations. It has appeal because it demonstrates its value in life. It offers non-Christians a God who grounds the worthwhileness of their lives and supplies believers with a basis of significance and a framework for living. As such, the open view can help us grow in relation to God and neighbor; it enhances

---

[55] J. Eareckson, *Joni*.

[56] J. Frame wrestles with the fact that for Van Til divine sovereignty extends to all things and, therefore, to evil and sin in *Cornelius Van Til: An Analysis of his Thought*, 83–6.

activities like prayer, evangelism, and works of charity. This is so because the open view corresponds with the kind of human being God made and the kind of being we experience ourselves to be. God made us free beings, capable of encountering God and responding to his word. We were made for relationship with God and for responding to the love that is offered. Berkhof writes

> By means of the freedom with which God endows him and the love to which he calls him, God begins a journey with him and involves him in a hazardous adventure and even involves himself in it. For by creating somewhere in the cosmos a free being, God limited his freedom and made room for a son, a partner, even a counter-player.[57]

Human beings are not the product of forces alien to them. They are free creatures capable of giving or refusing love. Ours is a finite freedom, a freedom situated in settings that both determine and limit us. Nevertheless, it is a freedom so real that we can genuinely respond and, to some extent, shape the world into which we were born. Unlike the animals, we are unfinished beings, created with potential that is not yet actualized. Our identity lies in front of us, not behind us.

The open view holds promise of being a theology for renewal because it corresponds so well with the freedom of the children of God. He has given us some 'say' in the outworking of the course of events. Each of us makes a difference. God has delegated spiritual authority and sends us forth to do mighty works in his name. We have authority to bind and loose, and to heal and cast out demons. Our faith can move mountains and prayer can change things. Not everything has been settled; therefore, our labor is not in vain. Our lives have a significant potential to count for God such that it is said that the angels are curious about it (1 Cor. 4:9; 1 Pet. 1:12). The outcomes are not foregone conclusions. We have the authority to act if we will use it, but we are accountable to God. Our authority can be thwarted by unbelief and disobedience. Let us seize the opportunities that God sets before us. What we decide makes a difference. God loves it when believers respond to his call with holy boldness. He loves to see a readiness on our part to receive the Spirit and gifts of the Spirit. God goes out on a limb with those who trust him and believe his promises. We should, therefore, attempt great things for God and expect great things from him.[58]

---

[57] Berkhof, *Christian Faith*, 184. A better witness to human freedom has been made by the Eastern churches since Irenaeus than by the Western churches.
[58] C.H. Pinnock, 'Divine Relationality: A Pentecostal Contribution to the Doctrine of God', *Journal of Pentecostal Theology* 16 (2000), 3–26.

Conclusion

I trust that we are all seeking to deepen our understanding of God in faithful and timely ways. I hope that the open view of God can contribute something to this quest in dialogue with other models. However excellent one's thought, the problems are not closed and the solutions complete. While the mystery may have been clarified somewhat, it has not become fully comprehensible: it remains open to further clarification and development. God is incomprehensible and his relationships with the created order cannot be fully comprehended. Here we see in a mirror dimly.

One hopes that, just as the Evangelical Alliance decided that the teaching of conditional immortality could stand alongside traditional belief in the nature of hell, so it might be possible that the open view of God might be accepted as a valid option for evangelicals. The open view is a research program, not a settled model clearly defined in every way. It will take time to consider how to handle certain questions and to discern the best path forward. Give the open view a little time to mature; other models have had centuries. Having raised a number of stimulating ideas, it is time now to ponder the implications.

Theologies seek root metaphors to help express their vision of God. Some make 'king' the key metaphor and generate a view of God in causal terms; others feature 'judge' and come up with a religious system of rights and duties. The open view is centered on God as a loving person and lifts up the personal relations God seeks to have with creaturely persons. God loves us and wants us to love him in return. What we do makes a difference to God; our sin grieves him and our obedience delights him. God does not exhaustively control what happens in the world but works flexibly with whatever happens. The open view is a model of love.[1] Being reformist in theology, rather than traditionalist, we keep the boundaries open and

---

[1] V. Brummer, *Model of Love*, ch. 1.

watch for new and possibly better ways of understanding the gospel.[2] But, in the course of our interpretations, we strive to do justice to all the 'names' of God, not just our favorites.[3]

There is no question that the debate between monergists and synergists over God's relationship with the world is an all-consuming and unresolved one in theology today. It seems now as if we are being asked to choose between a paleo-Calvinist package with meticulous providence, compatibilist freedom and exhaustive foreknowledge (a truly frozen world project) and the open view of God package with general providence, libertarian freedom, and a partly unsettled future (a truly dynamic world order). Startled by this stark alternative and aware of many criticisms of the open view, I wrote this book with a number of questions in my mind. Is the open view of God a legitimate option in evangelical theology? Does it represent enrichment or a declension? Does it represent growth in understanding or, in David F. Wells' words, an unraveling at the center?[4] How does the model fair when placed alongside conventional thinking? Is it a coherent alternative to the more dominant viewpoints? Can God be too big as well as too small, as J.B. Phillips suggested? On a personal level, I wonder why I have been so savagely attacked when I thought what I was doing was:

(a) Taking the Bible more seriously.
(b) Encouraging us all to think more profoundly.
(c) Addressing some important questions surrounding our cherished relationship with God.

Why the heated and often angry responses? Obviously, I have touched a raw nerve: the open view of God is different from the great tradition from Augustine and Calvin in many respects. I suppose it was inevitable that it would arouse strong feelings in opposition and raise the question in a new form as to whether the evangelical coalition is obligated to be Calvinist theologically or whether it is proper to call for reforms in that paradigm.

Vigorous debates about important matters are not unusual in the history of theology. Molinists have debated with Thomists and

---

[2] R.E. Olson distinguishes these two types of theological workers in 'The Future of Evangelical Theology' *Christianity Today* (9 February 1998), 40–50. My experience in this case strongly suggests that evangelicals prefer traditionalists to reformers. I think they worry that the reformers might be liberals in disguise. Curiously, their admiration for sixteenth-century reformers remains high.
[3] What we call biblical metaphors of God, older theologians called the names of God.
[4] Wells, *Modern Reformation* 9 (July, 2000), 12.

Calvinists with Arminians and theology has been enriched. Often there
has not even emerged a final interpretation of issues but the interaction
has been profitable nevertheless. There have always been, after all, different ways of looking at a number of things. The theological foundation – which is Jesus Christ – does not change, but there is room for
different ways to formulate doctrine. The complete truth has not been
given to any one person or school of thought, so there is always room to
grow in understanding God's word.

Why, given the rich diversity of theological paradigms over the centuries, does the openness proposal come as such a threat? It would, after
all, be possible to view it positively as fresh insight and as a possible contribution. One could say that, just as Calvinism was not built in a day,
why can the open view not be given a little time to look into things?[5]
Rancour could be lessened among us, if we:

(a) Would respect one another as believing scholars.
(b) Could observe the eschatological proviso of 1 Corinthians 13:12
    ('we know in part'), and not equate our opinions with the final truth
    of matters.
(c) Would refrain from caricaturing what the other is saying.
(d) Try to keep politics out of the discussion (is the opponent in or out of
    the evangelical movement?).

At the same time, I can understand why some want to rein in the reformist direction in theology because of the pluralism it fosters. It can give the
impression that theology is a flea market of ideas and terribly frag-
mented. I understand the counter trend towards clearer confessional
identity in a relativistic culture and why the open view, considered in
that light, might seem to be part of the problem and not part of the solution. I can even see why, even if a solid case were made for the open view,
some might prefer the status quo to any purported enrichment. Perhaps
what I am saying cannot be calmly considered at this time but must wait
for another time. I take the opposition seriously and ask myself what it
signifies. Is it the fundamentalist root of evangelicalism that is rigid
when it comes to rethinking issues? If we privilege the Augustinian tradition such that it is not capable of reform, clearly the open view of God is
illegitimate.[6] I get suspicious when the same people who want to protect

---

[5] On paradigm shifts, see Küng, *Christianity.*
[6] The spirit of fundamentalism is of course a universal phenomenon not limited
to evangelicalism; see P.L. Berger (ed.), *The Desecularization of the World:
Resurgent Religion and World Politics,* ch. 1.

God's sovereignty also want to keep women in their subordinate place. Why do they not see that the Father whom they claim to exalt is not the 'father' of patriarchal power but the God of Jesus Christ who woos us through his self-giving love?[7]

I suppose I am a 'liberal' in Barth's sense when he writes

> Being truly liberal means thinking and speaking in responsibility and openness on all sides, backwards and forwards, toward both past and future, and with total personal modesty. To be modest is not to be skeptical; it is to see what one thinks and says has limits. This does not hinder me from saying very definitely what I think I see and know. But I do this only in the awareness that there have been and are other people before and alongside me and still others who will come after. This awareness gives me an inner peace, so that I do not think I always have to be right even though I say definitely what I say and think. Knowing that a limit is set for me, I can move cheerfully within it as a free man.[8]

Rancour can be lessened if we adhere to a few simply values. We can decide to respect one another as believing students who are trying to do their best. We can observe Paul's eschatological proviso ('we know in part') and therefore not assume that we possess truth in its final form. We can refrain from caricature and we can leave ecclesiastical politics to one side.

The deepest objection to the open view of God raised by Bruce Ware is that it diminishes God's glory rather than enhancing it.[9] But we need to remember that, while God is certainly the 'most' and the 'best,' there are different kinds of goodness and greatness. Therefore, when we ascribe maximality to God we need to understand what is involved. We need to ask: wherein does God's glory consist? For example, is it divine perfection to be vulnerable or invulnerable? Is it God's perfection to suffer or not to suffer? The open view does not lessen God's glory if the gospel is true. Is it not to God's glory that he wants a relationship with his creatures, a partnership in which he makes himself vulnerable and suffers for sinners? Is it not conventional theism that lessens God's glory with its all-controlling and unconditioned deity? Lucas remarks

> Instead of the impassible Buddha, untroubled by the tribulations of mortal existence, Christians see God on a cross. Instead of the Aristotelian ideal of a

---

[7] The Southern Baptist Convention's revised 'Faith and Message' (2000).
[8] K. Barth, *Final Testimonies*, 34.
[9] Ware, 'God's Lesser Glory' and his subsequent book, *God's Lesser Glory*, 219–30.

self-sufficient God, who devotes his time to enjoying the contemplation of his own excellence, Christians worship a God who shared the human condition and came among us.[10]

What captures my mind and heart about his glory is the personal, dynamic, relational, and loving nature of God, to which Scripture attests but which the tradition (what our critics like to call 'orthodoxy') has so often obscured. My delight is in God who is a 'most moved mover' and in the power of his love. The open view of God does not diminish his glory because God's glory is self-sacrificing love, not all-controlling power. God's chosen way to be with us in the world is the way of faithful love. Most wonderfully God, though all-powerful, does not stand in isolation and does not aim at domination but enters intimate relationships. It is the Devil, not God, who, as Barth suggested, exists in solitary glory and is, in that sense, 'absolute'. The true beauty of God is his relativity. It is the self-emptying of God in love, his taking the form of a servant that makes God so great, not God's aloofness, as the tradition often implies?[11]

This is not to deny God's power. We are trying to describe more correctly how God's power expresses itself. His is not the kind of power spoken of in deterministic theologies, namely raw power, the power of the puppeteer, the power to make everything else surrender. God's power is a greater power than that; he makes free agents as creators and movers in their own right. What awesome power that requires! This act, the creation of such spirits, far from contradicting divine omnipotence presupposes it, for only omnipotence could bring about such a thing. Who but a most powerful being could create and govern the universe and press forward with his plans for it even when creatures disobey him and work against his will? God's is an omnipotence that is able not only to bring forth the most imposing of things, the world in its totality, but also the most delicate of things, a creature independent of it. God's omnipotence is capable not only of laying its hand heavily on the world but also of handling it so lightly that the creature has room to exist and flourish. Why would we suppose that total control is the best, or only, form of sovereignty? Is not shared sovereignty a truly wondrous thing? As Kierkegaard put it: 'It is only a miserable and worldly picture of power to say that it becomes greater in proportion as it compels and makes things dependent.'[12] Such a lot depends on how the discussion is

---

[10] Lucas, *Future*, 232.
[11] Barth, *Church Dogmatics* IV/1, 422.
[12] S. Kierkegaard, *Journal*, 113.

framed. If you start with exhaustive foreknowledge, you go straight to predestination and impassibility, but if you start with God's suffering love, you go straight to the open view of God as a real person.

I recognize conventional theism in its various forms as a brilliant interpretation and intellectual achievement of greatest magnitude.[13] It sought with the Greeks to transcend a naively anthropomorphic understanding of God and against the Greeks to keep hold of the personal God of the Bible. But, at the same time, it remained tied to Greek ideas such as unchangeability and unconditionedness, which blocked some biblical thinking. It could not shake itself loose from thinking of God as unmovable and existing in an eternity far apart from the temporal world, and as a static being unable to interact with changing history. Such forms of theism have had great appeal for earlier generations and even retain appeal for some today, but it has to be said that they are not the only legitimate renderings and that theology is open to discuss other models. It is possible that theology has confused the God of biblical revelation with the god of the philosophers and has created an unsound synthesis. It is possible that conventional theism owes a debt to philosophical ideas stemming from the pagan heritage and that reform in the doctrine of God is called for. It is possible that God's nature is deserving of sounder theological reflection, worthy of greater intelligibility, and capable of better existential fit. The open view of God may be a timely reform.

When a theological model is questioned people imagine that they have lost God when they have not. What they lose is a system of ideas that does not correspond with reality; they find God again, alive and very well, around the next bend. God is always greater than our opinions about him and God ever calls us to new beginnings even in theology. One may reject a model of God without rejecting the faith for which it claims to account.[14] The open view has opened some old wounds and fostered a fresh phase in the centuries-old debate between monergists and synergists, predestinarians and free will theists, Calvinists and Arminians. It has introduced to the discussion some new interpretations as well, for example the idea that the future is partly settled and partly unsettled, and that God is everlastingly eternal rather than timeless. It issues a challenge both to the Arminians to take their model further and to theological determinists to explain better what they propose. There is

---

[13] One cannot read a work like Thomas G. Weinandy's *Can God Suffer?* and not come away impressed by the great tradition in which he operates. It is intellectually dazzling and cannot be bettered by casual criticisms. Of such positions I have learned never to say, 'I have no need of you'(1 Cor. 12:21).

[14] H. De Lubac, *The Presence of God*, 167.

a lot of passion in the discussion because the issues matter profoundly but there can also be fruitful interaction.

A tension, which manifests itself here, exists between scholasticism and pietism in the evangelical movement. From a pietistic point of view, where doctrinal precision is not everything, a measure of theological pluralism is possible, such that an amicable dialogue between the open view of God and other models is possible. However, from the standpoint of a more scholastic orientation, where doctrinal exactness is more highly prized, dialogue, if it occurs at all, is often testy and the toleration of differences much more difficult. Nothing I can say is likely to alter this basic fact. I can only ask that discussion be permitted among evangelicals, that those who seek to define the movement theologically in their own terms do not silence the debate. I hope we will not let a vociferous minority call the shots and squeeze the whole movement into its mold. Surely evangelicalism is a much grander phenomenon than that.

I do not know what will happen. In the short term, a lot depends on the classical Arminians and whether they will allow room for the open view as an option or reject it along with the paleo-Calvinists. This would create an awesome opposition that would marginalize the open view among evangelicals for the time being. Obviously the open view of God will be a minority view among evangelicals; the real issue now is whether it will be tolerated as a legitimate option or chased away. A lot will depend on what the Arminians decide. One can only hope that, just as the minority view of conditional immortality has been accepted recently by the Evangelical Alliance as a legitimate option among evangelicals alongside the majority conventional view, so the open view of God will be regarded as an option. In the longer term, all bets are off, because of the power of the open view as an interpretation of Scripture which, over time, could work its way into Christian thinking and become commonplace. I wonder if some of the vehemence against the open view is due, not to strength of conviction, but to vulnerability; what appears to be a solid phalanx is, in fact, rather precarious.

Looking ahead, it would be good if open theists would ponder and explain better how far we wish to go with some of the exciting ideas we have lifted up. People have the right to know how much risk there is, how changeable, passible and lacking in foreknowledge God is. Similarly, our critics who have admitted that the open view has brought good insights forward, need to explain how they plan to integrate them into their own thinking.

Will the open view of God be widely accepted? Perhaps not, given the hostility of certain Calvinists and the suspicion of many Arminians. But even if it is not accepted, it is a good discussion we are having and the model can prove fruitful even if it does not entirely succeed. In words that our critics like to use: let the will of the Lord be done.

I close with words from a respected British evangelical theologian of the last generation and a friend, H.D. MacDonald:

> I prefer to see a dynamic not a deistic relation between God and the world, and consider God's sovereignty, not as having pre-arranged every detail in the universe. There is room for the free play of events, even though over every happening, God is in control. And such happenings of which he is not the cause and originator, he takes up into the fulfillment of his overall purpose. I (therefore) believe that God does change, not in his essential nature, but in his relationships with mankind. I cannot believe that Judas was brought into the world to be the cause of our Lord's death. He allowed himself to become the traitor and was so used by God to bring about his purpose for man's salvation. I do not accept the blueprint view of history – I believe that in general God's actions in history are contingent. God has not predestined everything and, while he does foreknow every possibility, he can only know a happening as a happening when it actually takes place. On the other hand, I do not believe in a completely haphazard universe. There are special events which God must bring about for the fulfillment of his purpose – to this I must refer prophecy. Thus, as I conceive it, there are some things that must happen and many things that may happen. And there are many things that just happen – things of which God is in no sense the cause. But, when they happen, his sovereignty is such that he can take them into his overall purpose for the world.[15]

---

[15] In a letter to Alex Brooks formerly of Bethany House.

Bibliography

Selected Titles

Adams, M.M., *Horrendous Evils and the Goodness of God* (Ithaca: Cornell University Press, 1999)

Brother Andrew, *And God Changed his Mind* (Grand Rapids: Chosen Books, 1999)

Anglin, W.S., *Free Will and the Christian Faith* (Oxford: Clarendon Press, 1990)

Armstrong, A.H., *Christian Faith and Greek Philosophy* (London: Darton, Longman & Todd, 1960)

Armstrong, J.H. (ed.), *The Coming Evangelical Crisis* (Chicago: Moody Press, 1996)

Baillie, J., *Our Knowledge of God* (New York: Charles Scribner's Sons, 1959)

Balentine, S.E., *Prayer in the Hebrew Bible: The Drama of the Divine-Human Dialogue* (Minneapolis: Fortress, 1993)

Barbour, I.G., *Issues in Science and Religion* (New York: Harper & Row, 1966)

—, *When Science Meets Religion* (San Francisco: HarperSanFrancisco, 2000)

Barth, C., *God With Us: A Theological Introduction to the Old Testament* (Grand Rapids: Eerdmans, 1991)

Barth, K., 'The Reality of God', *Church Dogmatics* II/1 (Edinburgh: T. & T. Clark, 1957)

Basinger, D., *The Case for Free Will Theism: A Philosophical Assessment* (Downers Grove: InterVarsity Press, 1996)

Basinger D. and R. Basinger (eds.), *Predestination and Free Will* (Downers Grove: InterVarsity Press, 1986)

Basinger, R., 'Evangelicals and Process Theism: Seeking a Middle Ground', *Christian Scholars Review* 15 (1986), 157-167

Bauckham, R., *God Crucified: Monotheism and Christology in the New Testament* (Grand Rapids: Eerdmans; Carlisle: Paternsoter, 1998)

Bauman, M., *Pilgrim Theology: Taking the Path of Theological Discovery* (Grand Rapids: Zondervan, 1992)

Beckwith F.J. and S.E. Parrish, *The Mormon Concept of God: A Philosophical Analysis* (Buffalo: Edwin Mellen Press, 1991)

Berkhof, H., *Christian Faith* (Grand Rapids: Eerdmans, 1979)

Bloesch, D.G., *God the Almighty: Power, Wisdom, Holiness, Love* (Downers Grove: InterVarsity Press, 1995)

Boettner, L., *The Reformed Doctrine of Predestination* (Grand Rapids: Eerdmans, 1941)

Boman, T., *Hebrew Thought Compared with Greek* (London: SCM Press, 1960)

Boyd, G.A., *Trinity and Process: A Critical Evaluation and Reconstruction of Hartshorne's Di-Polar Theism Towards a Trinitarian Metaphysics* (New York: Peter Lang, 1992)

—, *God at War: The Bible and Spiritual Conflict* (Downers Grove: InterVarsity Press, 1997)

—, *God of the Possible: A Biblical Introduction to the Open View of God* (Grand Rapids: Baker Book House, 2000)

—, *Satan and the Problem of Evil* (Downers Grove: InterVarsity Press, forthcoming)

—, *The Myth of the Blueprint* (Downers Grove: InterVarsity Press, forthcoming)

Bracken, J.A. and M. Suchocki (eds.), *Trinity in Process: A Relational Theology of God* (New York: Continuum, 1997)

Bray, G., *The Doctrine of God* (Downers Grove: InterVarsity Press, 1993)

—, *The Personal God: Is the Classical Understanding of God Tenable?* (Carlisle: Paternoster, 1998)

Brueggemann, W., *Theology of the Old Testament: Testimony, Dispute, Advocacy* (Minneapolis: Fortress, 1997)

Brummer, V., *What Are We Doing When We Pray?* (London: SCM Press, 1984)

—, *Speaking of a Personal God* (Cambridge: Cambridge University Press, 1992)

—, *The Model of Love: A Study in Philosophical Theology* (Cambridge: Cambridge University Press, 1993)

Butin, P.W., *Revelation, Redemption, and Response: Calvin's Trinitarian Understanding of the Divine-Human Relationship* (New York: Oxford University Press, 1995)

Calvin, J., *Concerning the Eternal Predestination of God* (Edinburgh: James Clarke, 1961)

Cameron, N.M. de S., *The Power and Weakness of God* (Edinburgh: Rutherford House, 1990)

Carson, D.A., *Divine Sovereignty and Human Responsibility: Biblical Perspectives in Tension* (Atlanta: John Knox Press, 1991)

—, *The Gagging of God: Christianity Confronts Pluralism* (Grand Rapids: Zondervan, 1996)

Case-Winters, A., *God's Power: Traditional Understandings and Contemporary Challenges* (Louisville: Westminster/John Knox Press, 1990)

Chadwick, H., *Early Christian Thought and the Classical Tradition* (Oxford: Clarendon Press, 1966)

Charnock, S., *The Existence and Attributes of God* (Ann Arbor: Cushing-Mallow, 1969)

Clarke, N.W., *The Philosophical Approach to God: A Neo-Thomist Perspective* (Winston-Salem: Wake Forest University Press, 1979)

Clayton, P., *God and Contemporary Science* (Grand Rapids: Eerdmans, 1997)

—, *The Problem of God in Modern Thought* (Grand Rapids: Eerdmans, 2000)

Cobb, J.B. and C.H. Pinnock, *Searching for an Adequate God: A Dialogue Between Process and Free Will Theists* (Grand Rapids: Eerdmans, 2000)

Cobb, J.B., *Grace and Responsibility: A Wesleyan Theology for Today* (Nashville: Abingdon Press, 1995)

Corey, M.A., *God the New Cosmology: The Anthropic Design Argument* (Lanham: Rowman & Littlefield, 1993)

Cottrell, J., *What the Bible Says about God the Creator* (Joplin: College Press, 1983)

—, *What the Bible Says about God the Ruler* (Joplin: College Press, 1984)

—, *What the Bible Says about God the Redeemer* (Joplin: College Press, 1987)

Craig, W.L., *The Only Wise God: The Compatibility of Divine Foreknowledge and Human Freedom* (Grand Rapids: Baker Book House, 1987)

—, *The Coherence of Christian Theism: Omniscience* (promised)

Creel, R.E., *Divine Impassibility: An Essay in Philosophical Theology* (Cambridge: Cambridge University Press, 1986)

Cullmann, O., *Christ and Time: The Primitive Christian Conception of Time and History* (London: SCM Press, 1951)

Davaney, S.G., *Divine Power: A Study of Karl Barth and Charles Hartshorne* (Minneapolis: Fortress, 1986)

Davis, S.T., *Logic and the Nature of God* (Grand Rapids: Eerdmans, 1983)

Edwards, R.B., 'The Pagan Dogma of the Absolute Unchangeableness of God', *Religious Studies* 14 (1978), 305-13

Erickson, M., *God the Father Almighty: A Contemporary Exploration of the Divine Attributes* (Grand Rapids: Baker Book House, 1998)

—, *The Evangelical Left: Encountering Postconservative Evangelical Theology* (Grand Rapids: Baker Book House, 1997)

Fiddes, P.S., *The Creative Suffering of God* (Oxford: Clarendon Press, 1988)

Flew, A., *God and Philosophy* (London: Hutchison, 1966)

Forster, R.T. and V.P. Marston, *God's Strategy in Human History* (Wheaton: Tyndale House, 1974)

France, R.T., *The Living God* (London: Inter-Varsity Press, 1970)

Franklin, S.T., *Speaking from the Depths: Alfred North Whitehead's Heremeneutical Metaphysics of Propositions, Experience, Symbolism, Language, and Religion* (Grand Rapids: Eerdmans, 1990)

Fretheim, T.E., *The Suffering of God: An Old Testament Perspective* (Minneapolis: Fortress, 1984)

Friesen, G., *Decision Making and the Will of God: A Biblical Alternative to the Traditional View* (Portland: Multnomah, 1980)

Geisler, N.L., *Creating God in the Image of Man? The New 'Open' View of God—Neotheism's Dangerous Drift* (Minneapolis: Bethany House, 1997)

—, *Chosen But Free* (Minneapolis: Bethany House, 1999)

Gilson, E., *The Spirit of Medieval Philosophy* (Notre Dame: University of Notre Dame Press, 1936)

Gonzalez, J.L., *Manana: Christian Theology from a Hispanic Perspective* (Nashville: Abingdon Press, 1990)

Gorringe, T.J., *God's Theatre: A Theology of Providence* (London: SCM Press, 1991)

Gray, T. and C. Sinkinson, *Reconstructing Theology: A Critical Assessment of the Theology of Clark H. Pinnock* (Carlisle: Paternoster, 2000)

Griffin, D.R., *God, Power, and Evil: a Process Theodicy* (Philadelphia: Westminster Press, 1976)

—, *Evil Revisited: Responses and Reconsiderations* (Albany: State University of New York Press, 1991)

Gruenler, R.G., *The Inexhaustible God: Biblical Faith and the Challenge of Process Theism* (Grand Rapids: Baker Book House, 1983)

Gruning, H., *How in the World Does God Act?* (Lanham: University Press of America, 2000)

Hallman, J.M., *The Descent of God: Divine Suffering in History and Theology* (Minneapolis: Fortress, 1991)

Hanson, R.P.C., *The Search for the Christian Doctrine of God: The Arian Controversy* (Edinburgh: T. & T. Clark, 1988)

Harrington, W.J., *The Prodigal Father: Approaching the God of Love* (Wilmington: Michael Glazier, 1992)

—, *The Tears of God: Our Benevolent Creator and Human Suffering* (Collegeville: Liturgical Press, 1992)

Hartshorne, C., *Omnipotence and Other Theological Mistakes* (Albany: State University of New York Press, 1984)

Hartshorne, C. and W.L. Reese (eds.), *Philosophers Speak of God* (Chicago: University of Chicago Press, 1953)

Hatch, E., *The Influences of Greek Ideas and Usages Upon the Christian Church* (London: Williams and Norgate, 1890)

Helm, P., 'The Impossibility of Divine Passibility' in N.M. De S. Cameron (ed.), *The Power and Weakness of God: Impassibility and Orthodoxy* (Edinburgh: Rutherford House Books, 1990), 125-37

—, *The Providence of God* (Downers Grove: InterVarsity Press, 1994)

Henry, C.F.H., *God, Revelation, and Authority* V: *God Who Stands and Stays* 1 & 2 (Waco: Word Books, 1982, 1983)

Hicks, J.M., *Yet Will I Trust Him: Understanding God in a Suffering World* (Joplin: College Press, 1999)

Hoitenga Jr., D.J., *John Calvin and the Will* (Grand Rapids: Baker Book House, 1997)

Horton, M., *We Believe: Recovering the Essentials of the Apostles' Creed* (Nashville: Word, 1998)

Hurtubise, D., 'Difficult Connections: Philosophical Process Theology and Christian Faith' (unpublished paper, Silver Anniversary International Whitehead Conference, Claremont, CA, 4-9 August, 1998)

Inbody, T.L., *The Transforming God: An Interpretation of Suffering and Evil* (Louisville: Westminster/John Knox Press, 1997)

Jantzen, G., *God's World, God's Body* (Philadelphia: Westminster, 1984)

Jenson, R.W., *Unbaptised God: The Basic Flaw in Ecumenical Theology* (Minneapolis: Fortress, 1992)

Johnson, E.A., *She Who Is: The Mystery of God in Feminist Theological Discourse* (New York: Crossroad, 1992)

Jones, M., *The Color of God: The Concept of God in Afro-American Thought* (Macon: Mercer Press, 1987)

Jüngel, E., *The Doctrine of the Trinity: God's Being is in Becoming* (Grand Rapids: Eerdmans, 1976)

—, *God as the Mystery of the World: On the Foundation of the Theology of the Crucified One in the Dispute Between Theism and Atheism* (Edinburgh: T. & T. Clark, 1983)

Kaiser, C.B., *The Doctrine of God: An Historical Survey* (Westchester: Crossway Books, 1982)

Kasper, W., *The God of Jesus Christ* (New York: Crossroad, 1986)

Kirkpatrick, F.G., *Together Bound: God, History, and the Religious Community* (New York: Oxford University Press, 1994)

Kitamori, K., *Theology of the Pain of God* (Richmond: John Knox Press, 1965)

König, A., *Here Am I! A Christian Reflection on God* (Grand Rapids: Eerdmans, 1982)

Küng, H., *Does God Exist?* (New York: Doubleday, 1980)

—, *The Incarnation of God: An Introduction to Hegel's Theological Thought As Prolegomena To A Future Christology* (Edinburgh: T. & T. Clark, 1987)

LaCugna, C.M., *God For Us: The Trinity and Christian Life* (San Francisco: HarperSanFrancisco, 1991)

Lakoff, G. and M. Johnson, *Philosophy in the Flesh: The Embodied Mind and Its Challenge to Western Thought* (New York: Basic Books, 1999)

Lee, J.Y., *God Suffers For Us: A Systematic Inquiry into a Concept of Divine Passibility* (The Hague: Martinus Nijhoff, 1974)

Lindstom, F., *God and the Origin of Evil: A Contextual Analysis of Alleged Monistic Evidence in the Old Testament* (Sweden: CWK Gleerup, 1983)

Lucas, J.R., *Freedom and Grace* (London: SPCK, 1976)

—, *The Future: An Essay on God, Temporality, and the Truth* (Oxford: Basil Blackwell, 1989)

MacGregor, G., *He Who Lets Us Be: A Theology of Love* (New York: Seabury Press, 1975)

MacLeod, D., *Behold Your God* (Rosshire: Christian Focus, 1995)

Macquarrie, J., *In Search of Deity: An Essay in Dialectical Theism* (London: SCM Press, 1984)

Maddox, R.L., *Responsible Grace: John Wesley's Practical Theology* (Nashville: Kingswood Books, 1994)

—, 'Seeking a Response-able God: The Wesleyan Tradition and Process Theology' (typescript, 2000)

Marshall, I.H., *Kept by the Power of God: A Study of Perseverance and Falling Away* (London: Epworth Press, 1969)

McDonald, H.D., *The God Who Responds: How the Creator Relates to his Creation* (Cambridge: James Clarke, 1986)

McLelland, J.D., *God the Anonymous: A Study in Alexandrian Philosophical Theology* (Philadelphia: The Philadelphia Patristic Foundation, 1976)

McSorley, H.J., *Luther: Right or Wrong? An Ecumenical-Theological Study of Luther's Major Work, The Bondage of the Will* (Minneapolis: Augsburg Publishing House, 1969)

McWilliams, W., *The Passion of God: Divine Suffering in Contemporary Protestant Theology* (Macon: Mercer University Press, 1985)

Mohler, A., et al., 'The Battle over the Doctrine of God', *The Southern Baptist Journal of Theology* (Spring, 1997)

Moltmann, J., *The Crucified God: The Cross of Christ as the Foundation and Criticism of Christian Theology* (London: SCM Press, 1994)

Morey, R.A., *Battle of the Gods: The Gathering Storm in Modern Evangelicalism* (Southbridge: Crown Publications, 1989)

Morris, T.V., *Our Idea of God: An Introduction to Philosophical Theology* (Downers Grove: InterVarsity Press, 1991)

Moscop, J.C., *Divine Omniscience and Human Freedom: Thomas Aquinas and Charles Hartshorne* (Macon: Mercer University Press, 1984)

Mozley, J.K., *The Impassibility of God: A Survey of Christian Thought* (London: Cambridge University Press, 1926)

Muller, R.A., *God, Creation, and Providence in the Thought of Jacob Arminius* (Grand Rapids: Baker Book House, 1991)

Murphree, J.T., *Divine Paradoxes: A Finite View of an Infinite God* (Camp Hill: Christian Publications, 1998)

Murphy N. and G.F.R. Ellis, *On the Moral Nature of the Universe: Theology, Cosmology, and Ethics* (Minneapolis: Fortress, 1996)

Nash, R.H., *The Concept of God* (Grand Rapids: Zondervan, 1983)

Ngien, D., *The Suffering of God According to Martin Luther's 'Theologia Crucis'* (New York: Peter Lang, 1995)

Nnamani, A.G., *The Paradox of a Suffering God: On the Classical, Modern-Western and Third World Struggles to Harmonise the Incompatible Attributes of the Trinitarian God* (New York: Peter Lang, 1995)

Norris, R.A., *God and World in Early Christian Theology: A Study in Justin Martyr, Irenaeus, Tertullian, and Origen* (London: Adam and Charles Black, 1966)

O'Donnell, J.J., *Trinity and Temporality: The Christian Doctrine of God in the Light of Process Theology and the Theology of Hope* (Oxford: Oxford University Press, 1983)

—, *The Mystery of the Triune God* (New York: Paulist Press, 1989)

O'Hanlon, G.F., *The Immutability of God in the Theology of Hans Urs von Balthasar* (Cambridge: Cambridge University Press, 1990)

Ogden, S.M., *The Reality of God and Other Essays* (New York: Harper & Row, 1966)

Owen, H.P., *Concepts of Deity* (New York: Herder & Herder, 1971)

Pailin, D.A., *God and the Processes of Reality: Foundations of a Credible Theism* (London: Routledge, 1989)

Pannenberg, W., 'The Appropriation of the Philosophical Concept of God as a Dogmatic Problem of Early Christian Theology' in *Basic Questions in Theology* II (Philadelphia: Fortress, 1971), 119-183

—, *Metaphysics and the Idea of God* (Grand Rapids: Eerdmans, 1988)

—, *Systematic Theology* volume one (Grand Rapids: Eerdmans, 1991)

Partridge, C., *H. H. Farmer's Theological Interpretation of Religion: Towards a Personalistic Theology of Religions* (Lewiston: Edwin Mellen Press, 1998)

Peters, T., *God as Trinity: Relationality and Temporality in Divine Life* (Louisville: Westminster/John Knox, 1993)

Pike, N., *God and Timelessness* (New York: Schocken Books, 1970)

Pinnock, C.H. (ed.), *Grace Unlimited* (Minneapolis: Bethany, 1975)

—, (ed.), *Grace of God, The Will of Man* (Grand Rapids: Zondervan, 1989)

—, *Flame of Love: A Theology of the Holy Spirit* (Downers Grove: InterVarsity Press, 1996)

—, 'Divine Relationality: A Pentecostal Contribution to the Doctrine of God', *Journal of Pentecostal Theology* 16 (2000), 3-26

Pinnock, C.H., R. Rice, J. Sanders, W. Hasker and D. Basinger, *The Openness of God: A Biblical Challenge to the Traditional Understanding of God* (Downers Grove: InterVarsity Press, 1994)

Piper, J., *The Pleasures of God* (Portland: Multnomah, 1991)

—, *The Justification of God* (Grand Rapids: Baker Book House, 1993)

Placher, W.C., *Narratives of a Vulnerable God* (Louisville: Westminster/John Knox Press, 1994)

—, *The Domestication of Transcendence: How Modern Thinking about God Went Wrong* (Louisville: Westminster/John Knox Press, 1996)

Prestige, G.L., *God in Patristic Thought* (London: SPCK, 1936)

Rice, R., *God's Foreknowledge and Man's Free Will* (Minneapolis: Bethany, 1985)

Sanders, J., *The God Who Risks: A Theology of Providence* (Downers Grove: InterVarsity Press, 1998)

Sarot, M., *God, Passibility and Corporeality* (Kampen: Pharos, 1992)

Schreiner, T.R. and B.A. Ware (eds.), *Grace of God, The Bondage of the Will* (Grand Rapids: Baker Book House, 1995)

Simons, G., *Is God a Programmer?: Religion in the Computer Age* (Brighton: Harvester Press, 1988)

Sproul, R.C., *Chosen By God* (Wheaton: Tyndale House, 1986)

—, *Not a Chance: The Myth of Modern Science and Cosmology* (Grand Rapids: Baker Book House, 1994)

—, *Grace Unknown: The Heart of Reformed Theology* (Grand Rapids: Baker Book House, 1997)

—, *Willing to Believe: The Controversy Over Free Will* (Grand Rapids: Baker Book House, 1997)

Stead, C., *Philosophy in Christian Antiquity* (Cambridge: Cambridge University Press, 1994)

Storms, C.S., *The Grandeur of God: A Theological and Devotional Study of the Divine Attributes* (Grand Rapids: Baker Book House, 1984)

Sweeney, L., *The Divine Infinity* (New York: Peter Lang, 1992)

Swinburne, R., *The Coherence of Theism* (Oxford: Clarendon Press, 1993)

—, *Providence and the Problem of Evil* (Oxford: Clarendon Press, 1998)

Taliaferro, C., *Contemporary Philosophy of Religion* (Oxford: Basil Blackwell, 1998)

Taylor, M.L., *God is Love: A Study in the Theology of Karl Rahner* (Atlanta: Scholars Press, 1986)

Tiessen, D.A., *The Openness Model of God: An Examination of Its Current and Early Expression in the Light of Hartshorne's Process Theism* (M.Div. Thesis, Providence Theological Seminary, 1998)

Tiessen, T., *Providence and Prayer: How Does God Work in the World?* (Downers Grove: InterVarsity Press, 2000)

Torrance, T.F., *The Christian Doctrine of God: One Being Three Persons* (Edinburgh: T. & T. Clark, 1996)

Tupper, E.F., *A Scandalous Providence: The Jesus Story of the Compassion of God* (Macon: Mercer University Press, 1995)

Vanstone, W.H., *The Risk of Love* (New York: Oxford University Press, 1978)

Varillon, F., *The Humility and Suffering of God* (New York: Alba House, 1983)

Vesey, G. (ed.), *The Philosophy in Christianity* (Cambridge: Cambridge University Press, 1989)

Ward, K., *Holding Fast to God* (London: SPCK, 1982)

—, *Rational Theology and the Creativity of God* (New York: The Pilgrim Press, 1982)

—, *Images of Eternity: Concepts of God in Five Religious Traditions* (Oxford: Oneworld Publications, 1987)

—, *Religion and Creation* (Oxford: Clarendon Press, 1996)

Ware, B.A., 'God's Lesser Glory: Open Theism's Diminutive Conception of Divine Providence' (Bueermann-Champion Lectureship, Western Seminary, Portland, Oregon, 5-7 Oct, 1999)

—, *God's Lesser Glory: The Diminished God of Open Theism* (Wheaton: Crossway Books, 2000)

Warfield, B.B., 'Predestination', *Biblical and Theological Studies* (Phillipsburg: P. & R. Publishing, 1952)

Watson, G., *Greek Philosophy and the Christian Notion of God* (Dublin: Columba Press, 1996)

Weinandy, T.G., *Does God Change?* (Still River: St Bedes Publications, 1985)

—, *Does God Suffer?* (Notre Dame: Notre Dame University Press, 2000)

Welker, M., *Creation and Reality* (Minneapolis: Fortress, 1999)

Wells, D.F., *God in the Wasteland: The Reality of Truth in a World of Fading Dreams* (Grand Rapids: Eerdmans, 1994)

Widdicombe, P., *The Fatherhood of God from Origen to Athanasius* (Oxford: Clarendon Press, 1994)

Williams, D.D., *The Spirit and the Forms of Love* (New York: Harper & Row, 1968)

Wink, W., *Engaging the Powers* (Minneapolis: Fortress, 1992)

Wolfson, H.A., *The Philosophy of the Church Fathers* (Cambridge, Mass.: Harvard University Press, 1970)

Wolterstorff, N., 'God Everlasting' in C. Orlebeke and L. Smedes (eds.), *God and the Good: Essays in Honor of Henry Stobb* (Grand Rapids: Eerdmans, 1975)

Wright, R.K.M., *No Place for Sovereignty: What's Wrong with Free Will Theism?* (Downers Grove: InterVarsity Press, 1996)

Zycinski, J.M., 'The Doctrine of Substance and Whitehead's Metaphysics', *Review of Metaphysics* 42 (1989), 765-81

Other Titles

Barth, K., *Final Testimonies* (Grand Rapids: Eerdmans, 1977)

Bartholemew, D.J., *God of Chance* (London: SCM Press, 1984)

Bauckham, R., *The Theology of Jürgen Moltmann* (Edinburgh: T. & T. Clark, 1995)

Berdiaev, N., *The Destiny of Man* (London: Geoffrey Bles, 1954)

Berger, P.L. (ed.), *The Desecularization of the World: Resurgent Religion and World Politics* (Grand Rapids: Eerdmans, 1999)

Berkhof, L., *Systematic Theology* (Grand Rapids: Eerdmans, 1941)

Beumer, J., *Henri Nouwen: A Restless Seeking for God* (New York: Crossroad, 1997)

Bloesch, D.G., *Holy Scripture: Revelation, Inspiration and Interpretation* (Downers Grove: InterVarsity Press, 1994)

Blumenthal, H.J. and R.A. Markus (eds.), *Neo-Platonism and Early Christian Thought* (London: Variorum Publications, 1981)

Boer, H.R., *An Ember Still Glowing: Humankind in the Image of God* (Grand Rapids: Eerdmans, 1990)

Bonhoeffer, D., *Letters and Papers from Prison* (New York: Macmillan, 1967)

Boyd, G.A., 'The Self-Sufficient Sociality of God: A Trinitarian Revision of Hartshorne's Metaphysics' in J.A. Bracken and M. Suchocki (eds.), *Trinity*

Bibliography

in Process: A Relational Theology of God (New York: Continuum, 1997), 73-94

Brown, P., *Augustine of Hippo: A Biography* (Berkeley: University of California Press, 1967)

Bruce, F.F., *In Retrospect: Remembrance of Things Past* (Grand Rapids: Eerdmans, 1980)

Brueggemann, W., *In Man We Trust: The Neglected Side of Biblical Faith* (Atlanta: John Knox Press, 1972)

Brunner, E., *The Christian Doctrine of God* (Philadelphia: Westminster Press, 1950)

Burson, S.R. and J.L. Walls, *C. S. Lewis and Francis Schaeffer* (Downers Grove: InterVarsity Press, 1998)

Buswell Jr, J.O., *A Systematic Theology of the Christian Religion* I (Grand Rapids: Zondervan, 1962)

Callen, B.L., *Clark H. Pinnock: Journey Toward Renewal. An Intellectual Biography* (Nappanee,: Evangel Publishing House, 2000)

Calvin, J., *Institutes of the Christian Religion* (ed. J.T. McNeill; 2 vols.; Philapdelphia: Westminster Press, 1960)

Canaday, A.B., 'Putting God at Risk: A Critique of John Sander's View of Providence', *Trinity Journal* 20 (1999), 131-63

Carasik, M., 'The Limits of Omniscience', *Journal of Biblical Literature* 119 (2000), 221-32

Clark, K.J., *Return to Reason* (Grand Rapids: Eerdmans, 1990)

—, 'Hold not Thy Peace at my Tears: Methodological Reflections on Divine Impassibility' in K.J. Clark (ed.), *Our Knowledge of God: Essays in Natural and Philosophical Theology*, (Dordrecht: Kluwer Academic Publishers, 1992), 167-93

—, *When Faith Is Not Enough* (Grand Rapids: Eerdmans, 1997)

Clarke, W.N., 'A New Look at the Immutability of God' in R. Roth(ed.), *God Knowable and Unknowable* (New York: Fordham University Press, 1973)

Cobb, J.B., *A Christian Natural Theology* (Philadelphia: Westminster Press, 1965)

Colyer, E.M. (ed.), *Evangelical Theology in Transition* (Downers Grove: InterVarsity Press, 1999)

Copan, P., 'Is *Creatio ex nihilo* a Post-Biblical Invention? An Examination of Gerhard May's Proposal', *Trinity Journal* 17 (1996), 77-93

Cottrell, J., 'Baptism in the Reformed Tradition' in David W. Fletcher, (ed.), *Baptism and the Remission of Sins* (Joplin, Mo: College Press Publishing, 1990), ch. 4.

Cross, T,L., 'The Rich Feast of Theology: Can Pentecostals Bring the Main Course or Only the Relish?' *Journal of Pentecostal Theology* 16 (2000), 7-47

Cullmann, O., *The Early Church* (London: SCM Press, 1956)

De Lubac, H., *The Presence of God* (London: Darton, Longman and Todd, 1960)

DeHart, P.J., *Beyond the Necessary God: Trinitarian Faith and Philosophy in the Thought of Eberhard Jungel* (Atlanta: Scholar's Press, 1999)

Demarest, B.A. and G.R. Lewis, *Integrative Theology: Knowing Ultimate Reality — The Living God* (Grand Rapids: Zondervan, 1987)

Dorrien, G., *The Remaking of Evangelical Theology* (Louisville: Westminster/ John Knox Press, 1998)

Dulles, A., *The Craft of Theology: From Symbol to System* (New York: Crossroad, 1996)

Dupuis, J., *Toward a Christian Theology of Religious Pluralism* (Maryknoll: Orbis Books, 1997)

Eareckson, J., *Joni* (Grand Rapids: Zondervan, 1976)

Erickson, M., *God in Three Persons: A Contemporary Interpretation of the Trinity* (Grand Rapids: Baker Book House, 1995)

Fackre, G., *The Christian Story: A Narrative Interpretation of Basic Christian Doctrine* (Grand Rapids: Eerdmans, 1984)

—, 'An Evangelical Megashift? The promise and peril of an 'open' view of God', *Christian Century* (3 May, 1995), 484–7

Fairbairn, A.M., *The Place of Christ in Modern Theology* (New York: Charles Scribner's Sons, 1983)

Fee, G.D., *Listening to the Spirit in the Text* (Grand Rapids: Eerdmans, 2000)

Finan, T. and V. Twomey (eds.), *The Relationship Between Neo-Platonism and Christianity* (Dublin: Four Courts Press, 1992)

Foster, R.J., *Celebration of Discipline* (San Francisco: HarperSanFrancisco, 1988)

Frame, J., *Evangelical Reunion: Denominations and the Body of Christ* (Grand Rapids: Baker Book House, 1991)

—, *Cornelius Van Til: An Analysis of his Thought* (Phillipsburg: P. & R. Publishing, 1995)

Fretheim, T.E., *Creation, Fall and Flood: Studies in Genesis 1-11* (Minneapolis: Augsburg, 1969)

—, *Exodus* (Louisville: John Knox Press, 1991)

Frye, N., *The Great Code: The Bible and Literature* (London: Routledge & Kegan Paul, 1982)

Godfrey W.R. and J.L. Boyd III (eds.), *Through Christ's Word* (Phillipsburg: Presbyterian and Reformed, 1985)

Goetz, R., 'The Suffering God', *Christian Century* 103 (1986) 385–9

Gray, T., 'God Does Not Play Dice', *Themelios* 24 (1999), 21-34

Grenz, S.J., *Revisioning Evangelical Theology: A Fresh Agenda for the 21ˢᵗ Century* (Downers Grove: InterVarsity Press, 1993)

Grudem, W., *Systematic Theology: An Introduction to Biblical Doctrine* (Grand Rapids: Zondervan, 1994)

Gunter, W.S., et al., *Wesley and the Quadrilateral: Renewing the Conversation* (Nashville: Abingdon Press, 1997)

Gunton C.E., *Becoming and Being: The Doctrine of God in Charles Hartshorne and Karl Barth* (Oxford: Oxford University Press, 1978)

—, *The One, The Three, and The Many: God, Creation and the Culture of Modernity* (New York: Cambridge University Press, 1993)

Hallman, J.M., *Theology* (Minneapolis: Fortress, 1991)

Harkness, G., *The Providence of God* (Nashville: Abingdon Press, 1960)

Hasker, W., *God Time and Knowledge* (Ithaca, NY: Cornell University Press, 1989)

Hays, R., *Echoes of Scripture in the Letters of Paul* (New Haven: Yale University Press, 1989)

Hebblethwaite, B., *The Ocean of Truth: A Defense of Objective Theism* (Cambridge: Cambridge University Press, 1988)

Heick, O.W., *A History of Christian Thought* I, (Philadelphia: Fortress, 1965)

Heim, S.M., *The Depth of the Riches: A Trinitarian Theology of Religious Ends* (Grand Rapids: Eerdmans, 2000)

Helm, P., *Modern Reformation* 6 (Nov/Dec, 1999)

Heppe, H., *Reformed Dogmatics: Set Out and Illustrated from the Sources* (London: George Allen & Unwin, 1950)

Heschel, A.J., *The Prophets* (New York: Harper & Row, 1955)

Hick, J., *Evil and the God of Love* (New York: Harper & Row, 1966)

Hodge, C., *Systematic Theology* I (London, 1871-3)

Hodgson, L., *The Doctrine of the Trinity* (London: James Nisbet, 1943)

Horton, M., 'Is the New News Good News? Shifting Views Concerning God in our Day', *Modern Reformation* 8 (1999), 11-12

House, P.R., 'Evangelical Christianity must re-assert its inerrantly-revealed biblical definition of God', *Southern Baptist Journal of Theology* 1 (1997), 4–5

House, G.A. and P.R. Thornbury (eds.), *Who Will Be Saved? Defending the Biblical Understanding of God, Salvation, and Evangelism* (Wheaton: Crossway Books, 2000)

Jenson, R.W., *The Triune Identity* (Philadelphia: Fortress, 1982)

Jeremias, J., *New Testament Theology: The Proclamation of Jesus* (New York: Charles Scribner's Sons, 1971)

Kantzer, K.S. and S.N. Gundry (eds.), *Perspectives on Evangelical Theology: Papers from the Thirtieth Annual Meeting of the Evangelical Theological Society* (Grand Rapids: Baker Book House, 1979)

Kaufman, G.D., *Systematic Theology: A Historicist Perspective* (New York: Charles Scribner's Sons, 1968)

Kenny, A., *The God of the Philosophers* (Oxford: Clarendon Press, 1979)

Kierkegaard, S., *Journal* (New York: Harper and Row, 1958)

Klein, W.W., *The New Chosen People: A Corporate View of Election* (Grand Rapids: Zondervan, 1990)

Knight, H.H., III, *A Future for Truth: Evangelical Theology in a Postmodern World* (Nashville: Abingdon Press, 1997)

Kraft, C.H., *Christianity With Power: Worldview and Your Experience of the Supernatural* (Ann Arbor: Servant Publications, 1989)

Kreeft, P., *The God Who Loves You* (Ann Arbor: Servant Books, 1988)

Kreeft, P. and R.K. Tacelli, *Handbook of Christian Apologetics* (Downers Grove: InterVarsity Press, 1994)

Küng, H., *Christianity: Essence, History, and Future* (New York: Continuum, 1996)

Kushner, H.S., *When Bad Things Happen to Good People* (New York: Avon Books, 1983)

Latourelle, R., *The Miracles of Jesus and the Theology of Miracles* (New York: Paulist Press, 1988)

Leahy, F.S., 'God's Coming Identity Crisis', *Review NOW* (April 1997)

Lee, S.H., *The Philosophical Theology of Jonanthan Edwards* (Princeton: Princeton University Press, 1988)

Levenson, J.D., *Creation and the Persistence of Evil: The Jewish Drama of Divine Omnipotence* (Princeton: Princeton University Press, 1994)

Lewis, C.S., *Mere Christianity* (London: Collins, 1952)

—, *Screwtape Letters* (New York: Macmillan, 1961)

Little, P., *Know Why You Believe* (Wheaton: Victor Books, 1987²)

Longenecker, R.N., *New Wine into Fresh Wineskins* (Peabody: Hendrickson, 1999)

Lovelace, R.F., *Dynamics of Spiritual Life: An Evangelical Theology of Renewal* (Downers Grove: InterVarsity Press, 1979)

Marsden, G. (ed.), *Evangelicalism in Modern America* (Grand Rapids: Eerdmans, 1984)

McCabe, L.D., *The Foreknowledge of God* (Cincinnati: Hitchcock & Walden, 1878)

—, *Divine Nescience of Future Contingencies a Necessity* (New York: Phillips & Hunt, 1882)

McDermott, G.R., *Can Evangelicals Learn From World Religions?* (Downers Grove: InterVarsity Press, 2000)

McGrath, A., *A Passion for Truth: The Intellectual Coherence of Evangelicalism* (Downers Grove: InterVarsity Press, 1996)

McGregor, R.K., *No Place for Sovereignty: What's Wrong with Free Will Theism* (Downers Grove: InterVarsity, 1996)

Meadows, P.R., 'Providence, Chance, and the Problem of Suffering', *Wesleyan Theological Journal* 34 (1999), 52-77

Merton, T., *Life and Holiness* (Garden City: Doubleday, 1964)

Migliore, D.L., *Faith Seeking Understanding: An Introduction to Christian Theology* (Grand Rapids: Eerdmans, 1991)

Moltmann, J., *God In Creation: A New Theology of Creation and the Spirit of God* (San Francisco: Harper & Row, 1985)

Morris, T.V. (ed.), *Philosophy and the Christian Faith* (Notre Dame: University of Notre Dame Press, 1988)

Ngien, D., 'Abraham Heschel's Theology of Divine Pathos in Response to the 'Unmoved Mover' of Traditional Theism' (forthcoming)

Nouwen, H., *Bread for the Journey* (San Francisco: HarperSanFrancisco, 1997)

—, *The Only Necessary Thing: Living a Prayerful Life* (New York: Crossroad, 1999)

O'Hanlon, G.F., 'Does God Change?', *Irish Theological Quarterly* 53 (1987), 161-83

Olson, R.E., *The Story of Christian Theology: Twenty Centuries of Tradition and Reform* (Downers Grove: InterVarsity Press, 1999)

Ostling, R.N. and J.K. Ostling, *Mormon America: The Power and the Promise* (San Francisco: HarperSanFrancisco, 1999)

Packer, J.I., *Evangelism and the Sovereignty of God* (Chicago, InterVarsity Press, 1967)

—, 'An Introduction to Systematic Spirituality', *CRUX* 26 (March, 1990), 2-8

Padgett, A.G., *God, Eternity and the Nature of Time* (New York: St Martins, 1992)

Pannenberg, W., *Basic Questions in Theology* II (Philadelphia: Fortress, 1971)

—, *An Introduction to Systematic Theology*, fn21/3

Paulsen, D., 'Must God be Incorporeal?', *Faith and Philosophy* 6 (1989), 76-87

Pelikan, J., *The Emergence of the Catholic Tradition (100-600)* (Chicago: University of Chicago Press, 1971)

Petersen, M.L., 'Orthodox Christianty, Wesleyanism, and Process Theology', *Wesleyan Theological Journal* 15 (1980), 45-58

Peterson, M., et al., *Reason and Religious Belief* (New York: Oxford University Press, 1991)

Picirilli, R.E., 'Foreknowledge, Freedom, and the Future', *Journal of the Evangelical Theological Society* 43 (2000), 259-71

Pinnock, C.H., *The Scripture Principle* (San Francisco: Harper & Row, 1985)

—, 'God Limits his Knowledge' in D. Basinger and R. Basinger (eds.), *Predestination and Free Will: Four Views of Divine Sovereignty and Human Freedom* (Downers Grove: InterVarsity Press, 1986), 143-62

—, 'Between Classical and Process Theism' in R. Nash (ed.), *Process Theology*, (Grand Rapids: Baker Book House, 1987), 313-27

—, 'Climbing out of a Swamp: The Evangelical Struggle to Understand Creation Texts', *Interpretation* 43 (1989), 143-55

—, *Tracking the Maze: Finding our Way Through Modern Theology From An Evangelical Perspective* (San Francisco: Harper & Row, 1990)

—, 'God's Sovereignty in Today's World', *Theology Today* (April, 1997), 15-21

—, 'Biblical Texts: Past and Future Meanings', *Journal of the Evangelical Theological Society* 43 (2000), 71-81

Plantinga, C., *The Hodgson-Welch Debate and the Social Analogy of the Trinity* (Princeton PhD, 1982)

Polkinghorne, J., *Serious Talk: Science and Religion in Dialogue* (Valley Forge: Trinity Press International, 1995)

—, *Quarks, Chaos, and Christianity* (New York: Crosssroad, 1996)

Robinson, H.W., *Suffering — Human and Divine* (New York: Macmillan, 1939)

Robinson, S.E. and C.L. Blomberg, *How Wide the Divide? A Mormon and an Evangelical in Dialogue* (Downers Grove: InterVarsity Press, 1997)

Ruthven, J., *On the Cessation of the Charismata: The Protestant Polemic on Postbiblical Miracles* (Sheffield: Sheffield Academic Press, 1993)

Schmid, H., *Doctrinal Theology of the Evangelical Lutheran Church* (Minneapolis: Augsburg, 1875)

Shank, R., *Life in the Son: A Study of the Doctrine of Perseverance* (Springfield: Westcott Publishers, 1960)

—, *Elect in the Son: A Study of the Doctrine of Election* (Springfield: Westcott Publishers, 1970)

Stackhouse, J.G. (ed.), *Evangelical Futures: A Conversation on Theological Method* (Grand Rapids: Baker, 2000)

Stevens, R.P., *The Other Six Days: Vocation, Work and Ministry in Biblical Perspective* (USA edition; Grand Rapids: Eerdmans, 2000; UK edition, *The Abolition of the Laity: Vocation, Work and Ministry in Biblical Perspective;* Carlisle: Paternoster, 1999)

Stone B. and T.J. Oord (eds.), *Nature and Thy Name is Love: Process and Wesleyan Theologies in Dialogue,* (Kingswood Press, forthcoming)

Suurmond, J.-J., *Word and Spirit at Play: Toward a Charismatic Theology* (Grand Rapids: Eerdmans, 1995)

Talbott, T., 'The Love of God and the Heresy of Exclusivism', *Christian Scholars Review* (1997), 99-112

Thielicke, H., *The Prayer That Spans the World: Sermons on the Lord's Prayer* (Cambridge: James Clarke, 1965)

Thorsen, D., *The Wesleyan Quadrilateral: Scripture, Tradition, Reason and Experience as a Model of Evangelical Theology* (Grand Rapids: Zondervan, 1990)

Tillich, P., *Systematic Theology* I (Chicago: University of Chicago Press, 1951)

Tozer, A.W., *The Knowledge of the Holy* (New York: Harper Row, 1961)

Travis, S., *I Believe in the Second Coming of Jesus* (Grand Rapids: Eerdmans, 1982)

Volf, M., *Exclusion and Embrace: A Theological Exploration of Identity, Otherness, and Reconcilation* (Nashville: Abingdon Press, 1996)

—, *After Our Likeness: The Church as the Image of the Trinity* (Grand Rapids: Eerdmans, 1998)

Volf, M., C. Krieg and T. Kucharz (eds.), *The Future of Theology: Essays in Honor of Jürgen Moltmann* (Grand Rapids: Eerdmans, 1999)

Wallis, R.T., *Neo-Platonism* (London: Duckworth, 1972)

Waltke, B.K., *Creation and Chaos* (Portland: Western Conservative Baptist Seminary, 1974)

Ware, B.A., 'An Evangelical Reformulation of the Doctrine of the Immutability of God', *Journal of the Evangelical Theological Society* 29 (1986), 431-46

—, 'On Opening What's Closed and Closing What's Open: Rethinking the Doctrine of God in the Light of the Openness Proposal', an unpublished ETS paper (November, 1995)

—, 'Despair Amidst Suffering and Pain: A Practical Outworking of Open The-
    ism's Diminished View of God', *Southern Baptist Journal of Theology* 4
    (Summer, 2000), 56-75
Ware, T. (now Kallistos), *The Orthodox Church* (London: Penguin Books,
    1963)
Wells, D.F., *Modern Reformation* 9 (July, 2000), 10–12
Wellum, S.J., 'The importance of the Nature of Divine Sovereignty for our View
    of Scripture', *Southern Baptist Journal of Theology* 4 (Summer, 2000), 76-
    90
Wilkinson, L., 'Post Christian Feminism and the Fatherhood of God', *CRUX*
    36 (2000), 16-30
Willard, D., *The Divine Conspiracy: Rediscovering Our Hidden Life in God*
    (San Francisco: HarperSanFrancisco, 1998)
Wolterstorff, N.P., *Lament for a Son* (Grand Rapids: Eerdmans, 1987)
—, 'Does God Suffer?', *Modern Reformation* 8.5 (1999)
—, 'God and Time', *Philosophia Christi* 2 (2000), 5-10
Wright, N.T., *The Climax of the Covenant: Christ and the Law in Pauline
    Theology* (Minneapolis: Fortress, 1992)
Wyschogrod, M., 'A Jewish Perspective on Incarnation', *Modern Theology*
    (April, 1996), 195-209
Yoder, J.H., *The Original Revolution* (Scottdale: Herald Press, 1971)

The Didsbury Lectures

* no longer available
† not published

1998   I...
        F...
1999   L...
        A...
2000   A...
        T...
2001   C...
        M...